An original philosophical study, this work focuses on two concepts — explaining and understanding — both of which have been neglected by philosophers of education. The book constitutes an inquiry into explaining something to someone and the understanding at which that explaining aims. It also inquires into the various roles which explaining and understanding play in education in general, and teaching in particular.

The purpose of Professor Martin's book is twofold: first, to provide a general clarification and illumination of the notions of explaining and understanding something; and second, the application of such general clarification and illumination to educational issues and questions. An attempt is made to clarify the structure of both explaining and understanding as viewed independently of any discipline or subject-matter field. Relevant literature — some from philosophy of history, some from philosophy of education, some from philosophy of science — is examined in an attempt to come up with a systematic and tenable account of explaining and understanding and some of the ways in which they enter education. Although this study of explaining and understanding is not bound to some theoretical context such as science or history, it is bound to the practical context of education.

Curriculum recommendations are made by the author, and she discusses the limitations of philosophical analysis as a basis for curriculum decisions. Questions of method and objectives, of what should be taught and learned, also arise within the discussions.

EXPLAINING, UNDERSTANDING, AND TEACHING

JANE R. MARTIN

Harvard University

McGRAW-HILL BOOK COMPANY
New York St. Louis San Francisco Düsseldorf
London Mexico Panama Sydney Toronto

To My Mother and Father

This book was set in Caslon by Vail-Ballou Press, Inc., and printed on permanent paper and bound by Vail-Ballou Press, Inc. The designer was J. E. O'Connor. The editors were Nat LaMar and Robert Weber. Peter D. Guilmette supervised the production.

EXPLAINING, UNDERSTANDING, AND TEACHING

Library of Congress Catalog Card Number 70-95815

1234567890 VBVB 79876543210

This book grew out of my doctoral dissertation, "Explaining, Understanding, and Teaching History: A Philosophical Analysis," but it is by now far removed from that work and bears only the slightest resemblance to it. Whereas the former work was primarily an essay in the philosophy of history, the present work is primarily an essay in the philosophy of education. It constitutes an inquiry into explaining something to someone and the understanding at which that explaining aims and also into the various roles which explaining and understanding play in education in general and teaching in particular. The purpose of the present study is twofold: first, general clarification and illumination of the notions of explaining and understanding something; second, the application of such general clarification and illumination to educational issues and questions.

To elaborate a bit, an attempt is made here to clarify the structure of both explaining and understanding independently of any discipline or subject-matter field. Most philosophical investigations of explanation have proceeded within the context of history or science or some other field of knowledge. This study ignores such boundaries, for the context within which it proceeds, namely education, cuts across fields of knowledge. In its determination to ignore subject-matter boundaries this study resembles contemporary analyses of teaching as well as, of course, analyses of what it is to know or believe something. Needless to say, general accounts of this sort leave certain questions unanswered. Yet if subject-matter differences affect teaching, knowing, believing, and also explaining and understanding in ways which general accounts may overlook, such general accounts may in turn illuminate problems which studies tied down to some specific subject matter ignore.

Although this study of explaining and understanding is not bound to some theoretical context such as science or history, it is bound to the practical context of education. This context, implicit in the first sections of the book, is made explicit in the last section. There the rather abstract discussions of explaining and understanding in the earlier chapters are related to practical educational issues. Questions of method and objectives, of what should be taught and learned, arise. Curriculum recommendations are made, suggestions for empirical research emerge, and the limitations of philosophical analysis as a basis for curriculum decisions are discussed. The application of the general findings to educational issues, then, takes a variety of forms. The relevance of philosophical analysis to educational practice may not be as direct and immediate as some would like, but it is more wide-ranging than many suspect.

I wish to thank the Milton Fund Committee of Harvard University for support which facilitated the preparation of the final manuscript, J. Theodore Klein for helping with that preparation, Elsie C. Fiore for typing the manuscript, and Timothy Leadbeater for helping with proofs and index. The doctoral dissertation out of which this book evolved was submitted to the Radcliffe Graduate School in 1961. Work on that dissertation was supported in part by a fellowship awarded me by *Pi Lambda Theta*. I want here to express my gratitude to *Pi Lambda Theta* and also to the Radcliffe Graduate School for scholarship aid during my years of doctoral study. The dissertation was written under the direction of Professors Israel Scheffler and Morton White. I cannot thank them enough for the help, guidance, and encouragement they gave me, not only in connection with the thesis, but throughout my graduate training. The study's final form owes a great deal to discussions about explanation and understanding I have had with students in one of my courses at the Harvard Graduate School of Education and to criticisms of earlier versions of the study by a number of readers. I am particularly indebted to Sylvain Bromberger for criticizing an earlier draft in great detail and for introducing me to his essay "An Approach to Explanation." That essay has without doubt improved and enriched my thinking about explaining, understanding, and teaching. One other reader of earlier versions must be singled out for special mention. Michael Martin has read each draft critically, has helped me work through various substantive questions, and has given me all the moral support I could possibly want.

Jane R. Martin

The author gratefully acknowledges the cooperation of the following publishers and authors for permission to reprint material from these sources:

Sylvain Bromberger: "An Approach to Explanation," in R. J. Butler (ed.), *Analytical Philosophy, Second Series,* Basil Blackwell & Mott, Ltd., Oxford, 1965.

Clarendon Press, Oxford, and William Dray: *Laws and Explanation in History,* 1957.

Cambridge University Press and D. H. Mellor (ed., *British Journal for the Philosophy of Science*): "Another Look at the Doctrine of Verstehen," by Jane R. Martin, *British Journal for the Philosophy of Science,* 20:53–67, 1969.

George Allen & Unwin Ltd.; Scott, Foresman and Company; and R. S. Peters: *Ethics and Education,* 1966.

Kingsley Price: "On 'Having an Education,'" by Kingsley Price, *Harvard Educational Review,* 28:320–337, 1958.

Hutchinson Publishing Group, Ltd.; Barnes & Noble, Inc.; and Gilbert Ryle: *The Concept of Mind,* 1949.

Charles C Thomas, Publisher, and Israel Scheffler: *The Language of Education,* 1960.

University of Minnesota Press and Michael Scriven: "Explanations, Predictions, and Laws," in Herbert Feigl and Grover Maxwell (eds.), *Minnesota Studies in the Philosophy of Science,* vol. III, 1962.

Contents

Preface　　　　　　　　　　　　　　　　　　　　　　*iii*

PART I INTRODUCTION　　　　　　　　　　*1*

Chapter One　The Legacy of the Antiregularists　　　*3*
Chapter Two　The Concept of Explanation　　　　　*12*
　1　Explaining and Explanations　　　　　　　　　*13*
　2　A Fivefold Distinction　　　　　　　　　　　　*17*
　3　The Need for Clarity　　　　　　　　　　　　　*25*

PART II EXPLAINING SOMETHING
　　　　　　　TO SOMEONE　　　　　　　　　*35*

Chapter Three　Explaining as Gap Filling　　　　　　*37*
　1　The Case of the Engine Seizure　　　　　　　　*38*
　2　The Continuous Series　　　　　　　　　　　　*41*
　3　Shifting the Question　　　　　　　　　　　　*44*
　4　Hat-doffingness　　　　　　　　　　　　　　　*49*

Chapter Four　Explaining as Question Answering　　　*60*
　1　An Approach to Explanation　　　　　　　　　　*61*
　2　The Truth Requirement　　　　　　　　　　　　*63*
　3　The Tutee's Predicament　　　　　　　　　　　*73*
　4　Hypothesis Five　　　　　　　　　　　　　　　*84*

Chapter Five　Explaining as Reason Giving　　　　　　*87*
　1　The Rationality Theory of Teaching　　　　　　*89*
　2　The Rationality Constraints Interpreted　　　　*95*
　3　A Rationality Theory of Explaining　　　　　　*103*

Chapter Six　Explaining as a Use of Language　　　　*111*
　1　A Linguistic Theory of Teaching　　　　　　　　*112*

2 A Linguistic Theory of Explaining   *116*

3 Conditions of Explaining Something to Someone   *123*

4 Explanations of Something for Someone   *128*

PART III UNDERSTANDING   *141*

Chapter Seven   Understanding as Seeing Connections   *143*

1 Understanding Something and Being Understanding   *143*

2 Competence in Performance   *147*

3 Internal and External Understanding   *152*

4 Analysis and Placing Things in Context   *159*

5 Seeing Connections   *163*

Chapter Eight   The Doctrine of *Verstehen*   *168*

1 Rational Explanation and the Agent's Point of View   *171*

2 A Theory of Understanding Actions   *174*

3 A Theory of Being Understanding toward Actions   *181*

4 A Theory of Historical Understanding   *185*

PART IV EXPLAINING AND UNDERSTANDING IN EDUCATION   *195*

Chapter Nine   Explaining as Method and Goal   *197*

1 Teaching by Explaining Something to Someone   *198*

2 Explaining as an Educational Objective   *206*

3 Learning to Explain and Learning by Explaining   *211*

Chapter Ten   *Verstehen* as an Educational Doctrine   *220*

1 Taking the Agent's Point of View   *221*

2 A Theory of Learning   *227*

3 Training in Performance   *231*

4 Knowing about Performances   *236*

5 Curriculum Decisions and the Nature of Understanding   *242*

Index   *247*

Part One

INTRODUCTION

☞ *Chapter I*

THE LEGACY OF THE ANTIREGULARISTS

The year 1957 marked a turning point in the study of explanation, for with the publication of William Dray's *Laws and Explanation in History* philosophers were forced to reexamine what had for some time been the "standard" theory of explanation. Dray's was neither the first attack on that theory nor the only attack to have impact on the philosophical community.[1] But I ven-

[1] See William Dray, *Laws and Explanation in History* (Oxford, London, 1957). Page references in this chapter are to this book.

For some representative criticisms of the standard theory which preceded Dray's book, see: Isaiah Berlin, *Historical Inevitability* (Oxford, London, 1954); W. B. Gallie, "Explanations in History and the Genetic Sciences," *Mind*, 64:160–181, 1955; Arthur C. Danto, "On Explanations in History," *Philosophy of Science*, 23:15–30, 1956; Alan Donagan, "Explanation in History," *Mind*, 66:145–164, 1957; P. H. Nowell-Smith, "Are Historical Events Unique?" *Proceedings of the Aristotelian Society*, 57:107–160, 1956–1957.

Among the criticisms with considerable impact are the above and also

ture to guess that his book was far and away the most influential single work attacking the standard theory of explanation. Whatever historians of ideas may eventually conclude on this score, there is no doubt that Dray packed into his book argument upon argument purporting to show the inadequacies of the standard theory, at least as a theory of explanation in history; that he presented these arguments in a most persuasive way; and that the work became a rallying point for those who were dissatisfied with the standard view.

Dray calls the standard theory of explanation, the one he subjects to sustained criticism, "the covering law model." I will be calling it the *regularity theory.* Others have called it "the deductive model," "the Hempelian theory," "the Popperian theory." Dray's label focuses attention on one necessary condition that the standard or regularity theory places on explanation, namely a set of laws.[2] This is by no means the only condition the theory places on explanation, but it is the condition which Dray and most other critics find particularly objectionable when the theory is held to be applicable to explanation in history.[3] In *Laws and Explanation in History* Dray argues that historical explanations—good, sound, solid ones—do not require laws and that even if they did, the laws they required would not function in an explanatory capacity (chaps. 2, 3).[4] As if this were not enough to clinch the case against the standard theory, he argues that the theory—especially

---

Michael Scriven, "Truisms as the Grounds for Historical Explanations," in Patrick Gardiner (ed.), *Theories of History* (Free Press, New York, 1959), pp. 443–475; Alan Donagan, "Historical Explanation: The Popper-Hempel Theory Reconsidered," *History and Theory,* 4:3–26, 1965.

[2] It should be noted that Dray's label is misleading in that it suggests that the theory requires a single law. The theory does not do this, as Dray himself acknowledges, *op. cit.,* pp. 52ff.

[3] For some significant formulations of the standard or regularity theory, see Carl G. Hempel, "The Function of General Laws in History," *The Journal of Philosophy,* 39:35–48, January, 1942; and Carl G. Hempel and Paul Oppenheim, "The Logic of Explanation," *Philosophy of Science,* 15:135–175, 1948, reprinted in Hempel, *Aspects of Scientific Explanation and Other Essays in the Philosophy of Science* (Free Press, New York, 1965); Karl R. Popper, *The Logic of Scientific Discovery* (Basic Books, New York, 1959); Ernest Nagel, *The Structure of Science* (Harcourt, Brace & World, New York, 1961).

[4] And in chap. 4 he argues that causal explanations are no exception.

the law requirement—is peculiarly inappropriate where the thing being explained is a human action, and he only rests his case after arguing for the inappropriateness of the theory when someone is explaining how possibly something could have happened (chaps. 5, 6).

Two philosophical traditions meet in Dray's work. According to the one tradition, history is a unique discipline: its methods, its interests, its standards of judgment are its own. This tradition is particularly concerned that history not be confused with science; it is dedicated to the proposition that history is as separate from science as any two human endeavors can be.[5] Dray's objections to the regularity theory of explanation in history, especially his objections to the law requirement, quite clearly fall in this tradition. The regularity theory is a theory of explanation in science, and it is this as much as anything that bothers Dray about it. He suspects "covering law theorists," as he calls them, of trying to make history scientific (chap. 1); he suggests that they have given a criterion of a technical sense of "explanation" found only in narrowly scientific discourse (pp. 76ff.); he attributes to them the assumption that historical explanations are simply woollier versions of scientific ones (p. 78). Throughout his attack and attacks like his on the regularity theory of explanation, one senses a fear of creeping scientism and a determination that history be seen as history and not just as one more instance of science.

According to the other tradition, a newer one, philosophers must concern themselves with ordinary language and ordinary practice: they must study the various uses of language and be sensitive to the context of utterances; they must stay close to everyday practice, describing it as it is rather than abstracting from it or prescribing for it.[6] Dray's work, in striking contrast to the work

[5] See, for example: R. G. Collingwood, *The Idea of History* (Oxford University Press, New York, 1956); Benedetto Croce, in Douglas Ainslie (trans.), *History: Its Theory and Practice* (Russell & Russell, New York, 1960); Wilhelm Dilthey, in H. P. Rickman (ed.), *Meaning in History* (G. Allen & Unwin, London, 1961); Wilhelm Windelband, in James H. Tufts (trans.), *A History of Philosophy* (Harper, New York, 1958).
[6] The classic work in this tradition is Ludwig Wittgenstein, in G. E. M. Anscombe (trans.), *Philosophical Investigations* (Macmillan, New York, 1953).
There have been numerous attempts to apply the methods of this tradi-

of others before him who have defended the uniqueness of history, falls directly in this tradition. He is interested in what the historian does and says, in his way of proceeding; he is interested in the context surrounding the historian's explanations, in "who says it to whom" and in what happens to the person to whom it is said; he is interested in the ordinary meaning of "explain" and deplores the covering law theorists' failure to recognize that it is a pragmatic term and not a term of formal logic (p. 11).

It is this second tradition that leads Dray to raise some important and interesting questions about explanation, questions such as the following: What makes a given statement an explanation for one person and not another? What does one have to do to get someone to understand something? What knowledge or competence does a person have to have to understand something? Proponents of the standard view had long ignored questions of this sort. If they did not actually believe these questions to be psychological rather than philosophical, they certainly considered them to be philosophically uninteresting, even trivial.[7] The very things that Dray, in adopting the Oxford ordinary-language approach to philosophy, latched onto as important in the study of explanation—actual practice, the context in which explanations are given—were the things that proponents of the standard view tended to dismiss out of hand as irrelevant to their purposes.

History repeats itself. In a book entitled *The Nature of Historical Explanation,* published in 1952, Patrick Gardiner set out to "consider the procedure historians in fact adopt to explain the events of which they treat."[8] Dray acknowledges his debt to Gardi-

---

tion to various fields. Some representative examples are: P. H. Nowell-Smith, *Ethics* (Penguin Books, London, 1954); H. L. A. Hart, *The Concept of Law* (Oxford University Press, London, 1963). See also the following anthologies: William Elton (ed.), *Aesthetics and Language* (Blackwell, Oxford, 1964); Donald F. Gustafson (ed.), *Essays in Philosophical Psychology* (Doubleday, Garden City, New York, 1964); Anthony Flew and Alasdair MacIntyre (eds.), *New Essays in Philosophical Theology* (Macmillan, New York, 1955).

[7] See, for example, May Brodbeck's answer to critics of the regularity theory, "Explanation, Prediction, and 'Imperfect' Knowledge," in Herbert Feigl and Grover Maxwell (eds.), *Minnesota Studies in the Philosophy of Science,* vol. III (University of Minnesota Press, Minneapolis, 1962), pp. 231–238.

[8] (Oxford University Press, London), p. 65.

ner's book and makes explicit his agreement with Gardiner over the kind of inquiry needed in the study of explanation in history (p. 21). But Gardiner disappointed Dray. Gardiner raised questions about historical practice which seem, at least to Dray, to create insurmountable difficulties for the regularity theory of explanation; yet instead of rejecting that theory, as Dray would wish, he modified it and remained "in essentials, a covering law theorist" (p. 18). From Dray's vantage point, Gardiner promised more than he produced, for he was not able to escape the standard view.

From our vantage point much the same can be said of Dray. Just as Gardiner raised questions about explanation in history which, at least from Dray's point of view, called for discussion outside the framework provided by the regularity theory, so Dray raises questions which, at least from our point of view, cry out for exploration in their own right. Yet Dray, too, is a prisoner of the standard view. To be sure, he rejects that view and is therefore not bound to it in the way that he thinks Gardiner is. Nonetheless, the regularity theory defines the limits of his discussion and the discussion of the many philosophers and historians who have taken up where he left off. The regularity theory is attacked, and the reader is forced to consider how *it* might be defended. The significantly new and interesting questions Dray asks about explanation and understanding are not really taken seriously. They become part of the ammunition of the history-is-unique movement and to this extent, of course, they do serve a purpose, albeit the negative one of rebutting the accepted doctrine. But they do not themselves attract inquiry. The promise is there; Dray opens up whole areas for discussion. But the lure of the standard view is too great for him and his followers, and we are left with a coherent and systematic attack on the regularity theory [9] and with relatively little enlightenment on the challenging issues which Dray put in the spotlight.

The present study will concentrate on some of these issues. It will be concerned with explanation as a pragmatic notion. In one

[9] But see, for example, the following counterattacks: Brodbeck, *op. cit.;* Hempel, "Aspects of Scientific Explanation," in *Aspects of Scientific Explanation and Other Essays in the Philosophy of Science,* pp. 331–496; Israel Scheffler, *The Anatomy of Inquiry* (Knopf, New York, 1963); Morton White, *Foundations of Historical Knowledge* (Harper & Row, New York, 1965).

sense it grows directly out of Dray's work: he and his followers brought to light the "pragmatic dimension" of explanation; we will try here to get clearer on the details of that dimension and on the relationship of that dimension to other dimensions. In another sense, however, this study parts company with the work of Dray and his followers, for it is not and ought not to be construed as an attack on the regularity theory of explanation. Indeed, and I will argue this at length in Chapter 2, the standard view of explanation has nothing to say about the pragmatic dimension of explanation. To discuss pragmatic questions, even to take a stand on them, is not in itself, then, to cast doubt on the regularity theory any more than it is to support that theory. For our purposes, the regularity theory of explanation is irrelevant. We will examine it in Chapter 2 just long enough to be convinced of the fact that we can dismiss it from our thoughts.

I have said that we will be concerned with explanation as a pragmatic notion. Actually our interest in explanation is more limited than this, for we will be concerned for the most part with just one pragmatic notion of explanation. In Chapter 2 a number of explanation notions will be distinguished, all but one of which will be seen to qualify as pragmatic. We will single out *explaining something to someone* for special attention on the grounds that this activity has particular significance for the educator. Chapter 2 will pave the way for the extended discussion of the activity of explaining something to someone contained in Chapters 3 to 6. We will then turn to an examination of the goal of this activity, namely *understanding*. Chapters 7 and 8 will be devoted to a discussion of this philosophically neglected but educationally crucial topic. In the last two chapters, Chapters 9 and 10, I will map out some of the ways in which explaining something to someone and understanding, as explicated in the preceding chapters, enter into education in general and teaching in particular.

The reader may well ask why a general discussion of explaining and understanding—and let me emphasize that our discussion of explaining and understanding is intended to be general—which purports to have something to do with the field of education, should take as seriously as this one does philosophical writings about history. What can philosophers of history conceivably have to say to the educator? The answer is simple. Philosophers of history have thought and written about explanation a good deal more than most people have. While their work is aimed at elucidating the nature of explanation in the historical context, much of what they have to say holds true, or at least seems as if it might hold true, quite generally. This is not to say that we are, after all, prepared to ignore context in our discussion of explanation. One sort of context, namely who says it to whom, will engage our interest throughout. We will, however, largely ignore another sort of context, namely the subject area within which the explainer and his explainee operate.

This approach no doubt has its limitations, for there may well be interesting and important things that hold true about explaining something in economics to someone, for example, which do not hold true for explaining something in physics or some other field to someone. Nevertheless the gains of this approach are great. For one thing, we may profit from the work already done on explanation in philosophy of history. For another, we may draw on philosophical discussions of teaching which are themselves neutral with respect to subject area. In recent years philosophers have paid a great deal of attention to the notion of teaching. We will find some of this work, as well as some work in philosophy of history, to be quite relevant both to the study of explaining something to someone and to the study of understanding.

Let us hope that philosophy of history gains something from its generosity in this instance; that our discussion of explaining something to someone and of understanding in general sheds at least some light on the specific problems of explanation and understanding in history. Indeed, since our interest here is quite general, that is to say is neutral with respect to subject area, I would hope that our discussion would have relevance for the study of explanation and understanding in any field. Be that as it may, there can be no doubt that an examination of the notions of explaining something to someone and of understanding has special relevance for education, for these are just as much educational notions as are teaching and learning.

I can imagine someone objecting at this point that "teaching" and "learning" are purely educational terms, whereas "explaining something to someone" and "understanding" are not: witness the interest of philosophers of history in the latter pair of terms, not the former pair, and the interest of philosophers of education in the former pair of terms, not the latter pair.[10] If one conceives of education as formal education, however—a narrow conception to be sure, but nonetheless a prevalent one—then I doubt very much that a case could be made for "teaching" and "learning" as purely educational terms any more than it could be made for "explaining something to someone" and "understanding." There can be learning without teaching; thus "learning" at least has applicability outside educational contexts. But "teaching" also does, for parents teach their children, sisters and brothers teach each other, and assorted individuals and groups ranging from music critics to statesmen teach all of us. On the other hand, if one conceives of education more broadly, as encompassing informal as well as formal contexts, then it seems that "explaining something to someone" and "understanding" can qualify as purely educational terms in the same way that "teaching" and "learning" do.

Suppose, however, that our critic is right and that "teaching" and "learning" have a special status in relation to education, one not shared by "explaining something to someone" and "understanding." The fact remains that the latter two terms enter into educational discourse in important ways and that they have not re-

[10] For some important analyses of teaching, see Israel Scheffler, *The Language of Education* (Charles C Thomas, Springfield, Ill., 1960), chaps. 4 and 5; Israel Scheffler, *Conditions of Knowledge* (Scott, Foresman, Glenview, Ill., 1965), chap. 1; Israel Scheffler, "Philosophical Models of Teaching," *Harvard Educational Review*, 35:131–143, Spring, 1965; B. Othanel Smith, "A Concept of Teaching," in B. Othanel Smith and Robert H. Ennis (eds.), *Language and Concepts in Education* (Rand McNally, Chicago, 1961), pp. 86–101; Thomas F. Green, "A Topology of the Teaching Concept," *Studies in Philosophy and Education*, 3:284–319, 1964–1965; William H. Hay, "On Green's Analysis of Teaching," *Studies in Philosophy of Education*, 4:339–345, 1966; B. Paul Komisar, "Teaching: Act and Enterprise," *Studies in Philosophy and Education*, 6:168–193. For analyses of learning, see B. Paul Komisar and C. J. B. MacMillan (eds.), *Psychological Concepts of Education* (Rand McNally, Chicago, 1967).

ceived their fair share of attention from philosophers whose special interest is education.[11] Educational theorists throughout the ages have wanted people to *understand* whatever it is they are being taught. They have argued, and they still do argue, that certain things must be studied in certain ways if people are to understand. In addition, *explaining* has been held to be a central task or function of the teacher. More and more we find the teacher being cautioned against telling, but being urged to take on the role of explainer. In view of the importance of the notions of explaining something to someone and understanding in educational theorizing it is surprising that so little philosophical energy has been devoted to clarifying them. This study should be viewed as a start toward such clarification. It will, perhaps, raise more questions than it answers, but this is no matter. Indeed, I would be surprised and somewhat dismayed if its effect were otherwise.

[11] However, brief discussions of explaining and understanding can be found in Jonas Soltis, *An Introduction to the Analysis of Educational Concepts* (Addison-Wesley, Reading, Mass., 1968), chap. IV; and in Reginald D. Archambault, "Teaching and Explanation," *Proceedings of the Philosophy of Education Society*, 21st Annual Meeting, 1965, pp. 19–24.

Chapter 2

THE CONCEPT
OF EXPLANATION

The terms "explanation" and "explain" are ambiguous, and the context in which they are used does not always render them unambiguous. Consider the statement, "Smith tried to explain why the Republicans lost the election but he did not succeed." Does the speaker mean that Smith was unable to come up with the correct reasons or causes for the Republican loss or that Smith, although he was well aware of the correct reasons or causes, failed to get them across to his audience? Or consider the directive a teacher gives his student: "Explain why war broke out between the North and the South." What precisely is the student being asked to do: investigate, for example, events leading up to the outbreak of hostilities between North and South in the hope of finding out why war broke out, or communicate what he knows about, for example, the causes of the Civil War to the teacher and his classmates?

We might expect philosophers, when discussing the general topic of explanation, to specify the senses in which they are using the terms "explanation" and "explain," but this has seldom been done. As a result philosophical analysis has suffered, and to the extent that educational theory has drawn upon philosophical analyses of the notion of explanation, it has suffered as well. The purpose of this chapter, therefore, is to sort out several different senses of the terms "explanation" and "explain" and to show the importance of keeping them distinct if some central questions about explanation and understanding and their role in education are to be clarified.

1   Explaining and Explanations

Let us start by pointing out what is perhaps obvious, namely that the verb "to explain" refers to something someone does. If there is any doubt about this, just consider that a perfectly good answer to the question "What did Jones do?" is "He explained why war broke out between the states" and a perfectly good answer to the question "What is that boy doing right now?" is "He's explaining to the rest of his class why dinosaurs became extinct." Just what sort of doing is at stake when we describe someone as having explained or as explaining remains to be seen. A first step toward clarity is taken if we simply recognize that to explain is to do something or other, just as to run, to study, to sit, to take the day off, or to find a needle in a haystack is to do something or other.

I say that this minimal account of "to explain" constitutes a step toward clarity, for once we recognize explaining as a doing of some sort we see that it is a very different sort of thing from an explanation. An explanation is not a doing at all. To be sure, one can do things *with* explanations and *to* explanations. One can give or present an explanation; arrive at, come up with, find, or discover an explanation; listen to, appreciate, ignore, or dismiss an explanation; and so on. But although the things one does with or to explanations may themselves be doings, the explanations one does things with or to are not doings. Explanations, then, are not something one does but are sentences or statements of some sort or other. Just what sort of sentences or statements constitute explanations remains to be seen.

It might be suggested at this point that there is really nothing to get clear about: we have two distinct terms—the verb "to explain" and the noun "explanation"—and two very different sorts of things in the world, one of which is picked out by the verb and the other of which is picked out by the noun. The situation is not, however, as neat as this account would make it. For one thing, people sometimes use the noun "explanation" in such a broad way that the distinction between some sort of doing and some sort of sentences or statements is obscured. Thus, for example, when a philosopher says he will discuss explanation in science he may be intending to limit himself to a discussion of a certain sort of account of the world; but one ought not to take this for granted, for he may be intending to consider some of the things scientists do (their explaining) as well as the accounts of the world they give (their explanations). He may, that is, consider both explaining and explanation to be cases of explanation.

But there is another reason why we cannot simply say there is such a thing as explaining and there are such things as explanations and leave it at that. The verb "to explain" is used to refer to at least two very different sorts of doings, while the noun "explanation," even if its range of application is restricted to sentences or statements, can be used in more than one way. Perhaps an example will help to bring to light the two sorts of doings that go under the name of explaining. Consider Freud's attempt to give an account of certain kinds of behavior, an attempt which involved him in research, theorizing, and the like. One of the things we can say about this is that Freud was trying to *explain* the behavior in question. Contrast this with the *explaining* in which the teacher of Freudian theory engages in order to get someone to understand the very sort of behavior Freud studied. The teacher's activity of explaining is not a matter of research, investigation, original theorizing, and the like, but a matter of pedagogy.

The verb "to explain" refers to doings which have close connections with two quite different areas of human endeavor: with research and inquiry on the one hand and with teaching and pedagogy on the other hand. For convenience's sake I will call the "inquiry-related" explaining *explaining something* and will use the subscript "R" when referring to it to remind the reader of its connection to *r*esearch of one sort or another. I will call the "pedagogy-related" explaining *explaining something to someone* and will use the subscript "T" when referring to it to remind the reader of the kinship between it and *t*eaching. The existence of different labels or names does not of course guarantee that there are different things to be named, and it might be objected that I have yet to show that what I am claiming are two very different sorts of doings are indeed different. It will soon become clear, however, that the sort of doing I am calling explaining$_R$ something and the sort of doing I am calling explaining$_T$ something to someone are in fact very different.

Like teaching or running a race or searching for a lost mitten, explaining$_T$ something to someone is an activity. It takes time, it requires effort, it is something one can engage in. Explaining$_R$ something is not like this at all. It is better compared to winning a race than to running one, to finding a lost mitten than to searching for one. Winning a race or finding a lost mitten is not an activity. We do not normally speak of someone as being engaged in winning a race (or finding a lost mitten), although we may say that he is trying to win (or find), and if he does win (or find) we will describe him as having won (or found). Similarly, we do not normally describe someone as being engaged in explaining something. We say that he is *trying* to explain$_R$ something or that he is *seeking* an explanation; and if he succeeds, we will describe him as having explained$_R$ something. "Explaining$_R$ something" is what Gilbert Ryle would call a success or achievement verb, whereas "explaining$_T$ something to someone" is what he would call a task verb.[1]

[1] *The Concept of Mind* (Hutchinson, London, 1949), pp. 130, 149–153. See Israel Scheffler, *Conditions of Knowledge* (Scott, Foresman, Glenview, Ill., 1965), pp. 31–33, for a criticism of Ryle's distinction between task and achievement verbs; and for a more refined classification of verbs than Ryle's, see Zeno Vendler, "Verbs and Times," *The Philosophical Review*, 66:143–160, 1957. Ryle's task-achievement distinction is adequate for the present purpose despite the problems with it, but the reader

Explaining$_R$ something and explaining$_T$ something to someone differ from one another, then, in that the latter is an activity and the former is not. They differ also in that one who explains$_T$ something to someone is trying to get that person to learn or understand something. He is imparting knowledge (or at least trying to do so), not seeking it. His problem is one of communication, of getting something across to someone. One who is trying to explain$_R$ something, on the other hand, is trying to find out something. He *is* seeking knowledge, or something approaching knowledge. His problem is *not* one of communication but of conducting the appropriate sort of inquiry. Explaining$_R$ something and explaining$_T$ something to someone are doings, in other words, which are related in that each is intimately connected with knowledge, but the connection with knowledge in the one case is that of imparting or communicating while the connection with knowledge in the other case is that of finding or discovering.

Now it may be argued that explaining$_T$ something to someone and explaining$_R$ something are not as different as I am claiming. Isn't inquiry ordinarily viewed as having as its goal understanding? But then, hasn't someone who has explained$_R$ something attained understanding? [2] To be sure, one who engages in explaining$_T$ something to someone may be primarily trying to get others to understand something while one who has explained$_R$ something may have produced understanding only in himself. But isn't this merely a difference in emphasis? Could not the latter have gotten others to understand and could not the former have gotten only himself to understand?

There is some force to this argument, for explaining$_R$ something and explaining$_T$ something to someone are by no means unre-

is urged to consult Sylvain Bromberger, "An Approach to Explanation" in R. J. Butler (ed.), *Analytical Philosophy,* 2d ser. (Blackwell, Oxford, 1965), pp. 72–105, for an application of Vendler's distinctions to the verb "to explain."

[2] Bromberger, *op. cit.,* p. 101, may be interpreted as taking this position. On his view, one who has explained$_R$ something has become able to explain$_T$ it to someone. Presumably he has become able to explain$_T$ it to someone because, having explained$_R$ it, he has attained understanding of it. For more on this point see Chap. 6, sect. 4.

lated and the notion of understanding provides one important point of contact between the two. Nevertheless, it seems to me to be a mistake to view explaining$_R$ something as necessarily involving understanding that thing. Granted that the two will often coincide, it is nonetheless possible for someone to have explained$_R$ a thing yet not to have understood it. Of course his explanation may make it *possible* for him and for others to understand the thing, but this is quite different from saying that it follows from the very fact of someone's having explained$_R$ something that he understands it. To understand something involves having certain relevant knowledge.[3] This is not required of explaining$_R$ something. One who has arrived on his own at conclusions expressible in statements meeting certain logical and empirical requirements may be said to have explained$_R$ something regardless of his state of mind.

In the interests of clarity, let us view the creation of understanding as one step removed from explaining$_R$ something. When this is done we see one who explains$_R$ something as producer of the explanations which constitute the raw materials used in explaining$_T$ something to someone. It also becomes clear that the problems of how to get someone to understand something, which take one into the areas of psychology and pedagogy, are not problems with which one who is *seeking* explanations of things must necessarily deal. Learning theory and child development are subjects which, if they have anything important to say at all, are presumably subjects worthy of study by the would-be explainer$_T$ and not normally by the would-be explainer$_R$.

2 A Fivefold Distinction

I just described one who explains$_R$ something as a producer of explanations. What can we say about one who explains$_T$ something to someone? Is he also a producer of explanations? No, for his is what may be called a practical activity as opposed to a theoretical activity. It is a practical activity in that its aim is not to find things out, not to add to our body of knowledge—as it would have

[3] The notion of understanding will be discussed at length in Chap. 7.

to be if we were to describe him as a producer of explanations—but to do things to people. In particular, one who explains$_T$ something to someone wants to get that person to understand something. To be sure, in the course of achieving his end he *gives* explanations, but his *giving* explanations does not qualify him as a *producer* of explanations in the sense in which one who explains$_R$ is a producer of explanations. The explanations he gives are not his product. His "product" if one wishes to speak in this way—a way which may well be misleading—is the understanding he creates when his explaining$_T$ is successful. The explanations the explainer$_T$ gives are his tools or means for "turning out" his product.

Now it could be the case that although explanations play different roles in relation to explaining$_R$ something and explaining$_T$ something to someone, in other important respects the explanations produced by the explainer$_R$ and the explanations given by the explainer$_T$ are one and the same. It could be the case but it is not in fact the case, for the explanations an explainer$_T$ gives are *for* someone while the explanations an explainer$_R$ produces are not—that is to say, not necessarily—for someone. To be sure, one who has explained$_R$ something may go on to explain$_T$ it to people—for example, he may write up his research for a scholarly journal—and if he does, he will give explanations that are for someone. Nonetheless, the explainer$_R$ qua explainer$_R$ has no audience to worry about. Some of his explanations may as a matter of fact be suitable for a given audience, but it is not necessary that they be in order for them to be adequate.

This difference between explanations that are for someone and explanations that are not for someone may not at first glance seem important enough to dwell on here. Yet anyone familiar with contemporary philosophical discussion of explanation must grant that this difference is of prime importance if clarity is to be attained. For we are told repeatedly that explanations are *for* someone and that accounts of explanation which do not take cognizance of this "pragmatic dimension" of explanation are mistaken. If, however, it is the case—and I am arguing here that it is—that some explanations are for someone and some are not, then it is an open question whether the accounts of explanation which are held to be mistaken are mistaken or whether they are not accounts of the sort of explanation of which their critics take them to be accounts. We would do well, therefore, to make the distinction between explanations that are for someone and explanations that are not explicit. For convenience's sake I will call the explanations given by an explainer$_T$ *explanations of something for someone*. To remind the reader that these explanations are part of the *d*iscourse of one who engages in explaining$_T$ something to someone I will use the subscript "D" when referring to them. And I will call the explanations given by an explainer$_R$ *explanations of something by someone*. Since these explanations embody the explainer's$_R$ *f*indings I will use the subscript "F" when referring to them.

Those who stress that explanation has a pragmatic dimension or that explanation is a pragmatic notion seem to be doing so on the grounds that explanations are for someone.[4] However, the matter is more complex than this. We have so far delineated what may be considered to be four distinct notions of explanation[5]: explaining$_R$ something, explaining$_T$ something to someone, an explanation$_F$ of something by someone, an explanation$_D$ of something for someone. If we formulate these clearly we will see that explanation does indeed have a "pragmatic dimension" but that this dimension is not everywhere the same. Let us therefore describe these four notions by the following forms, where "X" indicates a position occupied by some sentence or sentences, "E" indicates a position occupied by an expression through which some thing or things are mentioned,[6] and "A" and "B" indicate positions through which some person or persons are mentioned:

(R) A explains E.
(T) A explains E to B.
(F) X is an explanation of E given by A.
(D) X is an explanation of E for A.

---

[4] See for example William Dray, *Laws and Explanation in History* (Oxford, London, 1957), chap. 3.

[5] "Explanation" is here to be construed broadly, that is, as including explaining as well as explanations in the narrow sense of sentences or statements of a certain kind.

[6] "Thing" is to be interpreted broadly enough here to cover events, states, processes, actions, and just about everything else.

Let us call any notion that is relative to persons pragmatic. Explaining_R something, explaining_T something to someone, an explanation_F of something by someone, and an explanation_D of something for someone, then, are all pragmatic notions. It is not the case, however, that every one of the four notions involves communication with some audience, or "forness." Explaining_R something is a pragmatic notion because someone has to *do* the explaining; an explanation_F of something by someone is a pragmatic notion because someone has to *give* the explanation. If we want to lump all these notions together and speak of explanation as being a pragmatic notion (or having a pragmatic dimension) we can, but we must remember that it is pragmatic in two quite different respects (its pragmatic dimension has two aspects): it is pragmatic in that an audience or explainee may be involved; it is pragmatic in that an explainer may be involved.

Dray has claimed that a proper account of explanation cannot be given without bringing out its pragmatic dimension,[7] and Michael Scriven has claimed that explanation is not a syntactical notion.[8] In order to assess these claims we must consider Scriven's argument that the notion of an explanation "in the abstract" makes no sense. Scriven argues as follows:

> ... if there were no cases of this kind [explaining X to someone], there could be no such thing as "an explanation of X" in the abstract, whereas the reverse is not true. For it makes no sense to talk of *an explanation* which nobody understands now, or has understood, or will, i.e., which is not *an explanation for someone*. In the primary case, the level of understanding is that of the person addressed. The notion of "an (or the) explanation of X" in the abstract makes sense just insofar as it makes sense to suppose a standardized context.[9]

[7] Dray, *op. cit.*, p. 75.
[8] Michael Scriven, "Truisms as the Grounds for Historical Explanations," in Patrick Gardiner (ed.), *Theories of History* (Free Press, New York, 1959), p. 452.
[9] "Explanations, Predictions, and Laws," in Herbert Feigl and Grover Maxwell (eds.), *Minnesota Studies in the Philosophy of Science*, vol. III (University of Minnesota Press, Minneapolis, 1962), p. 205, author's italics.

Scriven does not distinguish between the notion of an explanation$_D$ of something for someone and the notion of an explanation$_F$ of something by someone as we have done. He might not be willing to grant this distinction, but it is well to note that he could grant it yet maintain as he does that explanation is, in effect, a context-bound affair; for explanations$_F$ of something by someone are context-bound, just as explanations$_D$ of something for someone are. Is he right, however, in his claim that the notion of an explanation of X in the abstract, that is to say, a context-free notion of explanation, makes sense just insofar as it makes sense to suppose a standardized context? It depends, of course, on what he means by this. If all he is saying is that a context-free notion of explanation will not correspond to actual cases of explanation, he is correct. It will not, any more than a context-free notion of deduction will correspond to actual deductive arguments or a context-free notion of proof will correspond to actual proofs.[10] But if he is saying that philosophers cannot discuss or analyze a context-free notion of explanation or else cannot discuss it without taking some context into account, he is, I think, mistaken. Philosophers do in fact deal with abstractions and artificial constructs—for example, a context-free notion of deductive argument—and, moreover, they have every right to do so. In this respect they are like scientists.

No one objects if a scientist abstracts from "reality," if he deals with constructs. It is difficult to see what objection there can be to a philosopher's doing this. So long as a philosopher does not claim to be talking about explaining$_R$ something, explaining$_T$ something to someone, an explanation$_F$ of something by someone, or an explanation$_D$ of something for someone—in other words about some context-bound notion of explanation—when he talks of an explanation "in the abstract" we would do well to ask not whether his account of the construct corresponds to our everyday experience—of course it will not—but whether the construct is a useful or fruitful one. If it is, concern with it would seem to be justified; if it is

---

[10] See May Brodbeck, "Explanation, Prediction and 'Imperfect Knowledge,'" in Feigl and Maxwell (eds.), *op. cit.*, pp. 237–238; Carl G. Hempel, "Aspects of Scientific Explanation," in *Aspects of Scientific Explanation and Other Essays in the Philosophy of Science* (Free Press, New York, 1965), p. 426, for discussions of this point.

not, the construct might better be abandoned. In either event, attempts to bind it to some context could seem to be misguided.

Scriven speaks of explanation as a *syntactical* notion (he denies that it is this); others have spoken of it as a *logical* or *formal* notion. These labels capture one important aspect of a context-free notion of explanation, but they are misleading, for they carry with them the suggestion that the aspect they capture is the only important aspect. As we will see in a moment, it is not. For convenience's sake, I will call the context-free notion of explanation that Scriven has attacked and that I am defending here an *explanation of something*. This notion can be described by a form of the sort used above, as follows:

X is an explanation of E.

This explanation notion involves simply a relation between a sentence or sentences, X, and some thing or things, E. No relation with persons is involved. Now since an explanation of something involves a relation between sentences and the world, considerations which are not strictly speaking syntactical or logical or formal arise: for example, one may ask whether the sentences X are true. Such considerations may be called empirical. To be sure, syntactical or logical considerations also arise, for E can itself be described in sentences so that an explanation of something may be said to involve a relation between sentences and sentences (the sentences X and a description of E), as well as between sentences and the world. For example, one may ask whether the sentence describing E follows deductively from the sentences X as well as whether the sentences X are true. But since an explanation of something has an empirical aspect as well as a syntactical or logical aspect, the ordinary labels will not do. Let us, therefore, call the notion of an explanation of something *semantic* rather than syntactic or logical or formal and let us use the subscript "S" when referring to an explanation of something to remind ourselves of its *semantic* nature.

In saying that an explanation$_S$ of something involves "simply" a relation between X and E, I do not mean to suggest that the relation between sentences and the things they describe is one that can be easily specified.[11] It should be noted, however, that the description of an explanation$_S$ of something by the form "X is an explanation of E" leaves open the question of the nature of this relation, just as it leaves open the question of the nature of the relation between X and the description of E. To say that empirical and logical considerations are relevant to the analysis of an explanation$_S$ of something is not to predetermine what empirical and logical requirements will be placed on it. I have said that it is appropriate to ask if the sentences are true, but I do not mean to suggest by this that I think they must be true if they are to constitute an explanation$_S$ of something.

An explanation$_D$ of something for someone, like an explanation$_S$ of something, involves sentences, yet it is a pragmatic notion since the sentences are for someone. In an explanation$_D$ of something for someone, unlike an explanation$_S$ of something, the sentences are directed to some audience. It is natural, therefore, that considerations that are totally irrelevant to the analysis of an explanation$_S$ of something will be relevant to any analysis which attempts to specify the conditions which must be met if something is to qualify as an explanation$_D$ of something for someone. Consider, for example, an explanation$_D$ of something for someone in French. To determine the adequacy of this explanation$_D$ we must, among other things, find out if the audience understands French. I am not suggesting that if the audience does understand French this explanation$_D$ is therefore adequate, or that if the audience does not understand French this explanation$_D$ is therefore inadequate; I am suggesting, however, that the language of X must be taken into consideration by one judging the adequacy of an explanation$_D$ of something for someone, whereas this is not the case in connection with an explanation$_S$ of something.

It would be a mistake to suppose, however, that because an explanation$_D$ of something for someone is a pragmatic notion, empirical and logical considerations are not relevant to its analysis. An

---

[11] For a discussion of the notion of *aboutness*, see Nelson Goodman, "About," *Mind*, 70:1–24, 1961; Carl G. Hempel discusses the puzzle of "about" in "Deductive-Nomological vs. Statistical Explanation," in Feigl and Maxwell (eds.), *op. cit.*, pp. 119–121.

explanation$_D$ of something for someone involves sentences X which bear some relation to something E and also to the description of E. It is not the case that any old relation between X and E or between X and the description of E will do; or to put it another way, it is not the case that all discourse directed toward an audience in the proper way—whatever that turns out to be—constitutes explanations$_D$ for that audience. Myths, lies, and irrelevancies, for example, might meet whatever pragmatic criteria we placed on an explanation of something for someone$_D$, yet on most —although, as I will argue in Chapter 4, not all—occasions they would not qualify as explanations$_D$ of something for someone. Logical and empirical, that is, semantic, criteria as well as pragmatic criteria must be met if discourse is to count as an explanation$_D$ of something for someone.

The distinction commonly made between sentences and statements may shed light on the distinction I am drawing between an explanation$_S$ of something and an explanation$_D$ of something for someone. According to John Austin, a statement is a "historic event," that is, an utterance by someone to an audience, whereas a sentence is a group of words independent of context.[12] Sentences are used to make statements. As we have seen, both an explanation$_S$ of something and an explanation$_D$ of something for someone involve sentences. But since the sentences of explanations$_D$ are *for* someone, explanations$_D$ involve the *use* of sentences. Strictly speaking, then, an explanation$_D$ of something for someone is a statement. Since an explanation$_S$ of something, on the other hand, is a nonpragmatic notion, it does not involve the use of sentences; by hypothesis the sentences of an explanation$_S$ of something are independent of any context. Thus an explanation of something is not a statement but a sentence or set of sentences.[13]

Those who see the pragmatic dimension of explanation as cen-

[12] "Truth," *Proceedings of the Aristotelian Society,* supp. vol. 24:111–128, 1950. Reprinted in George Pitcher (ed.), *Truth* (Prentice-Hall, Englewood Cliffs, N.J., 1964), see p. 20.

[13] It should be noted that Austin denies that the notion of truth applies to sentences ["Truth," in Pitcher (ed.), *op. cit.,* pp. 20ff.], yet I am claiming that an explanation$_S$ of something must meet certain empirical requirements, for example, a truth or high confirmation requirement. In Austin's view truth applies to statements, not sentences. It seems to me, however, that Austin has by no means proved his point and that the

tering on the "forness" of explanations, that is on their being *for* someone, may tend to overlook the fact that an explanation$_S$ of something and an explanation$_F$ of something by someone are two different things. To be sure, an explanation$_F$ of something by someone is like an explanation$_S$ of something in that it is not *for* anyone. Thus the very characteristic which distinguishes it so sharply from an explanation$_D$ of something for someone is one it shares with an explanation$_S$ of something. But an explanation$_F$ of something by someone is a statement, for it is a "historic event"— an utterance *by* someone although not necessarily *to* some audience. Thus it is quite distinct from and ought not to be confused with an explanation$_S$ of something. An explanation$_F$ of something by someone must, of course, meet logical and empirical, that is, semantic, criteria, for not any old utterance will constitute an explanation$_F$. But this is true also of an explanation$_D$ of something for someone, and no one doubts that an explanation$_D$ is distinct from an explanation$_S$ of something. Myths, lies, and irrelevancies will not, except perhaps under special circumstances, qualify as explanations$_F$ but this is not to say that an explanation$_F$ of E will "look" or "sound" like an explanation$_S$ of E. Considerations of context may militate against this sort of identity just as they may in the case of an explanation$_D$ of something for someone.

3 *The Need for Clarity*

In all, then, we have uncovered five distinct explanation notions, four of which are pragmatic and one of which is not pragmatic but is what I am calling semantic:

(R) A explains E.
(T) A explains E to B.
(F) X is an explanation of E given by A.
(D) X is an explanation of E for A.
(S) X is an explanation of E.

---

question of the real bearers of truth is still wide open. See Samuel Gorovitz and Ron G. Williams, *Philosophical Analysis: An Introduction to Its Language and Techniques* (Random House, New York, 1963), chap. IV, for a brief but illuminating discussion of this question.

There may well be other explanation notions besides these, for our fivefold distinction was introduced for purposes of clarification only and is not intended to be exhaustive. I hope that I have set forth here those explanation notions which are of particular theoretical importance for discussions of explanation in relation to education. Since discussions of explanation in education quite naturally look to philosophical accounts of explanation for guidance, the explanation notions I have singled out for attention are the ones which philosophers seem to have been talking about and too often tangling up in their discussions of explanation in noneducational contexts.

Some of the distinctions set forth here have of course been recognized by philosophers.[14] To my knowledge, however, only one writer has given a systematic analysis of "to explain" and "explanation," [15] and no one has stressed sufficiently the importance of maintaining these distinctions in talking about explanation and understanding. Yet the need for making such distinctions is great. Otherwise discussions of explanation may shift from one no-

---

[14] For example, Jonathan Cohen limits his discussion of explanation to the "logical category," in effect what I have called explanations$_S$ of something, and explicitly excludes the "psychological category"; "Teleological Explanation," *Proceedings of the Aristotelian Society*, 51:259–260, 1950–1951. William Dray, in discussing the ordinary meaning of "explain," distinguishes between giving "an explanation for so-and-so" and giving "the explanation"; his distinction may be taken as more or less parallel to my distinction between an explanation$_S$ of something and an explanation$_D$ of something for someone; *op. cit.*, p. 74. Jack Pitt, in distinguishing "the problem of explicating the concept of explanation, i.e., of clarifying the formal features of this concept, from the problem of investigating the empirical phenomena of explaining as an act of communication," in relation to some misunderstandings of the regularity theory, presumably has our distinction between an explanation$_S$ of something and explaining$_T$ something to someone in mind; "Generalizations in Historical Explanation," *The Journal of Philosophy*, 56:585, 1959. May Brodbeck, in defending the regularity theory, argues that its critics are discussing a "psychological sense" of "explain"—presumably our explaining$_T$ something to someone or our explanation$_D$ of something to someone—instead of a nonpsychological sense, presumably our explanation$_S$ of something; *op. cit.*, pp. 235ff. Carl G. Hempel distinguishes between a pragmatic and a nonpragmatic concept of explanation; "Aspects of Scientific Explanation," *op. cit.*, pp. 425ff.

[15] Bromberger, *op. cit.*

tion to another without warning and conclusions about one notion will be drawn on the basis of an analysis of another notion. The literature on explanation in history, for example, abounds with this sort of fallacious argument.

Let me illustrate the kind of mistake I am referring to with one brief example.[16] According to the regularity theory of explanation in history—the theory referred to earlier as the "standard theory" —explanations necessarily involve laws. One critic of this theory has argued against the law requirement on the grounds that historians do not use laws in arriving at their explanations. Now let us grant for the sake of argument that the critic's description of historical practice is correct. It does not follow from this fact about practice that the law requirement is a mistaken one, for the regularity theory does not purport to describe historical practice at all. In effect the critic has argued from an analysis of the pragmatic notion of explaining$_R$ something to the analysis of the semantic notion of an explanation$_S$ of something. But this is unwarranted.

Curiously enough, writers on education have tended to accept without question the very law requirement on explanation which philosophers have been vigorously attacking in recent years.[17] In their discussions of explanation in education these writers have made—or at least they appear to have made—the same sort of mistake that philosophers of history have made. For these educators, convinced that explanations involve laws,[18] have argued that the

[16] This illustration is taken from P. H. Nowell-Smith, "Are Historical Events Unique?" *Proceedings of the Aristotelian Society*, 57:107-160, 1956-1957. Instances of this sort of argument—that is to say, arguments from the nature of the historian's practice to the analysis of the notion of an explanation$_S$ of something—can be found in Dray, *op. cit.*; in Scriven, "Truisms as the Grounds for Historical Explanations"; and in almost every other criticism of the regularity theory of explanation in history.

[17] For attacks on and defenses of the law requirement, see n. 1, Chap. 1.

[18] See, for example, Leonard F. Swift, "Explanation," in B. Othanel Smith and Robert H. Ennis (eds.), *Language and Concepts of Education* (Rand McNally, Chicago, 1961), pp. 179-194; Byron G. Massialas and C. Benjamin Cox, *Inquiry in Social Studies* (McGraw-Hill, New York, 1966), pp. 100-103. See, however, Leslie R. Perry, "Objective and Practical History," *Proceedings of the Annual Conference* (Philosophy of Education Society of Great Britain, 1966), pp. 35-48, for a discussion of the teaching of history coupled with a rejection of the regularity theory of ex-

teacher should state—or else should have the students state—laws, and they have criticized the "traditional" classroom for failing on this count. It does not follow, however, from the fact—if it is one— that the explanations the regularity theory is concerned with involve laws, that laws need be or should be stated in the classroom. If the teacher is explaining$_T$ to the student, for example, why the North and South fought a war, he may cite a law in his explanation$_D$ for the student but he need not; if the teacher has the student explain$_R$ for himself why the North and South fought a war, the student may cite a law in his explanation$_F$ but he need not in order to have explained$_R$ something.

Since laws *need not* be cited in the explanations$_D$ the teacher gives or the explanations$_F$ the students arrive at, it surely does not follow that they *should* be cited. It is only when the semantic notion, the one the regularity theory provides an account of, and pragmatic notions of explanation are not clearly distinguished that such a conclusion even appears reasonable. Perhaps laws should be cited in the classroom by the student or the teacher, but if so this normative position needs to be argued for and cannot be supported simply by logical analysis.[19]

Now it is true that in stressing laws in explanation some writers are recommending not merely that laws be *cited* in the classroom but that they become a *focus* of study in, for example, social studies.[20] This curriculum proposal may or may not be a good proposal, but one must recognize that it is not justified solely by an appeal to the logical structure of explanation. Clearly, even if ex-

---

planation. Note that Perry seems to reject the regularity theory on the grounds that it does not describe the historian's procedure accurately. As we will see, advocates of the theory do not intend it as a description of actual practice. Perry may be viewed, then, as making the same sort of mistake as other critics of the theory, namely that of arguing from an analysis of some pragmatic notion of explanation to an analysis of a semantic notion.

[19] William K. Frankena has an illuminating discussion of educational reasoning in "A Model for Analyzing a Philosophy of Education," *The High School Journal*, 2:8–13, 1966; reprinted with author's revisions in Jane R. Martin (ed.), *Readings in the Philosophy of Education: A Study of Curriculum* (Allyn and Bacon, Boston, 1970).

[20] Massialas and Cox, *op. cit.*, for example.

planations$_S$ of something necessarily involve laws, it does not follow from that alone that laws should be emphasized in the curriculum. At the same time, in view of the barrage of criticism of the law requirement by philosophers of history, it is well to note that just as the curriculum proposal in question does not follow from the law requirement on explanation, so it does not depend on that requirement. Laws play a number of different roles in inquiry [21] and may well deserve an important place in the curriculum independently of any theory of explanation.

Unless the various notions of explanation are kept distinct, it is all too easy to move from one to another in discussion without realizing it. It is also all but impossible to understand, let alone evaluate, certain general claims about the role of explanation in education, for example that the function of education "is to get students to arrive at explanations and the grounds for making explanations on their own" [22] and that the educator's purpose is "to nurture the powers of explanation." [23] It should be equally clear that the distinctions must be maintained if various general claims about the notion of explanation and its proper analysis are to be understood and evaluated.

Consider Dray's claim, mentioned earlier, that a proper account of explanation cannot be given without bringing out its pragmatic dimension; or consider the related claim of Michael Scriven that explanation is not a syntactical but a pragmatic notion. The latter claim carries the implication that explanation is solely a pragmatic notion, but this is false for, as we have seen, an explanation$_S$ of something is a semantic notion. A literal interpretation of the former claim is not acceptable either, for an account of explanation which is limited to an explanation$_S$ of something, hence to its non-pragmatic features, is perfectly *proper;* it is simply not *complete.*

These claims, although literally false, may be construed as slogans to be evaluated in terms of their practical import rather than

[21] For a discussion of the roles played by laws in inquiry, see Israel Scheffler, *The Anatomy of Inquiry* (Knopf, New York, 1965), part I.
[22] Reginald D. Archambault, "Teaching and Explanation," *Proceedings of the Philosophy of Education Society,* 21st Annual Meeting, 1965, p. 24.
[23] Marc Belth, *Education as a Discipline* (Allyn and Bacon, Boston, 1965), p. 124.

their literal meaning.[24] As slogans, the claims direct attention to the notions of an explanation$_D$ of something for someone, explaining$_T$ something to someone, explaining$_R$ something, and an explanation$_F$ of something by someone, and direct attention away from the notion of an explanation$_S$ of something. Now it cannot be denied that philosophers have, until recently, ignored the pragmatic notions of explanation. Yet, valuable as it may be to call attention to these notions, there is no substitute for careful analysis of them and of their relationship to an explanation$_S$ of something. It is all too easy to mistake the function of slogans and to be misled by them.

Once we recognize the claim to legitimacy of what I am calling the semantic notion of explanation and accept these claims for what they are, we are able to place in perspective a vast amount of philosophical literature on explanation. I refer, of course, to the literature on the regularity theory of explanation. This theory stems from the work of such philosophers as Hume and J. S. Mill. It has been refined and set forth by a number of contemporary philosophers and attacked by many more.[25] One recurring criticism of the theory is that it does not provide an adequate account of the pragmatic dimension of explanation. The theory does formulate or describe logical and empirical conditions which explanations of events must meet.[26] It takes no stand, however, on whether there are pragmatic conditions to be met by explanations, let alone what they are *if* there are some. The theory, in other words, ignores questions of context. It is a theory of a context-free notion of explanation—a theory, if you like, of an explanation$_S$ of something.[27]

Unfortunately, too few students of the regularity theory have

[24] For a discussion of slogans, see Israel Scheffler, *The Language of Education* (Charles C Thomas, Springfield, Ill., 1960), chap. 2; B. Paul Komisar and James E. McClellan, "The Logic of Slogans," in Smith and Ennis (eds.), *op. cit.*, pp. 195–214.

[25] See n. 1, Chap. 1.

[26] Carl G. Hempel and Paul Oppenheim offer the theory as an account of the explanation of laws as well; "Studies in the Logic of Explanation," in Hempel, *op. cit.*

[27] "It is this nonpragmatic conception of explanation which the covering-law models are meant to explicate." Hempel, "Aspects of Scientific Explanation," p. 426.

realized that it gives an account not of one or more of our pragmatic notions of explanation but of our semantic notion. It is a common error to take the regularity theory to be an account of someone's practice. Those who criticize it as a theory of explanation in history are particularly prone to making this kind of mistake. Some argue from the nature of explaining$_R$ something to the falsity of the theory; others argue from the nature of explaining$_T$ something to someone to the falsity of the theory. Arguments of this sort are invalid since, even if a critic's analysis of explaining$_R$ something or explaining$_T$ something to someone is correct, nothing follows from such an analysis about the nature of explanations$_S$ of something, the very thing with which the regularity theory is concerned. Some critics, recognizing that the theory is not a description of practice at all, conclude that it is a prescription for practice and object to it as such. They are, in effect, making the same sort of mistake as those who consider it to be a description of practice, for they too take the theory to be a theory of one or more of the pragmatic notions of explanation. What both groups fail to recognize is that the theory is a theory of a nonpragmatic notion of explanation and hence constitutes neither a description of nor a prescription for practice.

A defense of the regularity theory of explanation is not my purpose here. Explaining$_T$ something to someone is the explanation notion of all those we have distinguished which has the closest ties to teaching and education, and it is on this notion that I want to focus. In passing, however, I would like to note two things about the regularity theory, or rather about criticisms of it. The first should by now be obvious. It is that criticisms of the regularity theory based on arguments from someone's practice miss their target. They need not, therefore, be taken seriously by advocates of the theory.[28] The second is that it is legitimate to ask whether the context-free notion of explanation on which regularity theorists have been spending their time and energy is worth the trouble (is it a useful or fruitful construct?) and also to ask how the context-free notion of explanation relates to the various context-bound notions of explanation. These two questions are, I think, related,

[28] Not all criticisms of the theory are of this sort, however.

for one way to show that an explanation$_S$ of something is a useful construct (theoretically useful, that is) is to show how it relates to the context-bound or pragmatic notions of explanation.

For example, consider for just a moment the context-bound notion of explaining$_R$ something. One way to view someone who is trying to explain$_R$ something is, in part at least, as seeking an explanation$_S$ of that thing, and one way to view someone who has succeeded in explaining$_R$ something is, in part at least, as having reached conclusions, produced results, come up with findings—that is to say, given an explanation$_F$—which can be formulated as or transformed into an explanation$_S$ of that thing. In Chapter 6 I will discuss the relationship between explaining$_T$ something to someone and an explanation$_S$ of something and also the relationship between an explanation$_D$ of something for someone and an explanation$_S$ of something. To put the matter very roughly but I hope not too misleadingly for the present, we may view one who is explaining$_T$ something to someone not merely as trying to get his explainee to understand the thing in question but as trying to get him to understand it in terms of some explanation$_S$ of it. Moreover, and again this is a very rough way of putting it, we may view the explanation$_D$ an explainer$_T$ gives his explainee as being identified with or transformable into an explanation$_S$ of the thing in question.

In Chapter 6 it will, I think, become clear that a semantic or context-free notion of explanation has theoretical value in that it not only helps us to understand the pragmatic or context-bound notions of explanation but also helps us to see relationships among them. However, a defense of a context-free notion of explanation is no more my purpose here than is a defense of the regularity theory. I have drawn attention to it and to the regularity theory simply to make it clear that the adequacy of this theory is not at issue here. The topic at hand is the nature of explaining$_T$ something to someone, and it is important to realize that we can satisfy ourselves about this without committing ourselves on the nature of an explanation$_S$ of something. To be sure, in Chapter 6 use will be made of the notion of an explanation$_S$ of something, but this in itself is compatible with neutrality about what constitutes an explanation$_S$ of something. Does an explanation$_S$ of something necessarily involve some law or laws? According to the regularity theory it does; according to some critics of the theory it does not. Fortunately we need not commit ourselves on this issue or, indeed, on the other substantive issues concerning the regularity theory, for it is possible to give an account of explaining something to someone which is compatible with the regularity theory but which in no way depends on the truth of that theory.

My reason for saying it is fortunate that we need not commit ourselves on these issues is that they are complex and difficult and were we to examine them adequately we might never get to the point of considering seriously the activity of explaining$_T$ something to someone. As a matter of fact, I wonder if this is not one reason why there has been so little attention paid to explaining$_T$ something to someone. Even those philosophers who have complained that the "pragmatic dimension" of explanation has been overlooked have put most of their energies into finding fault with the regularity theory of explanation rather than into developing a theory of one or more pragmatic notions of explanation. Let us put the regularity theory out of our thoughts, not because it is false—it may not be—but because it is irrelevant for our purposes. Let us examine explaining$_T$ something to someone and understanding each on its own merits and with an open mind, always remembering that whatever our findings, they will give comfort neither to the regularity theorists nor to the antiregularity theorists.

Part Two

EXPLAINING
SOMETHING
TO SOMEONE

Chapter 3

EXPLAINING
AS GAP FILLING

William Dray has proposed "the model of the continuous series" as an account of historical explanation.[1] Whether or not this model is intended as an account of explaining something to someone is difficult to say, but that is the way I will take it here.[2] In view of Dray's interest in "who says it to whom" it is certainly plausible to construe the model in this way, and Dray's lack of interest in the semantic "dimension" of explanation reinforces this

[1] *Laws and Explanation in History* (Oxford University Press, London, 1957), chap. 3. Page references in the text of this chapter will be to this book.
[2] The subscript "T" was introduced to help the reader distinguish talk about explaining something to someone from talk about other explanation notions. Since from now on the discussion will focus on explaining something to someone and the other notions of explanation will enter into it only occasionally, it will no longer be necessary to use the subscript "T." In those cases where one of the other explaining notions is at issue, we will of course use the appropriate identifying subscript.

interpretation of it. Moreover, the continuous-series model makes most sense when it is construed as an account of explaining something to someone. Indeed, despite the fact that the model as offered by Dray is held to apply to explanation in history—not to all explanation in history but to the explanation of some events—it illuminates crucial *general* features of explaining something to someone. We will examine the continuous-series model here, then, for what it has to say about explaining something to someone in general and will ignore the occupation of the explainer and the nature of the thing being explained even if we thereby go beyond Dray's own intent.

1 The Case of the Engine Seizure

The continuous-series model is presented mainly by means of an example, the engine seizure of a motorcar. The formulation of the model is, therefore, anything but systematic. We are left not only with the problem of determining exactly which notion or notions of explanation the continuous-series model is a model of, but also with the problem of determining exactly what Dray takes the criteria or conditions of adequacy of explanation to be.

Dray asks whether "It's due to a leak in the oil reservoir" is an explanation of the seizure and the reply he gives is, "It depends on who says it and to whom—or, to put the matter in more formal terms, it depends on what else is presupposed, or contextually supplied" (p. 67). To an assistant mechanic who knows about internal combustion engines, it may be an explanation, but to Dray, who knows little about engines, it is not one: "If I am to understand the seizure, I shall need to be told something about the functioning of an auto engine, and the essential role in it of the lubricating system. I shall have to be capable of a certain amount of elementary trouble tracing" (p. 67). An explanation, then, gives a continuous series of happenings; it breaks down an event into a sum of sub-sequences which lead up to the event. This series may be a temporal one but it need not be (p. 73); the happenings may be observable but they need not be (p. 80).

Now the sum of sub-sequences must "raise no further demand

for explanation in that particular context" (p. 69) ; they must be "hat-doffing" phenomena in that they do not puzzle us and we ask no questions about them. We have here what may be called a pragmatic condition of adequacy; pragmatic because what is hat-doffing or acceptable for one person may not be for another. We seek in vain, however, for some indication that the continuous-series model formulates any logical or empirical conditions of adequacy. If we give the model the benefit of the doubt, we can construe the notion of a continuous series of events leading up to an event in such a way that it rules out as explanations accounts of imaginary happenings, for example, a gremlin tinkering with Dray's engine, and actual but irrelevant happenings, for example, a famine in India: imaginary happenings would not be *events,* and irrelevant happenings, although events, would not *lead up to* the event in question. We can, then, view the model as acknowledging implicitly that explanations must meet semantic conditions. But even on this perhaps too generous reading, the model leaves open the question of the proper analysis of these conditions.

Dray insists that his model provides "objective standards" by which to judge whether or not something is an explanation (pp. 74–75) and it is well to recognize that there is no reason why pragmatic standards such as hat-doffingness cannot be objective. Indeed, they can be considered objective in at least two respects: objective in that there is wide agreement that they *are* standards which explanations must meet; objective in that when the standards are applied to particular cases, there is wide agreement about whether the particular cases are or are not explanations. But to say that pragmatic standards can be objective is not to say that they can replace logical and empirical standards. In his zeal to show that explanation really does have an irreducible pragmatic dimension, Dray more or less ignores the fact that it has another dimension. Yet as we saw in Chapter 2, explanation has both an irreducible pragmatic dimension and an irreducible semantic dimension. A single model or theory of explanation need not capture both, and the continuous-series model is not to be condemned if it fails to capture the semantic dimension; but it is always well to remember that both dimensions are there to be captured.

As we have seen, the regularity theory is limited in range of application to the semantic notion of explanation. I do not think Dray himself is clear on this point, however, for in presenting his continuous-series model he more than once gives the impression that it is in competition with the regularity theory (for example, pp. 72 ff.). But since the regularity theory focuses exclusively on logical and empirical criteria while the continuous-series model focuses exclusively on pragmatic criteria, it is difficult to see how the two could be in competition or in conflict. They might be *thought* to be in conflict by one who misunderstood the scope of the regularity theory or by one who wrongly supposed the whole endeavor of formulating logical and empirical conditions of adequacy for explanation to be misguided. If we avoid these errors, however, we find that the two theories are compatible with one another rather than in conflict. If the continuous-series model is to be considered a useful corrective to the regularity theory, it is not because it is an alternative to that theory or because it invalidates some portion of that theory; rather it is because it brings to our attention aspects of explanation which we have hitherto ignored.

In particular, the continuous-series model directs our attention to certain features of explaining something to someone. It brings to light the fact that for someone to understand something, for example, Dray's engine seizure, it is not sufficient that he have an item of information such as "There is a leak in the oil reservoir." The information must be connected or linked up with the topic in question clearly enough so that he can go from the item to the topic without encountering huge gaps. The continuous-series model, moreover, brings to light the fact that people vary in their ability to connect an event and an item of information. A series is something that can be shorter or longer; and just so, some people require a fuller explanation$_D$ than others if they are to link up some item of information to the topic in question.

As the continuous-series model is presented, however, the role of the continuous series itself in explaining something to someone is not entirely clear. Nor is it clear exactly what in any particular case is to be taken as the thing to be explained. Nor is the notion of hat-doffingness entirely clear. Let us consider each of these topics in turn in the hope that some conditions of explaining something to someone will emerge.

2 The Continuous Series

Recall that "It's due to a leak in the oil reservoir" may be an explanation for the assistant mechanic. Are we to assume that it may be an explanation because the two events, oil leak and engine seizure, constitute a continuous series for him? If so, then I think it fair to conclude that, according to the continuous-series model, an explanation$_D$ of something for someone must contain a description of a continuous series of events; and since we are assuming here that someone is explaining something to someone, it is fair to conclude further that the explainer must cite or mention a continuous series of events. Given this interpretation of Dray's model, the following necessary condition for saying that someone A explained something E to someone B can be abstracted:

Continuous-series Condition (*1*) : A cited a continuous series of events leading up to E to B.

This interpretation of the model carries a certain amount of plausibility. Dray does seem to be assuming that a continuous series of events would have to be *mentioned* in an explanatory account of the engine seizure and he speaks of the leak-to-seizure *sequence* (p. 68). No doubt a two-event series could be viewed as a limiting case of a continuous series. However, another interpretation seems to be consistent with many of Dray's remarks. According to this alternative view we may assume that the two events, oil leak and engine seizure, do *not* constitute a continuous series, yet we may take "It's due to a leak in the oil reservoir" to be an explanation for the assistant mechanic if he can himself connect the leak to the seizure by means of a continuous series of events. The assistant mechanic knows all about internal combustion engines; presumably he can do what Dray, a layman, can only do after he is given a more extended explanation$_D$, namely envisage a continuous series of happenings *"between* the leak and the engine seizure" (p. 68, italics added).

On this construal, a two-event sequence would not be a continuous series and the explainer need not cite a continuous series. The series would play a role in relation to his aim or goal rather than his discourse. Dray says, "It seems to me that my understanding of the engine seizure is very directly related to the fact that I can now *trace the course of events by which it came about"* (p. 68, author's italics). This suggests that being able to trace the course of events leading up to the seizure is to be conceived of as a criterion of understanding the seizure or else as a test or sign of understanding the seizure. In either case, we would have a necessary condition for saying that A explained E to B that would be very different from (1) above. We may formulate it as follows:

Continuous-series Condition (2): A tried to get B to be able to trace a continuous series of events leading up to E.

Continuous-series condition (2) is neutral on what A does and says to get B into this desirable state. A might or might not cite the continuous series which he wants B to be able to trace. Continuous-series condition (2), then, leaves the door open for A to cite a law or theory, and one suspects that Dray wants to avoid this. It must be remembered, however, that to allow A to cite a law or theory is not to require him to do so; and more important, even if A were required to do so, the regularity theory would not thereby receive support. We are concerned here with the explainer's discourse whereas the regularity theory is directed to something else altogether. If we interpret the continuous series as functioning in relation to the explainer's goal rather than his discourse, we must recognize that there may be a number of ways of achieving the goal, including citation of laws and theories. Perhaps not every way of trying to achieve the goal of B's being able to trace a continuous series of events leading up to E does constitute a case of A's *explaining* to B. But it does not follow that we must therefore adopt continuous-series condition (1). Other conditions may constrain A in the way he goes about trying to achieve his goal. Continuous-series conditions (1) and (2) can both be necessary conditions of explaining something to someone but need not both be. Either one can be a necessary condition of that activity independently of the other.

Let us put aside the question of whether continuous-series condition (1) or (2) or both capture Dray's intent, and examine these two conditions on their own merits. Consider continuous-series condition (1). It is too restrictive to be a condition of adequacy for explaining something to someone even where that something is an event. Surely if A does cite a continuous series of events he may be explaining E to B, but surely he can be explaining E to B if he does other things instead. For one thing, there is no good reason for requiring that A must cite *events*, let alone a continuous series of events, in order to explain E to B. Why can he not cite, for example, a state of a person or a condition of a society? But further, even if A does cite an event there is no good reason for requiring that he must supply a *series* of events to link that event to E in those cases where the two-event "sequence" is not a continuous series for B. Why cannot A, for example, connect the event to E by presenting a theory?

Continuous-series condition (2) can be criticized on similar grounds. Granted that in explaining E to B, A wants to get B to understand E, it does not seem that A must therefore be trying to get B to be able to trace a continuous series of events leading up to E. Dray is quite right that more is involved in understanding E, where E is due to something, C, than simply being aware that E *is* due to C: connections must be made, links envisaged, gaps filled between E and C. But it is a mistake to require that C be an event, or that, where C is an event, E and C must be connected by a continuous series of events. Suppose the event A is explaining to B is the outbreak of the Civil War. A might be trying to get B to be able to trace the course of events leading up to the Civil War. But could he not instead be trying to get B to be able to connect up the Civil War to, for example, various social and economic and geographic conditions? And need *these* connections be made by virtue of a continuous series of events?

Being able to trace a continuous series of events leading up to E is not a generally necessary condition for understanding E any more than it is a sufficient condition for understanding E. One may be able to trace a continuous series of events leading up to E yet not see the connection between them and E, for one may have learned quite mechanically to do such tracing. One may understand E yet not be able to trace a continuous series of events leading up to E, because E is not due to an event or is connected in some other way to an event. Both continuous-series condition (2) and continuous-series condition (1), then, must be rejected as necessary conditions of explaining something to someone.

But if the continuous series notion is too narrow to function as a necessary condition of explaining something to someone, it still should not be dismissed lightly, for in directing our attention to the crucial role that understanding plays in relation to explaining something to someone and to the importance in understanding of seeing connections between things, it points to what may in fact constitute a necessary condition of explaining something to someone.

3 Shifting the Question

One aspect of the continuous-series model deserves particular attention. In arguing against the regularity theory Dray says:

> The general law, "Whenever your oil leaks out your engine seizes up," does not explain the fact that my engine seized up *after my oil leaked out*—in the context of puzzlement envisaged. But reference to a series of facts constituting the story of what happened between the leakage of the oil and the seizure of the engine does explain the seizure (p. 70, italics added).

In an earlier passage he says, "But this would make me none the wiser as to *why an oil leak should have led to the seizure* . . ." (p. 67, italics added). Dray's original explanandum event [3] is the engine seizure, not the engine seizure after the oil leaked out or the oil leak's having led to the seizure. Dray seems to have shifted

[3] That is, the event to be explained.

explanandum events and in doing so shifted the question, a move he himself disparages (pp. 71–72).

One cannot tell whether Dray shifted the question intentionally or without realizing it. One might expect that had he done it intentionally he would have gone to lengths to show that his shift was not the sort of shift he himself was subjecting to criticism. Be that as it may, when seen from the standpoint of Dray's attack on the regularity theory, the shift in explanandum event from engine seizure to oil leak's having led to the seizure looks like a blunder of major proportions. For the regularity theory does not purport to give an account of the explanation of "causal facts." Thus to argue, as Dray seems to, that the regularity theory fails as an account of explanation because an explanation of the engine's seizing up which meets its conditions does not explain *why the leak led to the engine's seizing up,* is to argue that the theory does not do what it never was intended to do.[4] Of course Dray might want to deny that in criticising the theory for failing to do what it was never intended to do, he was committing a major blunder. "I know that the regularity theory was never intended as an account of the explanation of 'causal facts,' " he might say. "That's exactly what's wrong with it. An account of the explanation of 'noncausal facts' such as the engine's seizing up must contain an account of the explanation of 'causal facts' such as the leak's having led to the seizure or it will be inadequate. The regularity theory does not contain such an account. It is inadequate for this reason."

The issue of whether, from the standpoint of his attack on the regularity theory, Dray's shift in question is or is not a blunder is well beyond the scope of this study. And so, for that matter, is the

[4] Morton White, *Foundations of Historical Knowledge* (Harper & Row, New York, 1965), pp. 21–22. For general discussions of the continuous-series model as an attack on the law requirement of the regularity theory, see Arthur C. Danto, *Analytical Philosophy of History* (Cambridge University Press, Cambridge, England, 1965), pp. 214–215; Carl G. Hempel, "Aspects of Scientific Explanation," in *Aspects of Scientific Explanation and Other Essays in the Philosophy of Science* (Free Press, New York, 1965), pp. 452–453; Maurice Mandelbaum, "Historical Explanation: The Problem of 'Covering Laws,' " *History and Theory,* 1:239–241, 1961.

question of Dray's intent. Let us drop these matters, therefore, and pursue our original purpose in discussing the continuous-series model, which was to gain insight into explaining something to someone. If the question shift embedded in that model is viewed from the standpoint of a theory or analysis of explaining something to someone instead of from the standpoint of a theory of an explanation$_S$ of something, Dray's shift in question takes on special significance. For the aim of explaining something to someone is understanding, and there is surely a good deal of initial plausibility to the supposition that a shift in question is essential if understanding is to be achieved. Let us, therefore, interpret the continuous-series model as making question shifting a necessary condition of explaining something to someone. In doing so we may well be going far beyond Dray's intent, but we may also be on the track of something rather important.

Like the continuous series, the question shift in the continuous-series model can be viewed either in relation to the explainer's discourse or in relation to his goal. In other words, we may abstract from Dray's model either of the following as a necessary condition for saying that A explained E to B:

Question-shifting Condition (*1*) : A told B not merely that E was due to C but why C led to E.
Question-shifting Condition (*2*) : A tried to help B to know the answer to the question "Why did C lead to E?" and not merely to the question "Why did E occur?"

It should be noted that on question-shifting condition (1), if A only says to B, "It's due to a leak in the oil reservoir," he will not have explained the engine seizure to B even though Dray grants that this may be an explanation for the assistant mechanic. This does not in itself vitiate (1), for perhaps if A says no more to B than that E was due to C, he has *not* explained E to B. I myself am inclined to think that he has not; that he has told B the answer to a question of the form "Why did E occur?", that is, told him why E occurred, perhaps even given him an explanation$_D$ of E, but not explained E to B.[5] Something more is required of the explainer, I think, but for reasons given earlier, that something more need not be the citing of a continuous series of events, and for reasons which will become clearer in the next chapter, that something more need not be the answer to a question of the form "Why did C lead to E?"

It is often assumed that explanations are answers to "why" questions.[6] But although they can be answers to "why" questions, they need not be. One can explain *what* the significance of something is, *how* something could possibly have happened, etc. Thus for A to have explained E to B, A need not have tried to get B to know the answer to the question "Why did E occur?" let alone the question "Why did C lead to E?"; he need not have told B that E was due to C, let alone told B why C led to E. Consider that the explanandum event chosen by an explainer A is a ritual in a primitive culture and that A wants to explain to B what function this ritual serves in that culture. The "initial" question (I will be calling it the *underlying* question in the next chapters) in such a case would take the form "What is the function of E?" and not "Why E?" or "Why did E occur?" Presumably the answer to this question would take the form "The function of E is F." But then the initial question might legitimately be shifted to "How does E accomplish F?" Or consider that A has chosen a civil disorder as his explanandum event and that A wants to explain to B what this disorder is. In this case his initial question would be of the form "What is E?" Presumably the answer would take the form "E is (really) an X" (for example, "The civil disorder is

<hr/>

[5] This point will be discussed in Chap. 6, sec. 4.

[6] Carl G. Hempel and Paul Oppenheim appear to be making this assumption when they say: "To explain the phenomena in the world of our experience, to answer the question 'why?' rather than only the question 'what?' is one of the foremost objectives of empirical science"; "Studies in the Logic of Explanation," in Hempel, *op. cit.* Marc Belth in *Education as a Discipline* (Allyn and Bacon, Boston, 1965), p. 124, and many others also appear to be making it. For a penetrating discussion of "why" questions and their relationship to explanation, see Sylvain Bromberger, "Why-questions," in *Mind and Cosmos: Essays in Contemporary Science and Philosophy,* vol. III in the University of Pittsburgh Series in the Philosophy of Science (University of Pittsburgh Press, Pittsburgh, 1966), pp. 86–111.

the first stage of a revolution"). But then the initial question could legitimately be shifted to a question of the form "By virtue of what characteristics of E do you judge that E is an X?"

Suppose, however, that the initial question which A answers for B (or tries to get B to know the answer to) is of the form "Why did E occur?" Must the question in this case at least be shifted to a question of the form "Why did C lead to E?" I do not think so. Consider that A wants to explain to B why dinosaurs became extinct. His initial question is, "Why did dinosaurs become extinct?" His answer is, "It was because their food ran out." Now B is sophisticated enough to know that *if* their food had run out, dinosaurs would have become extinct, but he does not believe that the food *did* run out. A can try to answer (or get B to know the answer to) the question "Why did the food running out lead to dinosaurs becoming extinct?" but there is not much point in doing so. He would do better to try to answer (or get B to know the answer to) a different question, such as "What evidence is there for believing that the food ran out?" or, perhaps, "Why did the food run out?"

Question-shifting condition (1) is more liberal than its continuous-series counterpart in that it is compatible with various ways of linking C to E. Citing a continuous series of events leading from C to E is perhaps one way of answering the question "Why did C lead to E?" but it is not the only way. Presumably a theory could do the job; perhaps other things could too. But this condition is nonetheless too narrow: the explainer need not in his discourse shift from "Why did E occur?" to "Why did C lead to E?" Other shifts are available to him and so are other initial questions. This is not to say that in a given context any shift at all is available to an explainer. A shift from "Why did my engine seize up?" to "What was the highest temperature in Peru last year?" is surely illegitimate in the context envisioned by Dray, and so no doubt are any number of other shifts, including some shifts to questions which are related in subject matter to the initial question. Thus, in saying that question-shifting condition (1) is not liberal enough, we ought not to be construed as leaving open the door to any and all shifts.

Question-shifting condition (2) is also more liberal than its continuous-series counterpart. To try to get B to know the answer to the question "Why did C lead to E?" may be to try to get him to be able to trace a continuous series of events leading from C to E, but it need not be. But question-shifting condition (2) also is too narrow: events need not be explained in terms of antecedent events, and when they are not explained thusly, it makes no sense to try to get B to know the answer to a question of the form "Why did C lead to E?" although it may make sense to try to get him to know the answer to some other sort of question, for example, a question of the form "What is the connection between E and C?"

Just as the notion of the continuous series, which Dray built into his model, is too narrow to function as a necessary condition of explaining something to someone, so also the question shift embedded in his model is too narrow to serve this purpose. Yet as in the case of the continuous series, the notion that explaining something to someone involves a shift in question ought not to be dismissed lightly. It may well be that some shift in question, although not necessarily Dray's, is necessary for explaining something to someone. This issue will come up again in Chapter 4, where we find incorporated into another analysis of explaining something to someone—one which seems on the surface at least to be very unlike the one we are attributing to Dray—a condition requiring that instruction be given.

4 Hat-doffingness

Let us concern ourselves now with the hat-doffing notion mentioned earlier. According to Dray, for the "subevents" which are intended to explain the "gross event" to constitute a continuous series for someone, they must be acceptable or "hat-doffing" to him; that is to say, they must not puzzle him, he must ask no questions of them. Whether we have here a condition which relates to the explainer's discourse or his goal depends on our interpretation of the role played by the continuous series. Hat-doffingness is evidently a necessary condition for something's being a continuous series; whatever role the continuous series itself plays in explaining something to someone, it is a continuous series for someone, B, only if the subevents are hat-doffing for B.

Although the hat-doffing notion enters into Dray's account as a criterion of a continuous series of events, its significance for explaining something to someone goes beyond its role as a criterion of a continuous series. Suppose, as I argued above, that the explainer A need not try to get B to be able to trace a continuous series of events; it might still be the case that whatever state he tried to get B into, the things he would want B to have information about would have to be hat-doffing for B. Thus hat-doffingness could play a role in relation to the explainer's discourse or goal even if continuous-series conditions (1) and (2) were rejected. We would do well, therefore, to examine the notion further.

Hat-doffing phenomena do not puzzle us; we ask no questions of them. There is a familiar ring about this. One widespread but relatively unexamined assumption about explanation is that it aims at resolving puzzlement. Another related assumption is that demands for explanation arise in a context of puzzlement.[7] In making hat-doffingness a criterion for something's being a continuous series, is Dray incorporating these assumptions into his model? Fortunately we need not try to settle the question of Dray's intent here. The problem for us is to determine how the notions of puz-

---

[7] Max Black appears to be making this assumption when he says: "Explanations are demanded for unusual or exceptional or puzzling events, *i.e.*, events that do not conform to expectations . . ."; see *Critical Thinking* (Prentice-Hall, New York, 1946), p. 348. D. J. O'Connor also holds this view; see *An Introduction to the Philosophy of Education* (Philosophical Library, New York, 1957), p. 82. On p. 82, O'Connor makes the former assumption explicit. Stephen Toulmin appears also to be making that assumption when he says that the special function of scientific explanation is, if anything, "to bring our past experience to bear upon our present and future expectations, in such a way as to 'save appearances' and turn the unexpected, as far as possible, into the expected"; see *An Examination of the Place of Reason in Ethics* (Cambridge University Press, Cambridge, England, 1950), p. 88. And Max Black states that the "value of explanation is not merely the negative one of dispelling puzzlement concerning an unexpected phenomenon"; *op. cit.*, p. 350. On the topic of explanation and puzzlement, see John Passmore, "Explanation in Everyday Life, in Science, and in History," *History and Theory*, 2:105–123, 1962.

zlement and explanation demands function in the context of the continuous-series model, and whether they are adequate to the task assigned them.

One point that requires clarification at the outset is the relationship between the notions of lack of puzzlement and lack of explanation demands.[8] If puzzlement were defined independently of explanation demands, then there would seem to be no reason why someone might not be puzzled about something yet ask no questions and demand no explanations of it. For example, he might be shy or afraid; or, even if he were not, he might be so very puzzled about the thing that he found it impossible to formulate questions or explanation demands. On the other hand, someone might ask questions and demand explanations of something yet not be puzzled about it. For example, he might be trying to sidetrack the discussion or he might think that by asking questions he would make a good impression. Absence of puzzlement and absence of demands for explanation may or may not coincide. It is well, therefore, in examining the notion of hat-doffingness to consider that it includes two distinct requirements each to be judged on its own merits.

Let us consider these requirements in relation to the explainer's discourse. We appear to be able to abstract from Dray's hat-doffing notion two distinct necessary conditions for saying that A explained E to B:

Hat-doffing Condition (*1*): The phenomena referred to in A's discourse for B did not puzzle B.

Hat-doffing Condition (*2*): The phenomena referred to in A's discourse for B raised no demands by B for explanations.

One wonders, however, if these conditions are not too strong. Does the question of whether or not A has explained E to B really depend on B's reaction to A's discourse? Surely not. B may be the sort who makes a career out of puzzlement or out of asking questions; are we to say that because he always finds something that

---

[8] Actually there is another point: the relationship between asking questions and demanding explanations. Both these things enter into Dray's brief account of hat-doffing phenomena. They are not the same, but to simplify the present discussion I will treat them as if they were.

puzzles him or demands explanations, we can never explain anything to him?

Perhaps we have applied these conditions to the wrong notion. It will be recalled that explaining something to someone may or may not be successful; that A may or may not get B to understand E. It is plausible to suppose, then, that A can have explained E to B even though B is puzzled or demands further explanations but that in these circumstances he cannot have explained E to B successfully. Let us consider hat-doffing conditions (1) and (2), therefore, as stating necessary conditions for saying that A has explained E to B successfully, that is, has gotten B to understand E, rather than simply for saying that A has explained E to B.

It certainly makes sense, in determining whether A has successfully explained E to B, to take into account A's accomplishments and not merely his efforts. The question is whether lack of puzzlement and explanation demands on the part of B are the right sort of accomplishments. Is it necessary in order that A explain E to B successfully for A to put B into a state such that he is not puzzled and asks no questions? Let us consider this matter with reference to the series of events Dray posits as leading up to his engine seizure E:

(CSE$_1$) There is a leak in the oil reservoir.

(CSE$_2$) The oil runs out the underside.

(CSE$_3$) No oil is piped to the cylinder.

(CSE$_4$) The walls of the cylinder are dry.

(CSE$_5$) The piston doesn't move.

Suppose A cites series (CSE$_1$) to (CSE$_5$) to B and B, having been given this series, sees the connection between leak and seizure. Nonetheless (CSE$_1$) puzzles B: "Why is there a leak in the oil reservoir?" he asks, in effect demanding an explanation of (CSE$_1$). A in turn says, "There's a leak because there's a hole. Look and see for yourself." "Of course if there's a leak there must be a hole. That verges on a tautology. I'm puzzled about the leak because I can't imagine what made the hole," B replies. A says, "I have no idea what made the hole. I'm as puzzled about the leak as you are. But given that there is a leak, you can see that . . ." and here A cites the series again to B. But A doesn't need to repeat the series to B. B understood the engine seizure the first time A cited the series. B's puzzlement about (CSE_1) is real enough and so is his demand for an explanation of (CSE_1), but neither prevents B from having understood the seizure on the basis of A's explanation$_D$. And if A has gotten B to understand the seizure by citing the series to him, surely A has explained the seizure to B successfully.

Some puzzlement about and some demands for explanation of the phenomena A cites are, then, compatible with explaining E successfully to B, that is, with A's getting B to understand E. Thus hat-doffing conditions (1) and (2) are no more necessary conditions of successfully explaining something to someone than they are necessary conditions of explaining something to someone. The possibility remains, however, that although some puzzlement and some demands for explanation are compatible with explaining successfully, some are not; that although hat-doffing conditions (1) and (2) are not, as they stand, acceptable, a weaker version of each might be.

Thus, for example, it might be the case that although (CSE_1) can puzzle B yet B can understand E, the connection between (CSE_4) and (CSE_5) cannot puzzle B if B is to understand E; or it might be the case that although (CSE_1) can puzzle B yet B can understand E, E itself cannot puzzle B if B is to understand E. It might be the case but it isn't. B can, for example, understand why the engine seized up yet be puzzled about that seizure: "Why did it happen this morning and not last night?" he muses; "Does this mean that I'd better get myself a new car?" B can also understand why the engine seized up yet be puzzled about the connection between, for example, (CSE_4) and (CSE_5). "I just can't figure this out. Is the wall of the cylinder being dry a necessary condition for the piston not moving? Is the connection between the two things a causal connection?"

If *complete* understanding of E were at issue, perhaps the puzzlement and explanation demands I have cited as being compatible with B's understanding E would be ruled out. But complete understanding is not at issue. Understanding is at issue, and there are degrees and levels of understanding as well as all sorts of ways to understand a given thing. Thus, although it might be the case that someone who is told why there was a leak in the oil reservoir and that the connections between events in the series are causal is on his way to a better or deeper understanding of E than someone who is not told, it is nonetheless the case that one who is puzzled or asks questions about the events in the series or the connections between them can understand E. And although it might be the case that one who understands, for example, why the engine seized up this morning and not last night has greater understanding of the seizure than one who simply understands why it seized up, it is nonetheless true that one who understands why it seized up does understand it.

A's problem—if it is one—in explaining E to a puzzled soul, B, is not that he must work harder to accomplish his aim than if he were explaining E to an unpuzzled soul, as hat-doffing conditions (1) and (2) might lead us to believe, but rather that one thing leads to another where B is concerned, whereas dead ends are quickly reached with an unpuzzled soul. A will find himself involved in a new task of explaining without perhaps even recognizing that the original task is ended if B asks for an explanation of (CSE_1). But this is not to say that the original explaining task was not completed successfully. On the other hand, an unpuzzled explainee might cause A a great deal of trouble: he might ask no questions and be subject to no puzzlement because events (CSE_1) to (CSE_5) are all but meaningless to him; A has his work cut out for him if he is to succeed in explaining E to this sort of explainee.

Actually the connection between puzzlement and explanation demands on the one hand and understanding, be it complete understanding or not, on the other remains problematic unless we are clear on what these things involve. In Chapter 7 I will argue that understanding is a function of what one knows and the connections one sees, the latter being itself a matter of knowledge. But then, if puzzlement and demands for explanation are viewed, as they might well be, as "psychological phenomena," for example, if they are given a strictly behavioristic interpretation, there would be no reason to suppose them to be relevant to successful explaining in the way under discussion here. Only if the notions of puzzlement and of demands for explanation are interpreted at least in part in terms of knowledge is it reasonable to suppose that some puzzlement and some explanation demands are incompatible with understanding, let alone that all are. If, for example, someone who was puzzled about or demanded explanations of a given thing necessarily lacked knowledge about that thing and the knowledge he lacked was in turn necessary for understanding the thing, then the absence of that puzzlement or of the demands for explanation would be necessary for understanding the thing.

This is not the place to settle on the proper interpretation of the notions of puzzlement and demands for explanation. It is the place, however, to point out that understanding is open-ended in that different kinds of understanding of a given thing can be had, each involving rather different knowledge, and that no limits on the kinds of understanding that can be had can be set a priori. Thus even if an epistemic interpretation—that is, one in terms of knowledge—of the notions of puzzlement and demands for explanation is tenable, it does not follow that some one sort of puzzlement and demands for explanation would be incompatible with understanding in every case.

If understanding required some one sort of knowledge, then given an epistemic interpretation of these notions it could well be that the absence of some one sort of puzzlement and demands for explanation was generally necessary for understanding. But there is no such knowledge, or at least so I will argue in Chapters 7 and 8. Thus the most one could say about puzzlement and demands for explanation on the one hand and understanding on the other, even granting an epistemic interpretation of the former, would be that the absence of *some* puzzlement and demands for explanation would be necessary for understanding. The particular puzzlement or demands for explanation required to be absent if a person were to understand would vary from case to case. To determine what puzzlement or demands for explanation would be incompatible with understanding in any given case, one would have to have a rather detailed account of the understanding at issue.

We must conclude that hat-doffing conditions (1) and (2), even when given the benefit of the doubt in the form of an epistemic interpretation of the notions of puzzlement and demands for explanation and when applied to successful explaining something to someone, are untenable. Before we decide that Dray's notion of hat-doffingness is misguided, however, let us consider an interpretation of it rather different from the ones we have been discussing. I suggested earlier that Dray may be incorporating two rather widely held assumptions about explanation in his continuous-series model: the assumption that demands for explanation arise in a context of puzzlement and the assumption that the aim of explanation is to resolve puzzlement. Perhaps he also incorporates in the model the very common assumption that explanations reduce the unfamiliar to the familiar.[9] After all, one doffs one's hat to people who are familiar, not to strangers. Perhaps we should take Dray, then, to be insisting that the phenomena to which A refers when explaining E to B be familiar to B.

It is well to note in this regard that phenomena could be familiar to B yet puzzle him and that they could fail to puzzle him yet be unfamiliar. Thus, a familiarity interpretation of the hat-doffing condition on explaining would be independent of the puzzlement interpretation we have been discussing. Similarly, phenomena could be familiar to B yet raise demands by B for explanation; they could on the other hand raise no such explanation demands yet not be familiar to B. All of which is to say that the familiarity of phenomena and their failure to raise demands for explanation are two different things just as their familiarity and their failure to puzzle are. A familiarity interpretation of the hat-doffing condition on explaining something to someone would therefore be independent of an explanation-demands interpretation as well as being independent of a puzzlement interpretation.

[9] Dray, after citing with approval several philosophers who make this assumption, calls familiarity one important pragmatic requirement on explanation; *op. cit.*, pp. 75ff. John Hospers discusses some of the same literature more critically; "What Is Explanation?" in Antony Flew (ed.), *Essays in Conceptual Analysis* (Macmillan, London, 1956), pp. 96ff. For other discussions of this assumption, see Bromberger, *op. cit.*, pp. 95–96; Hempel, "Aspects of Scientific Explanation," pp. 430–433; O'Connor, *op. cit.*, pp. 84ff.; Passmore, *op. cit.*

One normally doffs one's hat to a person one is acquainted with, in the sense of having met him or at least seen him often. Are we to take hat-doffing phenomena, then, to be phenomena with which the person in question is acquainted in this sense? Consider the following necessary condition for saying that A explained E to B:

Hat-doffing Condition (*3*): B has firsthand experience with the phenomena referred to in A's discourse for B.

Surely this condition is too restrictive. B need not have looked under the hood of Dray's car or for that matter under the hood of any car in order to understand why the engine seized up, let alone in order for A to explain to him why it seized up. Perhaps more to the point, if this condition were correct, one could explain historical events in terms of other events only to a contemporary of those events and one could explain events in other countries and cultures only to one who had visited them. But this is absurd. We can and do explain things to people by citing phenomena with which they have had no experience themselves. Indeed, one might say that one of the functions of explaining something to someone is to supplant or make unnecessary firsthand experience.

Familiarity need not, however, be construed as acquaintance in this narrow sense. One who knows about or has heard about something may be said to be familiar with it, and it is perhaps this sort of familiarity that the hat-doffing notion incorporates. Consider, then, as a necessary condition for saying that A explained to B:

Hat-doffing Condition (*4*): B has knowledge about or at least has heard of the phenomena referred to in A's discourse for B.

In requiring some knowledge or experience of the phenomena in question but not necessarily firsthand knowledge or experience, this condition is clearly superior to hat-doffing condition (3). Yet hat-doffing condition (4), despite its liberality, is by no means broad enough. It requires the *phenomena* A cites in his explanation$_D$ for B to be familiar *prior* to A's explaining to B. Yet surely this is a mistake. Granted that when someone explains something to someone he must take into account his explainee's knowledge or lack thereof of the world, hat-doffing condition (4) overlooks the fact that he can "do things," so to speak, with the phenomena he cites.

Dray speaks of hat-doffing *phenomena* and in general seems to view hat-doffingness as a relation holding between some phenomena or sequence of phenomena and some person. The various interpretations we have given here of his hat-doffing condition preserve this feature of his account, but the conception of explaining that is implicit in this view of hat-doffingness is misleading, for it makes the explainer seem even more at the mercy of the state of the world and the state of the explainee's knowledge of the world than he really is. There is no reason to suppose that, given something E to be explained to someone B, the *relevant* phenomena will be hat-doffing in the sense of being familiar or unpuzzling, etc., for B *in themselves*. And if they are not, it does not follow that the explainer's task is hopeless. He can *make* phenomena hat-doffing for B in any of the senses discussed here by choosing his vocabulary carefully, by giving analogies and metaphors, by citing examples and illustrations. Hat-doffing condition (4), then, is no more a necessary condition of explaining something to someone than are hat-doffing conditions (1) to (3), for the *prior* hat-doffingness of the phenomena in question is not necessary for explaining something to someone.

Yet if all the hat-doffing conditions discussed here fail, we still ought not to dismiss this element of the continuous-series model too hastily, for Dray's hat-doffing notion points up the fact that the explainer must in some way or other take account of the explainee's state of knowledge in his explanation$_D$ for his explainee. This is a crucial aspect of explaining something to someone, one which we will pursue further in the next chapter.

To conclude our discussion of the continuous-series model, we may note that the conditions abstracted from it do not hold up as necessary conditions of explaining something to someone. Nonetheless, the model provides a good deal of insight into that activity: (1) The continuous-series notion points up the importance in explaining of getting someone to see connections between things. (2)

The question-shifting notion, in a real sense, brings out the complexity of the explanatory activity. (3) The hat-doffing notion highlights the fact that the explanations the explainer gives are *for* someone, so that what in one context enables an explainee to see connections may not in another.

Perhaps the most important contribution the continuous-series model makes to an analysis of explaining something to someone lies in its underlying conception of explanation as *filling in*. It is assumed that for explaining to take place there is some gap and that explaining involves filling that gap. It seems to me that this view of explaining something to someone is essentially correct. Where the model goes wrong is in its insistence that the filling in be of a certain sort. In a sense, the model is well conceived but not well executed. As we have seen, one can fill the gap by citing a continuous series of events leading from C to E but one need not; one can shift the question from "Why E?" to "Why did C lead to E?" but one need not. The filling in can take many more forms than are sanctioned by the continuous-series model itself.

If the continuous-series model in its emphasis on *filling in* contributes to our understanding of explaining something to someone, it must still be criticized for failing to make clear just what the gap that needs to be filled in is *between*. One gets the impression from Dray's account of the model that the gap holds between events: in the engine-seizure case, for example, there is a gap between leak and seizure, a gap which can be filled by the events (CSE_1) to (CSE_5) constituting the continuous series. But as an account of explaining something to someone this is surely mistaken. Although the job of one who explains$_R$ something may perhaps be viewed at least in part in this way, the job of one who explains something to someone is not to fill in a gap between the phenomena under discussion. Rather, his job is to fill in the gap between his audience's knowledge or beliefs about some phenomena and what he takes to be the actual state of affairs. For a more sophisticated account of the gap-filling aspect of explaining something to someone and other aspects as well, let us now turn to the work of Sylvain Bromberger.

Chapter 4

EXPLAINING
AS QUESTION
ANSWERING

Dray gives us insight into explaining something to someone but in no sense provides us with a systematic account of that activity. In contrast Sylvain Bromberger provides us with a careful and detailed analysis of explaining something to someone.[1] He proceeds by setting forth a series of hypotheses each of which purports to state the essential characteristics of what he calls "explaining episodes." He finds defects in all but the last hypothesis; the last one —Hypothesis Four—he believes contains conditions such that every explaining episode must meet them and such that any episode meeting them is an explaining episode. Our task will be to examine Hypothesis Four to see whether these claims are justified. Even if they are not, I think we will find that Bromberger's general ap-

---

[1] "An Approach to Explanation," in R. J. Butler (ed.), *Analytical Philosophy*, 2d ser. (Blackwell, Oxford, 1965), pp. 72–105. Page references in the text of this chapter will be to this essay.

proach to explanation is instructive and that his specific analysis of explaining something to someone contains several important insights.

1 An Approach to Explanation

For purposes of analysis Bromberger conceives of explaining something to someone in terms of episodes in which a tutor answers some question for his tutee. The question may be a "why" question, but it need not be; it may actually have been asked, but it need not have been. Bromberger asks what it is for someone to explain something to someone where the "something" can be specified by means of an *indirect question*. Thus, he asks what the truth conditions are for a statement such as "John is explaining to Rosalie how ozone differs from ordinary oxygen," where "how ozone differs from ordinary oxygen" is an indirect question (the corresponding direct question would be "How does ozone differ from ordinary oxygen?") (p. 73). Bromberger recognizes that when we describe someone as having explained something to someone we do not always specify an indirect question (pp. 98–100). "Sam explained Hector's behavior to Rebecca" is a case in point. But he sees this as posing no problem for his analysis, and I think he is right. In every case of explaining something to someone there is *some* question which the explainer—or, to use his terminology, the tutor—may be viewed as having answered or tried to answer even though it may not always be obvious what the question is. For example, given an episode where Sam explained Hector's behavior to Rebecca, Sam may be taken to have explained to her, for example, *why Hector behaves as he does.*

Two technical terms play an important role in Bromberger's analysis: "p-predicament" and "b-predicament." Briefly, someone A is in a *p-predicament* with regard to any question Q if and only if, on A's views, Q admits of a right answer but A can think of no answer to which, on A's view, there are no decisive objections (p. 82). Now when A is in a p-predicament with regard to Q he may also be in a b-predicament with regard to it, but he need not be; and similarly, when he is in a b-predicament with regard to Q he may also be in a p-predicament with regard to it, but he need not be. For A is in a *b-predicament* with regard to Q if and only if Q admits of a right answer, but that answer is beyond what A can conceive, think of, imagine (p. 90).

It is worth noting, if only because of the predicament letters chosen by Bromberger, that a person in a p-predicament need not be puzzled or perplexed and a person in a b-predicament need not be baffled or bewildered. What is at issue in these predicaments is the person's view of the soundness of the question and his repertoire of answers, that is to say his cognitive state and not his feelings and discomforts. Thus the introduction of the notion of a predicament is not to be taken as an indication that Bromberger subscribes to the assumptions about puzzlement and explanation demands mentioned earlier. He does not. If there is any connection between his analysis and these assumptions, it is that in his analysis of explaining something to someone, he attaches great importance to the recognition of the tutee's state of mind and that these assumptions draw our attention to that same factor.

Bromberger's Hypothesis Four follows:

The essential characteristics of explaining episodes are the following:

(a) the question is sound, i.e. admits of a right answer;

(b) the tutor is rational and knows the right answer to the question at the time of the episode;

(c) during the episode the tutor knows, or believes, or at least assumes that at the beginning of the episode the tutee was in a p-predicament with regard to the question,

or that, at the beginning of the episode the tutee was in a b-predicament with regard to the question,

or that, at the beginning of the episode, the tutee was in either a p-predicament or a b-predicament with regard to the question;

(d) in the course of the episode the tutor presents the facts that in his opinion the tutee must learn to know the right answer to the question;

(e) in the course of the episode the tutor also provides the tutee with such instruction as he (the tutor) thinks necessary to remove the basis of whichever of the states mentioned in (c) he deems the tutee to be in;

(f) at the end of the episode all the facts mentioned in (d) and
(e) have been presented to the tutee by the tutor (pp.
94–95).

2 The Truth Requirement

Hypothesis Four requires of an explaining episode that the question admit of a right answer [condition (a)]. Bromberger recognizes (p. 80) that loose usage countenances statements such as the following, "Max explained to Alonso why the Gödel incompleteness theorem is of no epistemological significance," that is, it countenances episodes whose questions are based on false presuppositions. He chooses nevertheless to limit his analysis to what he calls strict usage. Hypothesis Four also requires that the tutor know the right answer [condition (b)]. Again Bromberger recognizes a difference between strict and loose usage: strict usage requires that the tutor utter verities; loose usage allows the tutor's view about the truth of what he says to prevail over the view of someone who describes the tutor as having explained to his tutee. But again he chooses to limit his analysis to strict usage and seems to think that the loose usage in both cases is of little interest (p. 80, n. 1).

On the contrary, it seems to me that what Bromberger calls "loose" usage *is* of interest, or at any rate *should be* of interest, to those concerned with the notion of explanation. Presumably when a person, for example, a teacher or a historian or a bank clerk or a lawyer, engages in explaining something to someone, he selects as his questions only those he *takes* to be sound,[2] but there is no reason at all to suppose that they *really are* sound. A sound question, that is, one that admits of a right answer, is a question which is not based on a false presupposition. Yet there may be no way of his knowing, at the particular time or place at which he engages in his activity, that a question he assumes is not based on a false presupposition really is based on one. Similarly, we may presume that the person *thinks* he knows the answer to the question he selects, but

---

[2] Would he be explaining something to someone if he knew that his question was not sound yet he proceeded in the usual manner? I think not. We would describe him as *pretending* to explain or *acting as if* he were explaining, thereby distinguishing his activity from explaining itself.

there is surely no reason to suppose that he *really does* know. If we are only interested in those cases of explaining something to someone in which the question is sound and the person knows the right answer to it, our analysis will shed less light than it would otherwise on an activity so basic to teaching, history, and numerous other fields.

Perhaps it is important to distinguish the "loose" cases of explaining from the "strict" ones, but even if it is important, the "loose" ones may engage our interest as much as the "strict" ones do. An analysis of explaining something to someone which accounts for both the "strict" and the "loose" usages distinguished by Bromberger is, therefore, to be preferred over one that does not. Thus conditions (a) and (b) of Hypothesis Four need to be amended. Consider, instead of (a),

(a') the question is sound, i.e., admits of a right answer, or the tutor believes, or at least assumes, that the question is sound, i.e., admits of a right answer.

Consider, instead of (b),

(b') the tutor is rational and knows the right answer to the question at the time of the episode, or thinks, or at least assumes, he knows the right answer to the question at the time of the episode.

Now I can imagine someone objecting to (a') and (b') on the grounds that explaining is like knowing: we only say that Jones *knows* that $2 + 2 = 4$ if $2 + 2$ *does* equal 4; similarly, we say that Jones *explained* to Smith why the engine seized up only if the engine *did* seize up and only if Jones' answer to the question "Why did the engine seize up?" *is* the right answer. This objection, however, does not hold up under examination. For granted that explaining has something to do with knowledge, the question at issue is what exactly explaining has to do with knowledge. In many respects explaining something to someone is like teaching rather than like knowing. Perhaps you have to be trying to tell the truth or thinking that what you are telling is the truth in order to be teaching, but you certainly can be teaching although you do not in fact tell the truth. I think we would say without hesitation that people in John Stuart Mill's day were taught that tuberculosis is not contagious; I think we would say without hesitation that Columbus and his contemporaries were taught that the world is flat. What I am arguing here is that, other things being equal, we would in similar fashion say without hesitation that someone explained to Mill and his contemporaries why tuberculosis is not contagious and that someone explained to Columbus and his contemporaries what the shape of the world is, although (so far as we know), in the Mill case the question was not sound and in the Columbus case the answer was not right.

I should point out that in arguing for what may be called a modified or weak truth condition on explaining, I am leaving open the question of whether there is a truth condition and, if so, what sort of truth condition there is on other explanation notions. Perhaps an explanation$_S$ of something must be true. But if so, it does not follow that there is a truth condition on explaining something to someone. Moreover, there is some controversy among those philosophers who purport to be giving an account of the notion of an explanation$_S$ of something over the question of whether explanations$_S$ must meet a truth condition.[3] Thus, far from its being obvious that explaining something to someone is like knowing in this crucial respect, it is not even obvious that the explanation notion, which one would expect, because of its context-free nature, to be the most likely candidate for a truth condition, has a truth condition on it.

Of course, our imaginary objector might agree that we sometimes say that someone explained something to someone although the question was not sound or the answer not right. He might insist, however, that we label this usage "loose" or "unusual" or "secondary" and that we, like Bromberger, attend to the "strict"

[3] Carl G. Hempel, for example, disagrees with himself. Compare "The Function of General Laws in History," p. 232; "Studies in the Logic of Explanation," p. 248; "Aspects of Scientific Explanation," p. 338; all in *Aspects of Scientific Explanation and Other Essays in the Philosophy of Science* (Free Press, New York, 1965).

or "usual" or "primary" usage. I prefer not to invoke or lean on this sort of distinction here for the basis on which the distinction would be drawn is far from clear to me. It might be suggested that we look to see when we qualify our description that someone has explained something to someone and that we in fact qualify it only in cases like the Mill and Columbus ones. Thus, for example, we say, "He was wrong about tuberculosis" after we say "He explained why tuberculosis is not contagious." Yet this will not do. We qualify our statement that someone explained something to someone if we think *our audience* is mistaken in its own judgment of the soundness of the question or rightness of the answer, not if we think the tutor in the explaining episode is mistaken on this score. Thus we say "He (the tutor) was wrong about tuberculosis" not because he was wrong (although he was) but because our audience doesn't realize he was wrong: our audience also thinks tuberculosis is not contagious. We would be just as apt to qualify our statement "Jones explained why tuberculosis is contagious" (by saying "And of course it is contagious") if we thought our audience believed that tuberculosis was not contagious even though the tutor in the case had given a right answer to a sound question. So far as I can see, the burden of making clear the soundness or unsoundness of the question and the rightness or wrongness of the answer falls on the one who describes someone as having explained and not on the word "explain" or the notion of explaining.

If (a′) is substituted for (a) and (b′) for (b), then a host of cases otherwise ruled out by Hypothesis Four are accommodated, cases in which the tutor himself would say he was explaining something to someone, in which an observer at the time of the episode would say so, and in which I think we too would say so. For example, if, according to the state of knowledge at the time an episode takes place, the question the tutor thinks sound is indeed sound, then the episode qualifies as an explaining episode, other things being equal. Similarly, if, according to the state of knowledge at the time an episode takes place, the answer the tutor takes to be correct is indeed correct, then the episode qualifies as an explaining episode, other things being equal. But now the question arises whether too many cases are accommodated by the substitution of (a′) for (a) and (b′) for (b). For (a′) and (b′) seem to countenance as explaining episodes not only episodes in which the tutor takes the question to be sound or takes his answer to be correct and is justified in so doing, but also cases in which these assumptions or beliefs of his may be quite arbitrary and may have no backing at all.

According to Bromberger, loose usage allows the tutor's views about the truth of what he is saying (and, presumably, about the soundness of the question) to prevail over the views of the user of a statement of the form "someone explained W to someone" where "W" occupies the position taken by an indirect question.[4] If this is so, then loose usage countenances cases in which the tutor's views of the question and answer are not justified. I myself am not clear on what loose usage allows and doesn't allow. But usage aside, I do think it is important to distinguish between those cases in which the tutor's views of the soundness of the question and the correctness of the answer are justified from those cases in which they are not. The latter sort of case does not seem to me to qualify as a case of explaining something to someone whereas the former sort of case does, other things being equal. If an "objective" standard, namely that the question *be* sound and that the tutor *know* the right answer, is too strong, a standard made relative to the tutor's view of the question and answer is, I think, too weak, for the tutor may be incompetent or deluded. I would suggest that a standard made relative to the view of a competent observer *at the time of the explaining episode* is perhaps neither too strong nor too weak.

Whether (a′) and (b′) do in fact accommodate the cases I am saying should be ruled out by an analysis of explaining something to someone depends on how one interprets the stipulation in (b), retained in (b′), that the tutor must be rational. Bromberger never makes explicit his reasons for including this stipulation in

---

[4] Compare Israel Scheffler's position with regard to teaching. He proposes a secondary or "subjective" notion of success to supplement the primary or "objective" notion according to which "we assume that the truth of the doctrine taught is to be judged from the teacher's point of view"; *Conditions of Knowledge* (Scott, Foresman, Glenview, Ill., 1965), p. 12.

Hypothesis Four; it is, indeed, the only part of Hypothesis Four which does not clearly grow out of his observations on his earlier hypotheses. But this is perhaps beside the point. What is to the point is to ask whether a tutor could be rational yet not be justified in his beliefs or assumptions about the question or answer. I think not. That is to say, I think that the requirement of the tutor's rationality serves to bar the cases I have been worrying about when (a') is substituted for (a) and (b') for (b).

Perhaps this rationality requirement was included in Hypothesis Four because Bromberger recognized a problem in relation to conditions (d) and (e) analogous to the one I have been raising in connection with (a') and (b'). For (d) and (e) involve the tutor's beliefs or opinions, and the question therefore arises whether these need to be circumscribed in any way. (d) requires that the tutor present the facts that in his opinion the tutee must learn to know the right answer. It is possible for someone to know the right answer to a question and meet the requirements of condition (c), yet have an absolutely wild idea of what the tutee must learn to know the right answer. But surely, if the facts he thinks the tutee must learn are totally unconnected to what he takes the right answer to be and to the state he deems the tutee to be in, we would not describe the episode as an *explaining* episode. Similarly (e) requires that the tutor provide such instruction as he thinks necessary to remove the basis of the state he deems the tutee to be in. He might have a wild view of what is necessary to remove the state he deems the tutee to be in, so wild we would say he had not explained to the tutee. Presumably a rational tutor *could not* have a wild view of what the tutee should learn or of what instruction is necessary; hence (d) and (e) do not accommodate cases which they shouldn't but which, on the face of it, they might seem to.

One obvious defect of (d) is that it fails to reflect the changes made in Hypothesis Four when (a') is substituted for (a) and (b') for (b). If it is required that the tutor only believe or assume that he knows the right answer, surely it is too much to require that he present the *facts;* he may be justifiably mistaken about the facts just as he is about the soundness of the question and the correctness of his answer. Thus (d) must be amended so that it allows him to present what he takes to be the facts and not necessarily the facts themselves. And so that there is no ambiguity, (d) must also be amended to allow the tutor to present what he thinks the tutee must learn to know what he, the tutor, takes to be the right answer. Consider, then, (d') :

> (d') in the course of the episode the tutor presents the facts or what he believes or at least assumes to be the facts that, in his opinion, the tutee must learn to know the right answer or the answer the tutor believes or assumes is right.

Condition (f) has a similar defect and must also be amended so as to accommodate not only facts but what the tutor believes or assumes to be facts. Consider, then, (f') :

> (f') at the end of the episode all the facts or what the tutor believes or at least assumes to be facts mentioned in (d') and (e) have been presented to the tutee by the tutor.

Even now, conditions (d') and (f') are only acceptable if the notion of a fact is given a liberal interpretation. Facts are often contrasted with value judgments, moral principles, general laws, theories, and the like. Yet a tutor can explain to his tutee, for example, why the schools ought to be desegregated. And although facts in the narrow sense may indeed be relevant generally to the question "Why ought the schools be desegregated?", in a particular explaining episode, for example, one in which the tutor thinks the tutee knows the facts but is in a p-predicament nonetheless, the tutor may think it necessary to assert relevant moral principles rather than the facts.

Given a broad construal of the notion of a fact, (d) still presents a problem. Suppose that the question is sound, and that the tutor knows the right answer, is rational, and knows what facts the tutee must learn to know the right answer. One can imagine episodes in which nonetheless the tutor does not present the facts the tutee must learn to know the right answer: episodes in which he does not present them because he knows or at least assumes that the tutee could not possibly grasp them at his present stage of development. To be sure, condition (e) requires him to give instruction to the tutee and Bromberger clearly envisions this instruction as, at least in many cases, an attempt to bring the tutee up to a level where he can grasp the facts. But the facts may be so far beyond the tutee that such instruction would take years to provide, and it would be absurd to call the result an explaining episode. Now it might be argued that in such a case there could be no explaining episode. Yet I would maintain that explaining something to someone does sometimes involve simplification, omission of too difficult material, and even something very much like fabrication and myth.

Thus I would maintain that I explained to my very young son why the Pilgrims came to Massachusetts when I told him that they wanted to worship as they pleased and [the instruction of condition (e)] told him that in England the Pilgrims were forced to worship in a way they did not like—the way the King said—while in Massachusetts there was no one to tell them what to do. But I would also maintain that in my explaining this to him I did *not* present the facts which in my view he needed to learn to know the right answer. Some facts, yes. But not enough facts. I omitted, for example, the fact that the Pilgrims did not intend to come to Massachusetts but got blown off their course and ended up there. I take this to be something he needs to learn to know the right answer since otherwise he will think that they came to Massachusetts in order to worship as they pleased, whereas strictly speaking they came to the New World, but not specifically to Massachusetts, for that reason.

Some might say I gave my son a mixture of fact and story; others that I gave a partial account of the facts.[5] Whatever the description of the case, what seems clear is that I did explain but did not meet condition (d). What also seems clear is that explaining something to someone is like teaching in another important respect.

---

[5] See, in this connection, Ralph Beatley's discussion of the use of spurious or "slippery" reasons in teaching arithmetic, "Reason and Rule in Arithmetic and Algebra," in Israel Scheffler (ed.), *Philosophy and Education* (Allyn and Bacon, Boston, 1958), pp. 205–218.

We talk of a "spiral curriculum," and one of the things we mean is that we can teach the same thing at different levels. At one level we simplify, at another we complicate. So too with explaining. One can imagine a spiral curriculum for explaining episodes centering around some one indirect question, such as why the Pilgrims came to Massachusetts. The explainer weaves a fact-story for his child one Thanksgiving season; tells him about the intent to go to Virginia the next; discourses on the state of religious freedom in France, Spain, and Holland the next; and so on.

This is not to say that anything goes in explaining. Nor is it to say that the explainer is forever stuck with the same indirect question. Needless to say, one can stop explaining why the Pilgrims came to Massachusetts and go on to something else. I am simply suggesting that another sort of loosening up of Bromberger's analysis is required; that there is, to use Bromberger's terminology, another distinction between "strict" and "loose" usage which needs to be drawn, a distinction which has been overlooked by Bromberger. If on "strict" usage the tutor must present the facts he thinks the tutee must learn, on "loose" usage, in situations where the tutee is young or a beginner in a field, a good deal of leeway in what is actually presented is allowed. It is important to recognize that the "loose" usage I refer to here differs from the "loose" usage Bromberger discusses (p. 80). Bromberger's "loose" usage allows the tutor's view of the truth to prevail over ours. This "loose" usage allows what the tutor presents to the tutee to diverge from the tutor's view of the truth.[6] It seems to me to be important for an account of explaining something to someone to take cognizance of this "loose" usage. Suppose, then, we substitute (d″) for (d) in Hypothesis Four:

> (d″) in the course of the episode the tutor presents the facts or some of the facts, or what he believes or at least

[6] In analyzing the notion of explaining something to someone, one must maintain a distinction between the tutor's knowledge (or what on his view is knowledge) and the tutor's *utterances* to his tutee. I am not sure that Bromberger does this. Even if one requires the tutor to *know* the answer, one need not require him to *say* it to the tutee if there are good pedagogical reasons against saying it.

assumes to be the facts or some of the facts, that, in his opinion, the tutee must learn to know the right answer or the answer the tutor believes or assumes is right,

or he presents material that he knows, or believes or at least assumes, is not the facts, but that in his opinion is sufficiently related to the facts and is pedagogically helpful to the tutee in learning an answer to the question which the tutor knows, or believes, or at least assumes, is not the right answer, but which is sufficiently related to the right answer, or the answer he believes or at least assumes is right, so that it is pedagogically justified.

Let us also substitute (f″) for (f) in Hypothesis Four:

(f″)   at the end of the episode all the facts, or what the tutor believes or at least assumes to be facts, mentioned in (d″) and (e) or the material that in his opinion is related to the facts in the way outlined in (d″) have been presented to the tutee by the tutor.

(d″) can undoubtedly be improved upon. If nothing else, the notion of material being sufficiently related to the right answer requires clarification. I will not attempt such clarification here, however, for it would lead us too far afield. It is enough for the present purpose to point out that these notions serve to "counterbalance" the requirements that the material be pedagogically helpful and that the answer be pedagogically justified. In effect, they place constraints on what is to count as an explaining episode. It is not the case, after all, that every episode in which the tutor intentionally departs from the facts or from what he takes to be the facts is an explaining episode. Although mythmaking and storytelling may on occasion enter into explaining something to someone, explaining something to someone must not be confused with either.

I can imagine someone objecting to (d″) not so much in its details as in principle. A condition of this type, it might be argued, is misguided in that a perfectly reasonable pedagogical consideration is given (wrongly) the status of logical condition. Granted that in an explaining episode a tutor must adjust what he says to his tutee's predicament, the conditions for saying truly that someone has explained something to someone ought not to be confused with good pedagogy. But this sort of objection to (d") is itself based on a confusion. We are indeed trying to determine the conditions for saying truly that someone explained something to someone, and one may, if he wishes, call these *logical* conditions. But we must distinguish between conditions which are logical in the sense that they have to do with the "logic" of a term or concept and conditions which are logical in the sense of being formal, that is, in specifying relations holding between statements. The conditions we seek are logical in the first sense, but to say this is to say nothing about whether they are logical in the second sense. There is no reason in principle why some of the "logical" conclusions of explaining something to someone may not be "pedagogical" in the sense that they incorporate into the analysis of explaining something to someone what might normally be called pedagogical conditions.

3 *The Tutee's Predicament*

Bromberger built a truth requirement into conditions (a), (b), and (d), and it is this requirement I have been objecting to. Interestingly enough, conditions (c) and (e) embody a weaker requirement than a truth requirement: the tutor need only *believe* or *assume* that the tutee was in a particular predicament, he need not *know* it; the tutor need only provide such instruction as he *thinks* necessary, he need not *know* what is necessary. But if conditions (c) and (e) are praiseworthy on this count, there is nonetheless an important defect in each. Condition (c) requires that the tutor deem the tutee at the beginning of the episode to be in a p-predicament or a b-predicament or in either one or the other with regard to the question. I see no reason, however, why the tutor might not deem the tutee to be in a different predicament and, other things being equal, still be explaining something to someone. Condition (e) requires that the tutor provide such instruction as he thinks necessary to remove the basis of the state he deems the tutee to be in. I do not think this is necessary in every case. I will consider these points in turn.

Imagine that I am in the following state or predicament in relation to the question "Why did my engine seize up?": I think that the question is sound; I can think of the right answer, namely "There is an oil leak," but on my view there are decisive objections to it; I can think of another answer which, although not the right one, I take to be the right one and I can think of no decisive objections to it. Let us call this predicament and any predicament like it an *m-predicament*.[7] It seems to me to be perfectly possible for someone who knows that I am in this predicament with regard to the question "Why did my engine seize up?" to explain to me why my engine seized up. If it is, then condition (c) is too restrictive; it would have to be amended to accommodate m-predicaments as well as p- and b-predicaments.

It might be argued that the predicament which I have imagined I am in with regard to the question "Why did my engine seize up?" and which I have called an m-predicament is really a b-predicament (or perhaps a p-predicament) with regard to a different question, for instance "Why are the objections you take to be decisive not really decisive?" This objection to my example of an m-predicament brings out clearly that a person who is in a given sort of predicament relative to question Q_1 will often, although not necessarily always, be in a different sort of predicament relative to question Q_2. But it does not show that someone cannot explain something to someone if he thinks the tutee is in an m-predicament with regard to the question at issue.

The tutor's intent or purpose seems to be the crucial factor here. In the situation envisioned the tutor may see his task simply as showing his tutee why the latter's objections to the right answer

---

[7] The "m" of "m-predicament" is intended to remind the reader that the person in the predicament is *m*istaken. It should be noted that Bromberger is well aware that a person can be in a predicament other than a p- or a b-predicament; his point is simply that if a tutor has taken his tutee to be in some predicament other than a p- or a b-predicament, there will have been no explaining episode. One reason for this limit on predicaments is that a host of cases which Bromberger thinks ought to be ruled out by Hypothesis Four are thereby ruled out. So far as I can determine, the trouble Bromberger sees with these cases is that they are cases of telling, not explaining. Such cases ought, of course, to be ruled out. But the limitation on predicaments of Hypothesis Four is not the only way to rule them out, and it has the serious defect of ruling out cases which are cases of explaining and not merely telling.

are not decisive after all. If so, then we do not have a bona fide explaining episode in which the tutee is taken to be in neither a b- nor a p-predicament. What we have is an episode in which the question is "Why are the objections the tutee takes to be decisive not really decisive?" and the tutee is taken to be in a b- or perhaps a p-predicament—an episode, in other words, which conforms to Hypothesis Four.

The tutor may see his task differently, however. Granted that he perceives that his tutee rejects the right answer and accepts the wrong answer to the question "Why did the engine seize up?" he may nonetheless see his task as showing the tutee why the engine seized up. To succeed in this task he might have to show the tutee why the objections the tutee takes to be decisive are not really decisive. But the tutor would in this instance see this latter task as subsidiary to his overall or primary one and not as replacing it. If such be the case—and I see no reason why a rational tutor could not see his task in this way—we would have a bona fide explaining episode which did not conform to Hypothesis Four; that is, an episode where the tutor perceived his tutee to be in neither a b-predicament nor a p-predicament.

Consider now the following predicament: I can think of the right answer to Q, "Why did my engine seize up?" and have no objections to it, but I can also think of another answer to Q, a wrong one, to which I see no objections. Let us call the predicament I am in relative to Q or any predicament like it an *a-predicament*.[8] Bromberger describes an episode in which the tutee is in an a-predicament: A prisoner escapes from a jail by digging a tunnel; the jailors entertain alternative hypotheses, one of which is correct, as to the manner of disposing of the dirt; when the prisoner is captured he informs the jailors of his manner of disposing of the dirt; the one hypothesis is now confirmed and the other rejected. According to Bromberger this is a clear case of a nonexplaining episode since the tutor merely settles for the tutee which means of escape had been used (pp. 78–79).

In the situation Bromberger envisions, the prisoner merely tells

---

[8] The "a" of "a-predicament" is intended to remind the reader that the person in the predicament cannot decide between *a*lternatives.

his jailors that he dropped the dirt out the window into the moat. Consider, however, a situation somewhat different from the one just described. Suppose the prisoner wants his jailors to understand how he disposed of the dirt and recognizes his jailors to be in an a-predicament relative to the question "How did he (the prisoner) dispose of the dirt?" He proceeds to tell them in great detail how he got the dirt to the window, how he opened the window, how he got the dirt out of the window, how the dirt dropped into the moat. I submit that in this case he has explained how he disposed of the dirt even though he takes the jailors to be in an a-predicament.

Bromberger's interest in the jail case is primarily to distinguish between explaining something to someone and telling something to someone. Fortunately that distinction does not stand or fall on our ruling out a-predicaments from explaining episodes. One who explains something to someone must be trying to get that person to understand the thing in question; one who tells something to someone need not be trying to get him to understand. One who explains something to someone must take into account that person's predicament or state (or what on his view is that predicament or state) relative to the topic at hand; one who tells something to someone need not do this. One who explains something to someone must give that person what Bromberger refers to as instruction; one who tells something to someone need not give him instruction. There is no danger, then, that by opening the door to a-predicaments or, for that matter, to other predicaments, the line between explaining and telling (or between explaining and describing, explaining and informing, explaining and reporting, and so on), will be blurred.

Consider now the following predicament: I conceive of the right answer to Q without objections and I conceive of no other answer to Q or no other answer for which I do not have decisive objections. Let us call this predicament or any predicament like it an *r-predicament*.[9] Bromberger recognizes that it is possible for an

---

[9] The "r" of "r-predicament" is intended to remind the reader that the person in the predicament has the *r*ight answer to Q. I suppose it might be argued that having the right answer to Q would disqualify a person

explaining episode to take place in which the tutor knows or believes the tutee knows the answer to Q. He includes the words "or at least assumes" in condition (c) to allow for cases of this sort. The tutor according to condition (c) must know or believe or *at least assume* that the tutee was in a p- or a b-predicament. "Assume" here may be interpreted as "go on the assumption that," and of course, one may go on the assumption that such and such is the case without believing, let alone knowing, that it is the case (p. 86, n. 1). Thus a student in taking an examination is supposed to go on the assumption that his examiner is ignorant of the subject although the student presumably knows or believes otherwise. We may well wonder, however, whether the tutor need go on the assumption that his tutee is in a p- or b-predicament given that he knows or believes the tutor to be in an r-predicament. Can there really be no explaining episode if he not only believes but goes on the assumption that his tutee is in an r-predicament relative to Q?

Recall again the case of the engine seizure. Suppose our tutee knows the right answer to the question Q "Why did the engine seize up?" namely that it was due to an oil leak. Suppose he has no objections to this answer and conceives of no other answer. Suppose also that he has not the faintest idea how the leak led to the seizure; he simply does not see any connection between seizure and leak. Surely a tutor who took him to be in this state with regard to Q (an r-predicament) could explain why the engine seized up to him. To be sure the tutor would not be explaining why the engine seized up to him if all he did was tell him that it was due to an oil leak. But if he filled in the gap for his tutee—be it by citing a continuous series or something else—then, other things being equal, I see no reason why he would not be explaining why the engine seized up to his tutee. It might be argued, of course, that in the case envisioned the question underlying the episode would be Q_1 —"Why did the leak lead to the seizure?"—not Q and that the tutor would not be taking the tutee to be in an r-predicament with

from being in a predicament with regard to Q. But to be in a predicament with regard to Q, in the sense in which "predicament" is used here, involves having (or not having) some answer to Q and some view of the soundness of Q. Thus someone having the right answer to Q qualifies as being in a predicament.

regard to Q_1. Yet this need not be so. The tutor *could* be trying to get his tutee to understand why the engine seized up and could think that to do so the tutee must know more than the answer to Q. If so, and if the tutor tried to fill things in for the tutee, I think we would have to say that there had been an explaining episode with Q as the underlying question in which the tutor knew and acted on the assumption that his tutee was in an r-predicament with regard to Q.

Bromberger's predicaments seem to involve two different dimensions. One dimension is that of the person's view of the soundness of Q: one who is in a p-predicament, it will be recalled, takes Q to be sound. A second dimension is that of the person's state, so to speak, with respect to the right answer to Q: one who is in a b-predicament cannot conceive of the right answer to Q; one who is in a p-predicament can, but not an answer that is free of objections. Given these two aspects or dimensions of predicaments it becomes clear that the b-, p-, m-, a-, and r-predicaments by no means exhaust the predicaments a person can be in, relative to a given question Q. Only one other predicament, however, is of importance to us here. We will discuss it briefly and simply take note of a whole class of predicaments which cannot figure in explaining episodes.

Consider the following predicament: Q is sound but I take Q to be unsound and can conceive of no answer to Q. Let us call this predicament and any predicament like it an *f-predicament*.[10] Note that this predicament, although like a b-predicament in that the person cannot conceive of the right answer to Q, is distinct from (although compatible with) the b-predicament in that the b-predicament is neutral on the issue of the person's view of the question while the f-predicament is not. When we consider that what is at stake in explaining, according to Hypothesis Four, is not the tutor's actual predicament but rather the tutor's view of that predicament, we realize the need for separating f- from b-predicaments. A rational tutor might well proceed in one way with a tutee he took to be viewing Q as unsound and in quite a different way with

[10] The "f" of "f-predicament" is intended to remind the reader that the person in the predicament is under a *f*alse presupposition.

a tutee whose view of Q was unknown. But can there be an explaining episode in which the tutor takes his tutee to be in an f-predicament? I do not see why not. He would along the way have to try to convince the tutee that the question was after all a sound one but in each case we have examined there has been, so to speak, a subsidiary task for the explainer to perform as well as the underlying task of explaining whatever it is that is being explained.

We must distinguish an f-predicament from other predicaments in which the person takes Q to be unsound. A person might, for example, believe Q to be unsound yet conceive of answers to Q. (Right ones, wrong ones, with objections, without objections. Different predicaments could be distinguished but there is no need for us to do so.) Unless he were, despite his belief, acting on the assumption that Q were sound, for example, in order to exercise his imagination or develop his powers of creativity, I think we would call him irrational. Now Hypothesis Four requires the tutor of an explaining episode to be rational but says nothing about the tutee's rationality. Perhaps for good reason, for it is surely possible to explain something to someone who is irrational. The question remains, however, whether it is possible for a tutor to explain to his tutee if he *takes* the tutee to be irrational. The tutee might in fact be irrational without the tutor realizing it. The tutor's task might be difficult, if not futile, in such a case, but it could (logically speaking) be undertaken. It could also be undertaken if the tutor, although he believed the tutee to be in a predicament of the sort under discussion, hence to be irrational, nonetheless acted on the assumption that the tutee did not take Q to be unsound or did not conceive of answers to Q, for example, was in a b-predicament. But if the tutor proceeded on the assumption that his tutee was irrational, an explaining episode could not get off the ground.[11]

The matter of the tutee's rationality and the tutor's treatment of the tutee in this respect will be discussed at some length in the next chapter. For the present we need only say that insofar as one

---

[11] If the tutor took the tutee to believe Q to be false but to be thinking up answers to Q as, for example, an exercise in imagination, he could explain to his tutee. But again he would have to act as if his tutee were in some other predicament, for example, a p- or an f-predicament.

who is in a given predicament must thereby be considered to be irrational, that predicament cannot figure in an explaining episode. To simplify our discussion, let us call any predicament of that sort *irrational* and any other predicament *rational*. M-, a-, r-, and f-predicaments would then be rational predicaments, as would b- and p-predicaments. Consider, now, as a substitute for condition (c), condition (c'):

(c') during the episode the tutor knows, or believes, or at least assumes that at the beginning of the episode the tutee was in some rational predicament with regard to the question.

Condition (e) requires that the tutor provide such instruction as he thinks necessary to remove the basis of the state he deems the tutee to be in. It is important, therefore, to be clear on the range of these states, for presumably the instruction will vary depending on the state the tutor perceives the tutee to be in.[12] Two problems arise in connection with (e), however. First, is it not too strong to require that the tutor give such instruction as he thinks necessary to remove the basis of the tutee's predicament? To be explaining something to someone, one may have to provide instruction of the sort Bromberger has in mind, but one does not have to think that instruction is *necessary* to remove the basis of the state he deems the tutee to be in. Suppose alternative courses of instruction are available, each of which will in all likelihood remove the presumed basis of the predicament but none of which is necessary for so doing. A tutor who thought that any one of these would achieve his goal and who provided his tutee with any one of these would, other things being equal, be explaining to the tutee. Let us substitute (e') therefore for (e):

(e') in the course of the episode the tutor also provides the tutee with such instruction as he (the tutor) thinks is necessary

---

[12] Actually, as Bromberger points out (p. 103), it will vary depending on the *basis* of that state, since two people may be in the same predicament for different reasons.

to remove the basis of whichever of the states mentioned in
(c') he deems the tutee to be in,

or is effective in removing the basis of whichever of the
states mentioned in (c') he deems the tutee to be in,

or is helpful in removing the basis of whichever of the
states mentioned in (c') he deems the tutee to be in.

Second, the whole notion of providing instruction to remove the
basis of the tutee's state poses a problem. Consider the following
example. The question is "Why should the schools be desegregated?" The tutor recognizes that the tutee is in a b-predicament
relative to the question and that he is in it because he is going
under the false assumption that the question is unsound. He also
recognizes that what is necessary, or effective, or helpful for removing the false assumption is not simply providing facts or theory
but changing basic attitudes. Yet surely it is not necessary for the
tutor to engage in *this* in order to be explaining to the tutee why
the schools should be desegregated. We may, in the situation envisioned, want to require that a case designed to show that the tutee's assumption is false and should be revised be presented; but
this is quite different from requiring that, for example, therapy to
change deep-seated attitudes be given. A tutor may recognize that
his tutee needs therapy, but surely he need not provide it in order
to be explaining to the tutee.

Condition (e) is included in Hypothesis Four in order to rule
out from the class of explaining episodes those episodes in which
the tutor simply gives the answer to the question (p. 95). This is
all to the good, for, as we saw in the last chapter, explaining something to someone involves more than simply telling someone the
answer to a question. Condition (e), however, seems to err in another direction, for it seems to require that on certain occasions
basic personality change be undertaken by the explainer. But if explaining something to someone is not telling the answer, neither
does it necessitate therapy or character education. If this is a problem with condition (e), it holds, I might add, not only for episodes in which the underlying question involves a value judgment.
In the case of some nonvalue questions, too, the tutor may think

that in order to remove the basis of the tutee's predicament it is necessary to change his attitudes.[13]

I say that condition (e) *seems* to err in this respect, for (e) can be understood in such a way that the supposed counterexample offered here loses its force. If we interpret the notion of instruction as some philosophers have, that is, as "at heart" involving giving reasons, weighing evidence, and the like,[14] as being "essentially a rational process," both at the giving, and insofar as it is successful, at the receiving end,[15] then the problem I have posed disappears. The tutor would not, on this view of instruction, be required to use therapy or the like for removing the basis of his tutee's state even if in his view therapy, say, were necessary or effective or helpful for achieving this end. Condition (e) requires the tutor to give instruction; as long as instruction is understood in a relatively narrow way, it does not demand too much of the tutor.

Bromberger's analysis conceives of explaining episodes as answering *a single* question—the question referred to in conditions (a) to (d). This question governs the episode as a whole; hence I have been calling it the *underlying question*. I propose that we interpret condition (e) as imposing on explaining episodes some *shift* in question—a shift of the sort we discussed in the last chapter although not necessarily the particular shift embedded in the continuous-series model. I propose, in other words, that the instruction required by condition (e) be viewed along the lines in which Bromberger views an explaining episode as a whole, namely in terms of question answering. The question or questions answered in what Bromberger has called instruction would be *subsidiary* to the underlying question. The underlying question and its answer, together with the tutor's view of the tutee's predicament with regard to the underlying question and his view of what he must do

[13] For example, cases in which the tutor takes the tutee to be in a p-predicament with regard to Q because the tutee on his view has a psychological block.

[14] See Thomas F. Green, "A Typology of the Teaching Concept," *Studies in Philosophy and Education,* 3:288, 1964–1965.

[15] See R. F. Atkinson, "Instruction and Indoctrination," in Reginald D. Archambault (ed.), *Philosophical Analysis and Education* (Humanities Press, New York, 1965), p. 172.

about that predicament, would to a degree at least determine the nature of these questions. Answering these *subsidiary questions,* as I will call them, is not the primary task of the explainer; the primary task—insofar as it is to be viewed in terms of question answering—is to answer the underlying question of the episode. Yet this is not to say that it is not essential for the explainer to answer at least one subsidiary question. It is an essential task albeit a subsidiary one.

Notice that condition (e) when interpreted in terms of question answering would no more specify the subsidiary question or questions of an episode than conditions (a) to (d) specify the underlying question. The tutor's view of the tutee's predicament along with his knowledge of the subject would determine what subsidiary questions he must try to answer, just as the tutor's view of his task determines what question underlies a given episode. Notice also that the objection just raised to condition (e), namely that in certain contexts therapy and the like would seem to be required in explaining episodes, dissolves. For if the tutor's instructional task is conceived of as answering questions, therapy and similar methods no longer enter into the picture: to answer questions is one thing; to give therapy or the like is something quite different and is in no sense to be assimilated to question answering. Consider, then, condition (e″):

(e″) in the course of the episode the tutor also provides or attempts to provide the tutee with answers to such subsidiary questions as he (the tutor) thinks are necessary to remove the basis of whichever of the states mentioned in (c′) he deems the tutee to be in,
  or is effective in removing the basis of whichever of the states mentioned in (c′) he deems the tutee to be in,
  or is helpful in removing the basis of whichever of the states mentioned in (c′) he deems the tutee to be in.

Explaining something to someone does after all, then, involve shifting the question. It involves shifting from the underlying question of an episode to one or more subsidiary questions. Needless to say, the shift need not be a continuous-series shift. But there must be *some* shift if an episode is to count as an explaining episode, the exact nature of the shift depending on the tutor's view of the tutee's predicament and his view of the underlying question and its answer. It should be noted that there is no necessary temporal order for the shift: the tutor may tackle the subsidiary question before the underlying question or after it, or he may interweave his answers so that no temporal priority can be determined. The shift is a logical requirement; the best way to execute it is a pedagogical problem.

4 *Hypothesis Five*

Here is a new hypothesis to supplant Bromberger's Hypothesis Four:

HYPOTHESIS FIVE

The essential characteristics of explaining episodes are the following:

(a) the underlying question is sound, i.e., admits of a right answer, or the tutor believes, or at least assumes, that the underlying question is sound, i.e., admits of a right answer;

(b) the tutor is rational and knows the right answer to the underlying question at the time of the episode,

or thinks, or at least assumes, he knows the right answer to the underlying question at the time of the episode;

(c) during the episode the tutor knows, or believes, or at least assumes that at the beginning of the episode the tutee was in some rational predicament with regard to the underlying question;

(d) in the course of the episode the tutor presents the facts or some of the facts, or what he believes or at least assumes to be the facts or some of the facts, that, in his opinion, the tutee must learn to know the right answer or the answer the tutor believes or assumes is right

or he presents material that he knows, or believes, or at
least assumes, is not the facts, but that in his opinion is
sufficiently related to the facts and is pedagogically helpful
to the tutee in learning an answer to the underlying question which the tutor knows or believes or at least assumes, is
not the right answer, but which is sufficiently related to the
right answer, or the answer he believes or at least assumes
is right, so that it is pedagogically justified;

(e) in the course of the episode the tutor also provides or
attempts to provide the tutee with answers to such subsidiary questions as he (the tutor) thinks are necessary to
remove the basis of whichever of the states mentioned in
(c) he deems the tutee to be in,

or are effective in removing the basis of whichever of the
states mentioned in (c) he deems the tutee to be in,

or are helpful in removing the basis of whichever of the
states mentioned in (c) he deems the tutee to be in;

(f) at the end of the episode all the facts, or what the tutor
believes or at least assumes to be facts, mentioned in (d)
or the material that in his opinion is related to the facts in
the way outlined in (d) have been presented to the tutee
by the tutor and the answers or what the tutor takes to be
answers mentioned in (e) have been provided.

Bromberger can think of no episode that fits all the clauses for
Hypothesis Four and is not correctly described by a statement of
the form "someone explained W to someone" where "W" occupies
a position occupied by an indirect question, nor can he think of an
episode that is so describable but that does not fit all the clauses of
Hypothesis Four (p. 97). The burden of our discussion of Hypothesis Four is that contrary to Bromberger's belief, none of the
conditions in Hypothesis Four is a necessary condition of explaining something to someone. Hypothesis Five is an improvement on
Four in this respect, but as we will see in the next chapter, neither
Hypothesis Four nor Hypothesis Five contains a set of sufficient
conditions.

The objections to Hypothesis Four brought forth here and in

the next chapters should not, however, blind us to its virtues. If we compare it to the continuous-series model of explaining something to someone, we find it a great improvement in several respects. For one thing it makes explicit the need for a truth requirement—or something approaching it—on explaining something to someone whereas the continuous-series model either ignores this aspect of that activity or takes it for granted. Second, it recognizes the importance in explaining something to someone of the explainer's *view* of the explainee's state in a way that the continuous-series model does not. The continuous-series model brings out well that explanations$_D$ are *for* some audience. But this is only a beginning. What Hypothesis Four makes clear is that the explainer's perception of the explainee's state rather than that state itself is what matters. Finally, Hypothesis Four, in requiring that instruction be given, takes a larger view of explaining something to someone than does the continuous-series model. The continuous-series model allows one sort of instruction only, namely filling in a continuous series of events; Hypothesis Four is more generous and in this respect therefore it provides a more adequate account of explaining.

Chapter 5

EXPLAINING AS REASON GIVING

The tutor-tutee terminology used by Bromberger in his analysis of explaining something to someone is handy, but it is not without hazards. Tutoring is in important respects quite different from explaining even though it may sometimes involve explaining, and unless one recognizes this, the tutorial analogy suggested by this terminology can be downright misleading. For one thing, the tutor-tutee relationship is a much more direct and personal one than the explainer-explainee relationship. While tutoring, the tutor is normally face to face with his tutee, but this presumption does not hold for the explainer who may do his explaining when not in the presence of his explainee, for example, while writing a book or speaking on television. Hand in hand with this goes the fact that a tutor normally tutors one person or a small group of people at a time whereas there are no limits on the size of the explainer's audience: someone may explain something to one person, a small group of people, or to hundreds, thousands, or even millions of people.

Moreover, "tutorial" has either remedial or Oxonian overtones whereas explaining something to someone has neither. Someone who is backward in a subject is tutored in the hope that he will catch up. Explaining can serve a remedial function but such a function is not especially characteristic of it.[1] To be sure, one who explains something to someone must perceive some lack in that person relative to the question at hand and must try to remedy it, and in this respect I suppose explaining involves catching someone up. But a real tutee is backward in two respects: he is backward relative to a given question or subject and also relative to some reference group's position vis-à-vis that question or subject, for example, relative to his fellow classmates' mastery of French. An explainee may be backward in this double respect, but there is no presumption that he is. On the other hand, the explainee is not normally in the position of a tutee of the Oxford variety. This sort of tutee is not backward in the double respect just described. In the Oxford sense, the "tutorial" method is a particular way of teaching to be contrasted, for example, with the lecture method. Its purpose is in no sense remedial. However, there is the direct, personal relationship between tutor and tutee which need not be present in explaining, and there is also a procedure which, in emphasizing that the tutee draw conclusions for himself, is, as we shall presently see, in some ways the antithesis of explaining.

Whatever its defects, the tutorial analogy is a good antidote to the temptation to assimilate explaining something to someone into telling or informing.[2] The explainer must take his audience into account in a way that the tutor must but the teller and informer need not; his aim, like the tutor's but unlike the teller's and the informer's, is to get his audience to know or understand something. In these respects, of course, explaining is also like teaching. Indeed, it is in some respects closer to teaching than tutoring since teaching does not have the remedial connotations of tutoring and need not

[1] W. B. Gallie, however, attributes to explanations in history what might be called a remedial role; *Philosophy and the Historical Understanding* (Schocken Books, New York, 1964), chap. 5.
[2] Michael Scriven, for example, calls explaining "the appropriate piece of informing"; "Explanations, Predictions, and Laws," in Herbert Feigl and Grover Maxwell (eds.), *Minnesota Studies in the Philosophy of Science,* vol. III (University of Minnesota Press, Minneapolis, 1962), p. 176.

involve a one/one or one/small-group relationship. If teaching as a matter of fact is usually carried on face to face, so perhaps is explaining; neither activity need be, however, and that is what matters here.

Although philosophers have by and large ignored the notion of explaining something to someone, they have paid a good deal of attention to the notion of teaching. Indeed, in recent years a body of philosophical literature devoted to the analysis of teaching has grown up. Since teaching and explaining do seem to be similar, we might do well to examine some of this literature here. Analyses of teaching may shed light on aspects of explaining something to someone which neither Hypothesis Four and its attendant tutorial analogy nor the continuous-series model illuminates sufficiently.

1 The Rationality Theory of Teaching

Analyses of teaching have increasingly given a central role to reason and rationality. I will call the view of teaching which puts primary emphasis on reason and rationality the *rationality theory* of teaching and will discuss this theory in some detail, for it must be clarified and interpreted before we can see its relevance for the analysis of explaining something to someone. In the next chapter I will discuss a view of teaching which gives language a central role. I will call this view the *linguistic theory* of teaching and will discuss one version of it.

The view of teaching I am calling the rationality theory has gained wide acceptance among philosophers.[3] Rather than discuss

---

[3] See, for example, Israel Scheffler, *The Language of Education* (Charles C Thomas, Springfield, Ill., 1960); Israel Scheffler, *Conditions of Knowledge* (Scott, Foresman, Glenview, Ill., 1965); Israel Scheffler, "Philosophical Models of Teaching," *Harvard Educational Review*, 35:131–143, 1965; R. S. Peters, "Education as Initiation," *Studies in Education* (University of London Institute of Education, 1964); R. S. Peters, *Ethics and Education* (G. Allen, London, 1966); Thomas F. Green, "A Topology of the Teaching Concept," *Studies in Philosophy and Education*, 3:284–319, 1964–1965; and also, "Teaching, Acting, and Behaving," *Harvard Educational Review*, 34:507–524, 1964; R. F. Atkinson, "Instruction and Indoctrination," in Reginald D. Archambault (ed.), *Philosophical Analysis and Education* (Humanities Press, New York, 1965).

one writer's version of the theory here, a task which might become unwieldy since there is no neat and systematic formulation of the rationality theory, I will treat as a whole the literature that assigns a central role in teaching to reason and rationality and will abstract from it what I take to be its basic theses about teaching. It is well to note that in referring to the views set forth in these writings as a *theory,* I am very likely going beyond the intent of the writers themselves. It is perfectly legitimate to do this, but it must be remembered that the philosophers whom I am grouping together as rationality theorists have in fact said very different things about teaching, and that giving them a label may obscure important differences among them.

Israel Scheffler was one of the first to stress rationality in connection with teaching. Let me therefore introduce the rationality theory by quoting from *The Language of Education.* Teaching, Scheffler pointed out in that work, may proceed by various methods but not by any method at all:

> To teach, in the standard sense, is at some points at least to submit oneself to the understanding and independent judgment of the pupil, to his demand for reasons, to his sense of what constitutes an adequate explanation. To teach someone that such and such is the case is not merely to try to get him to believe it: deception, for example, is not a method or a mode of teaching. Teaching involves further that, if we try to get the student to believe that such and such is the case, we try also to get him to believe it for reasons that, within the limits of his capacity to grasp, are *our* reasons. Teaching, in this way, requires us to reveal our reasons to the student and, by so doing, to submit them to his evaluation and criticism.[4]

To teach is thus, says Scheffler, "to acknowledge the 'reason' of the pupil, i.e. his demand for and judgment of reasons, even though such demands are not uniformly appropriate at every phase of the teaching interval." [5] These remarks are elaborated on in Scheffler's later work and in the works of many other philosophers.

---

4 Scheffler, *The Language of Education,* p. 57.
5 *Ibid.,* p. 58.

It is important to clear up one possible misunderstanding of the rationality theory of teaching at the outset, a misunderstanding which can easily arise when teaching is referred to as rational because of the ambiguity inherent in the notion of a rational process or activity. When a political scientist or sociologist calls an institution, for example, a bureaucracy, rational or irrational, he is concerned with questions such as the following: How well does it do the job it is supposed to do? Are the methods employed the ones best suited to attaining the desired ends? If he answers this sort of question affirmatively, he calls the institution "rational"; if he answers it negatively he calls it "irrational." [6] This sort of judgment is analogous to the judgment that a given action was rational. Broadly speaking, says Carl Hempel, an action will qualify as rational "if, on the given information, it offers optimal prospects of achieving its objectives." [7] In other words an action, like an institution or a process, is judged to be rational if it is deemed well suited to attaining certain objectives.

Let us call the notion of rationality just delineated rationality$_E$ where the subscript "E" is intended to remind the reader that what is at issue in these determinations of rationality may roughly be thought of as the *effectiveness* or *efficiency* of the action or institution or process, etc. There are problems with this notion of rationality$_E$, but these need not concern us here.[8] For insofar as philosophers who contribute to the theory under discussion may call teaching or instruction a rational process or activity, they are *not* making a judgment about the suitability of the process or activity of teaching or instruction for achieving certain results or objectives. Nor are they claiming that the teacher must act in ways which on his view, at least, are well suited to attaining the desired end. What, then, are they saying about teaching or instruction?

In his discussion of the concept of a rational action Hempel points out that even in very simple cases some courses of action

---

[6] See, for example, Robert K. Merton, *Social Theory and Social Structure*, rev. ed. (Free Press, New York, 1957).

[7] Carl G. Hempel, "Aspects of Scientific Explanation," in *Aspects of Scientific Explanation and Other Essays in the Philosophy of Science* (Free Press, New York, 1965), p. 464.

[8] For a discussion of some of the problems, see *ibid.*, pp. 463ff.

which are available to an actor and are likely to bring about the desired end state may nevertheless be ruled out for him because they violate certain "general constraining principles," for example, moral or legal norms, social conventions. We may construe the rationality theory of teaching as formulating some of the general constraining principles that govern teaching, in particular those which require that the pupil's rationality be acknowledged. Just what exactly these are, according to the theory, remains to be seen. Whatever their exact nature, however, we may grant or deny that they govern teaching without taking any position at all on the rationality$_E$ of teaching. If teaching is rational in the sense that it must acknowledge the pupil's rationality—let us call this rationality$_P$ where the subscript "P" is used to remind the reader that the *p*upil's reason is at issue here—it does not follow that it is rational$_E$, although of course teaching could be both rational$_E$ and rational$_P$.

Hempel, in making the point that actions judged to be rational$_E$ are aimed at achieving the end state without violating certain general constraining principles, gives as examples of such principles moral or legal norms, contractual commitments, social conventions, the rules of the game.[9] All these sorts of constraining principles govern teaching but not all in the same way. That they do not comes out clearly if one asks what happens when these various sorts of principles are violated. If a legal constraining principle is violated, a teacher may be in trouble with the police, but he can still be teaching and his teaching might even be good teaching; if a moral constraining principle is violated, a teacher can also still be teaching. Rationality theorists are claiming that if the constraints to be discussed here are violated, the teacher is not teaching at all, for they profess to be discussing the "standard sense" of "teach." Thus we may say that the constraining principles they formulate have *logical* status: like rules of the game, rather than like norms or social conventions, they define the activity of teaching so that if someone violates them, he is not and cannot be teaching.[10]

[9] *Ibid.,* p. 465.
[10] For an interesting discussion of rules which define practices, see John Rawls, "Two Concepts of Rules," *The Philosophical Review,* 64:3–32, 1965.

According to the rationality theory, rationality and reason enter into teaching in at least two distinct ways: one relates to the *manner* in which teaching proceeds; the other relates to the *learning* at which teaching aims. Rationality theorists argue that not every way of getting someone to behave according to some norm is teaching. Some ways of getting people to do things may be very effective but they are not therefore ways of teaching, for teaching requires us to do such things as reveal our reasons to the student and submit our views to his judgment.[11] To adapt Hempel's terminology to our purposes, we might say that the theory proposes that a *general constraining principle on manner* governs teaching. Since the constraining principle has logical status, we may alternatively view the theory as proposing a necessary condition for saying that someone has taught something to someone.

It should be clear that the rationality theory's constraint on manner is not itself a principle of teaching on the normal construal of the latter notion, that is, it does not constitute a recommendation on how to teach. It functions as a criterion against which *any* method of teaching must be tested: if a method fails to meet the criterion it is *not* a teaching method at all. We may formulate the rationality constraint on manner (RCM) so as to make this clear:

(RCM) Whatever method you use, the pupil's reason must be acknowledged or you won't be teaching.

When the theory is so formulated, one can easily see that an activity, although rational$_P$, might not be rational$_E$: numerous methods might be used which did acknowledge the pupil's reason but were nonetheless quite ineffective in achieving the desired goals.[12]

In addition, the rationality constraint on manner should not be

[11] Scheffler, *The Language of Education*, p. 57.
[12] The question that remains is whether there is not some sort of rationality$_E$ requirement on teaching even though rationality theorists have not been concerned with it. In the last chapter we saw that there is good reason for requiring that the tutor in an explaining episode be rational. It might be argued on similar grounds that the teacher must be rational. A rationality requirement on the teacher would, in effect, place a rationality$_E$ requirement on teaching.

mistaken for a constraint on the learning which is the goal of teaching. It constrains the *way* in which teaching must proceed and not *what* teaching aims at. The rationality theory does hold that the pupil's rationality must be acknowledged in relation to the kind of learning which teaching aims at as well as in relation to the manner in which it proceeds, for it holds that the intent of teaching is not merely that the pupil acquire beliefs, even true ones, but that he also have backing for them. But the *general constraining principle on learning* which is presumed to govern teaching is independent of the constraining principle governing manner. Either rationality constraining principle could govern an activity without the other governing it. Thus someone could proceed so as to acknowledge his pupil's rationality yet aim only that his pupil acquire, for example, beliefs without backing; and conversely, someone could try to get his pupil to acquire beliefs with the sort of backing rationality theorists have in mind yet fail to acknowledge his pupil's reason in the course of so doing. Rationality theorists would claim that someone who acknowledged the pupil's rationality in one of these ways but not the other was not teaching. My point is simply that someone *could* do this, hence that according to the theory two distinct rationality constraining principles govern teaching.

It should perhaps be emphasized also that the general constraining principle on learning or, as I will call it, the rationality constraint on learning does not constitute a recommendation on what students ought to learn. Its function is analogous to that of the rationality constraint on manner: it serves as a criterion against which specific aims or objectives are tested without itself dictating specific aims or objectives. Thus although the rationality theory holds that to be teaching one must intend that one's pupil gain a certain kind or level of learning, it leaves the question of what it is that they should learn at this level wide open. We may formulate the rationality constraint on learning (RCL) so as to make this clear:

(RCL)   Whatever you want your pupil to learn, you must intend him to achieve a level of learning or mastery such that his reason is acknowledged or you will not be teaching.

2 The Rationality Constraints Interpreted

Some clarification of the rationality constraining principles on manner and learning is necessary if the rationality theory is not to be accused of absurdity and dismissed out of hand. If these constraints are interpreted as governing teaching at every moment or point, they doubtless rule out as teaching everything we normally take to be teaching. For the rationality theory to begin to be acceptable, these constraints must be interpreted as applying to teaching *as a whole*.[13] On this holistic interpretation someone might be teaching although at a particular moment he was trying to get his pupil to believe something without backing or was proceeding without due regard to his rationality. One would, therefore, have to look beyond the particular moment, or even the particular lesson, to the whole "episode" before judging that the general constraining principles on manner and learning were not functioning.

Granted that the rationality constraints on manner and learning govern teaching as a whole, it is necessary to get clear on just what they involve. One way to interpret the constraint on manner is that dialogue or conversation must take place in the course of teaching, for these notions are given prominence by rationality theorists.[14] Yet we can all think of cases of teaching—clear cases at that—which do not at any point involve dialogue or conversation. I see no reason why teaching could not proceed without language. But even if some language must be used in teaching when taken as a whole, the discourse need not take the form of dialogue or conversation. For example, one can teach by lecturing and entertaining occasional questions, but lecturing is not conversation

---

[13] To teach, says Scheffler, "is *at some points, at least,* to submit oneself to the understanding and independent judgment of the pupil . . ."; *The Language of Education,* p. 57, italics added.
[14] See, for example, Scheffler, *Conditions of Knowledge,* chap. 1; Green, "A Topology of the Teaching Concept," *op. cit.,* pp. 288ff.

and the asking and answering of questions is not necessarily dialogue.

Perhaps, however, it does the rationality theory an injustice to interpret its constraint on manner as requiring that conversation or dialogue need *actually* take place. If the theory *is* interpreted in this way, then I think it simply does not provide an analysis of the standard sense of "teach." The theory might then be viewed as providing a persuasive or programmatic analysis of "teach," and the question before us would be to decide whether the recommendations embodied in the analysis were good ones.[15] I myself would be inclined to reject the proposal that dialogue or conversation must or even should actually take place, at least at some points, in teaching. Surely one could teach typing, or French, or mathematics, for example, without there occurring a conversation or dialogue between teacher and student, and I am by no means convinced that there would be anything wrong with doing so.

The theory may, however, be interpreted as requiring not that dialogue or conversation *actually* take place but that the teacher *allow* it to take place if the occasion should arise, or, perhaps, that it be *possible* for it to take place. Some teachers lecture and do not permit dialogue or conversation to take place, while some physical setups, for example, television, do not provide the possibility for it to take place. Such lecturer-teachers might be considered mean or peculiar, and such television teachers might be considered unfortunate, but I am not sure that they would not still be teaching in the standard sense of "teach," particularly if they gave evidence, reasons, etc., for their views, had their material very well organized, and had built into their lessons answers to the questions they ex-

[15] In a review of *The Language of Education*, Elizabeth Flower argues that Scheffler has given a "programmatic explication of an effective use of the term [teaching]" and not a description of the way the term is used; in *Studies in Philosophy and Education*, 4:132–133, 1965. Scheffler, however, denies this in his "Reply to Elizabeth Flower," *Studies in Philosophy and Education*, 4:135, 1965. On this same point and for other criticisms of the rationality theory as it is contained in Scheffler's work, see Joan Cooper, "Criteria for Successful Teaching: or An Apple for the Teacher," *Proceedings of the Annual Conference,* The Philosophy of Education Society of Great Britain, 1966, pp. 5–18.

pected their students to have. This weaker version of the dialogue-conversation interpretation of the rationality constraint of manner has the same defects as the stronger version.

A better case can be made for the rationality theory if in trying to understand its constraint on manner we dismiss the notions of dialogue and conversation and take seriously instead the notions of questioning and justification—the asking for and giving of reasons —which also figure prominently in the writings of rationality theorists.[16] We may then interpret the constraint on manner as requiring that, in the course of teaching, justifications be given and questions be entertained. To require that the teacher be the one to give the justifications would be a mistake, of course, since someone who tried to get his pupil to figure out the relevant reasons for himself and therefore did not give them to him could still be teaching. It would also be a mistake to require that the pupil ask the questions since for pedagogical or practical reasons, for example, a very shy pupil, someone who was teaching might ask the relevant questions himself. The rationality constraint on manner must be understood, then, as allowing the questioning and reason giving to be done by either the teacher or the pupil.

Exactly what in teaching must be subject to questioning and justification? Many many things in teaching can be the subject of questioning and justification: the teacher's selection of content, his organization of content, his choice of teaching method, his choice of teaching materials, etc. Are we to construe the rationality constraint on manner as requiring that *everything* in teaching which can be justified and questioned must actually be justified and questioned at some points? Or that *some things* in teaching which can be justified and questioned, but no particular ones, must be at some points? Or that *some particular things* in teaching must be justified and questioned at some points? The writings of rationality theorists are not entirely clear on this issue. On one point, however, the theory is unambiguous: insofar as teaching aims at the ac-

---

[16] See, for example, Scheffler, *The Language of Education,* pp. 57–58; Scheffler, *Conditions of Knowledge,* chap. 1; Green, "A Topology of the Teaching Concept," *op. cit.,* pp. 288ff.; Atkinson, *op. cit.,* pp. 172ff.

quisition of beliefs (*teaching that*), the beliefs which the teacher is trying to get across must be the subject of questioning and justification.[17]

Teaching is concerned with more than the acquisition of beliefs, however. Skills, methods, propensities, and the like can be taught. One wonders just how the rationality constraint on manner applies to the teaching of these things since they are not primarily matters of belief. An example may make clear the way in which the constraint on manner when interpreted in terms of questioning and justification can apply in these areas, the areas of *teaching how* and *teaching to*. Whether this is what rationality theorists have in mind I do not know.

Suppose someone is teaching someone to play the guitar and is devoting a lesson to the G chord. The pupil questions the fingering for the chord—"Why must I use my little finger when it's so much easier to use my fourth finger?" The teacher justifies this way of playing the G chord by pointing out that it is much easier to move to other chords if this fingering is used and that once the pupil learns to play it in this way it will be as easy for him as any other fingering. Actions, methods, choices, and so on can be justified in this sort of way. If we construe the notion of content or subject matter broadly so as to include skills, methods, propensities and the like—indeed, whatever the teacher is trying to get across —then we may simply understand the constraint on manner as requiring that the subject matter or content of teaching be open to questioning and justification.

There is a difference between questioning and justifying some subject matter—"Is belief B really true?" "Is method M really the best way to do such and such?"—and questioning and justifying someone's having to study or learn that subject matter—"Why should pupil P have to learn that B is true?" "Why should P have to study M?" To justify someone's having to study or learn something may require, among other things, reference to the sort of life he will one day lead or want to lead, to the state of the society he will live in or want to live in, to general normative principles. It is of course very important that decisions or judgments about what

17 Scheffler, *The Language of Education*, p. 57; Green, *ibid.*, pp. 290ff.

should be studied and learned be questioned and justified, but questioning and justifying this sort of curriculum decision is not a necessary part of teaching. Someone can teach without engaging in questioning or justification of this kind.

A teacher may want to open up to his pupils for questioning and justification the many educational and pedagogical decisions—decisions of curriculum and methods and the like—which enter into teaching, but he surely is not required to do so in order to be teaching. The rationality constraint on manner is best understood as requiring questioning and justification in relation to the content of teaching and not in relation to the teacher's actions or decisions. Justifying these things to one's pupil would count as acknowledging his rationality, but it does not follow from this that someone must do so in order to be teaching. In holding that teaching must acknowledge the pupil's rationality, the rationality theory should not be interpreted as maintaining that every way of acknowledging a pupil's rationality is teaching; nor should it be interpreted as maintaining that teaching must acknowledge the pupil's rationality in every respect in which the pupil's rationality can be acknowledged.

The question still remains whether someone could not teach something although no questions about subject matter were asked and no justifications attempted. Suppose someone wanted his pupil to learn, organized the subject matter so as to maximize the likelihood of his learning, tried to get the pupil to want to learn, provided him with varied assignments and classroom activities, and helped him when he needed help, but in all of this no justifying or questioning occurred. Would we not still describe him as teaching? What seems to me to be essential to teaching is not that questioning and justifying occur but that it could occur if the appropriate situation were to arise. I am not at all sure that the "standard sense" of "teach" is sufficiently clear to enable us to decide on the basis of it alone between a categorical and a dispositional view of the rationality constraint on manner. The dispositional interpretation—that is, the "if the appropriate situation were to arise" interpretation—allows more things to qualify as teaching than the categorical, and this I count in its favor.

One basic difficulty I see with the rationality theory is that, unless one takes pains to construe it liberally, it rules out large areas of the educational scene—past, present, and future—as areas in which teaching is possible. Rationality theorists are motivated in part by the desire to differentiate teaching from indoctrination, brainwashing, strict conditioning, and kindred activities or processes. They are, therefore, very interested in ruling out certain things as teaching and thus might object to this loosening up of their constraint on manner. The problem with the theory, however, is that unless the constraint on manner is loosened up, it rules out much too much: the straight lecture approach, the traditional assign-recite pattern, television teaching, and various kinds of machine approaches are made to fall outside the boundaries of teaching, and this is surely a mistake if the original intent, namely to provide a descriptive analysis of teaching, is to be preserved.[18]

The rationality constraint on learning needs also to be examined. The interpretation of the constraint which is most plausible in light of the writings of rationality theorists is that to be teaching one must aim not simply at the acquisition of beliefs by the pupil but at the acquisition of beliefs together with proper backing for them, that is, backing that is integral to the subject at hand and whose force is appreciated.[19] If we take the notion of proper backing to exclude appeals to such authorities as the teacher and the textbook, as I think rationality theorists intend us to, we are in danger of ruling out much of what has normally been called teaching. We may deplore the fact that teachers have tried to get their

[18] Actually, this is an overstatement of the case. If the rationality constraint on manner is conceived of as governing the whole of teaching and not each part of it, these things and all sorts of other things which rationality theorists apparently want to ban from teaching are able to creep back in. Suppose, for example, that someone is teaching arithmetic: from time to time he gives reasons and entertains radical questions and hence he meets the constraint on manner; but he also gives his students a "long-division" pill. As far as I can see, the constraint on manner does not rule pill giving, open force, etc., out of teaching unless their use makes it impossible for the teacher even *at some points* to acknowledge the student's rationality. I do not know whether rationality theorists would find this consequence of the application of the "at-some-points" clause objectionable or not. It seems to me to be quite all right.

[19] Scheffler, *Conditions of Knowledge,* pp. 66–74.

pupils to believe things merely because they or the textbook say so, but I see no reason for saying that anyone who has set his sights no higher than this has *ipso facto* not been teaching.

Appeals to the "standard sense" of "teach" are not really decisive with regard to this issue, first because the "standard sense" of "teach" is by no means clear, and second because rationality theorists do not purport to be giving an analysis of the "standard sense" of *all* senses of "teach." Their concern is with teaching as an activity, that is, with an activity sense of "teach" and they are willing to grant that there are other senses of "teach," for example, a role sense which presumably encompasses what teachers in fact do in their institutional role. But this means that they can reject the sort of argument I have been adducing to show that the rationality constraint on learning is too narrow if the notion of proper backing is taken to exclude appeals to the authority of the teacher and textbook, on the ground that the teachers described have been fulfilling the *role* of teaching but nonetheless have not been engaging in the *activity* of teaching.

We may agree that there is an activity sense and a role sense of "teach" and that someone called a teacher may do many things besides teaching; indeed, if we take the message of *Up the Down Staircase* seriously, we will have to grant that in some school situations one whose role is teacher may find it all but impossible to engage in the activity of teaching.[20] Yet from the fact that there is more than one sense of "teach," it does not follow that the activity sense is governed by a narrow rationality constraint on learning. I simply do not think that the "standard sense" of the activity sense is clear enough for us to tell whether it is or not. What to my mind is crucial and what leads me to reject a narrow interpretation of the rationality constraint on learning is that such an interpretation builds into the analysis or definition of "teach" a decision which ought to be backed up by arguments showing that the sort of learning in question really is desirable.

The kind of learning which on a narrow interpretation of the rationality constraint on learning is built into the analysis of

[20] Bel Kaufman, *Up the Down Staircase* (Prentice-Hall, Englewood Cliffs, N.J., 1964).

"teach" is tantamount to what people who advocate learning with understanding as opposed to "rote learning" have in mind.[21] But I take it that they normally are making a recommendation for teachers or curriculum planners and not a conceptual point about teaching. In any event, although learning with understanding is doubtless a good thing, that teaching should in general aim at achieving it is still not self-evident, let alone that it necessarily does aim at achieving it. I can at least imagine contexts in which the particular combination of subject matter, pupil proficiency, and level of schooling combine to make something less than learning with understanding a suitable aim for teaching. An analysis of teaching should therefore be open enough to include as teaching at least those cases in which for good reasons something less than learning with understanding is aimed at.

The rationality constraint on learning can be loosened up by allowing appeals to the authority of the teacher, the textbook, and the like to qualify as "proper backing." But if this is done, one of the main purposes of the rationality theory, namely to distinguish teaching from such activities as indoctrination, is in danger of being defeated. Suppose someone actively and over the whole of his activity tries to prevent a pupil from acquiring any backing for the beliefs he is trying to get him to acquire except the say-so of an irrelevant authority. Surely he is not teaching but is doing something else, for example, indoctrinating. In allowing appeals to authority to enter into teaching, then, we must try not to blur the line between teaching and indoctrination. A construal of the rationality constraint on learning, parallel to our construal of the constraint on manner, gets around this problem. Instead of broadening the rationality theorists' restricted view of proper backing so as to include appeals to irrelevant authorities, we may interpret the constraint on learning dispositionally, that is, as requiring that the teacher try to get his pupil to acquire beliefs with proper backing *if*

[21] See Hugh G. Petrie, *Rote Learning and Learning with Understanding,* unpublished Ph.D. dissertation, Stanford University, 1965; Hugh G. Petrie, "Learning with Understanding," in Jane R. Martin (ed.), *Readings in the Philosophy of Education: A Study of Curriculum* (Allyn and Bacon, Boston, 1970).

the appropriate situation were to arise. This would allow one who was teaching to aim at something less than learning with understanding yet go part of the way at least toward differentiating his activity from indoctrination.

A dispositional construal of the rationality constraint on learning seems particularly apt when we consider that the rationality theory is intended as a theory of all of teaching and not just as a theory of *teaching that.* If the rationality theory were interpreted as requiring that the teacher aim at the acquisition of proper backing for beliefs, it would seem not to apply to *teaching how* and *teaching to.* However, if the constraint on learning is viewed simply as holding that the teacher aim at proper backing where it is appropriate, this problem disappears. For indeed, one who did not aim at this when appropriate—for example when the pupil was able to understand the reasons for a procedure and would clearly benefit from having them—would not be teaching how or teaching to but doing something else entirely.

In sum, the rationality theory of teaching is tenable only if it is given a rather liberal interpretation. The pupil's rationality must indeed be acknowledged in teaching, and the theory is valuable if for no other reason than that it points this up. But the two constraints on teaching contained in the theory must be taken as applying to the underlying content of teaching and are best viewed as dispositional, that is, as containing an "if the appropriate situation were to arise" clause. Moreover, the dialogue and conversation notions which figure in the writings of rationality theorists are not to be taken literally. Whereas one sometimes suspects that the linguistic theory to be discussed in Chapter 6 takes its cue from the lecture method, one wonders if the rationality theory in its stress on dialogue and conversation does not take its cue from the seminar method or the so-called Socratic method of teaching.

3 A Rationality Theory of Explaining

I am aware of the philosophical problems which arise when the rationality constraints on learning and manner are interpreted dispositionally.[22] What I have attempted to do here is at one and the same time to clarify the rationality theory and to construe its main theses in such a way that they are not overly restrictive. If a neater way of liberalizing the two constraints is available, that will be all to the good. Whether or not my clarification and interpretation of the theory are acceptable to those philosophers I have been calling rationality theorists I do not know. In view of their interest in differentiating teaching from indoctrination [23] it is quite possible that they would look askance at my efforts to loosen up the constraints which according to them govern teaching. Yet this loosening up seems necessary if justice is to be done to the wide range of things we call "teaching." If teaching does, as they say, involve acknowledging the pupil's rationality—and I think it does—the sense in which the pupil's rationality must be acknowledged is a good deal weaker than their writings at times lead one to believe.

What bearing has this theory of teaching on explaining something to someone? Briefly stated it is this: just as the teacher must acknowledge his pupil's rationality, so the explainer must acknowledge the explainee's rationality. Indeed, like teaching, explaining something to someone is governed by a rationality constraint on manner and a rationality constraint on learning. Let us consider first the constraint on manner.

In ruling out of explaining episodes what I called irrational predicaments, condition (c) of Hypothesis Five, formulated at the end of the last chapter, in effect places a rationality constraint on manner on explaining something to someone, for it requires the explainer to *treat* the explainee as being in a rational predicament, that is, as rational at least with regard to the underlying question Q. It does not require that the explainee *be* rational; nor does it

[22] See, for example, Rudolph Carnap, "Testability and Meaning," *Philosophy of Science,* 3:420–468, 1936. See also, among others, Carl G. Hempel, "The Theoretician's Dilemma," in Herbert Feigl, Michael Scriven, and Grover Maxwell (eds.), *Minnesota Studies in the Philosophy of Science,* vol. II (University of Minnesota Press, Minneapolis, 1958), pp. 37–98; Arthur Pap, "Disposition Concepts and Extensional Logic," in *ibid.,* pp. 196–224; Israel Scheffler, *The Anatomy of Inquiry* (Knopf, New York, 1963), part II.
[23] Scheffler, *The Language of Education,* pp. 57–58.

require that the explainer *know* or *believe* that the explainee is rational. The explainer need simply go on the assumption that the explainee is rational regardless of the explainee's actual state or the explainer's view of that state. And this, of course, is what the rationality constraint on manner is all about. The teacher, according to the rationality theory, must *treat* his pupil as rational; he must *acknowledge* his pupil's reason in the way he proceeds. This is not to say that the teacher must believe his pupil to be rational in relation to the topic at hand, nor is it to say that the pupil must be rational in that regard.

Condition (e) of Hypothesis Five may also be said to place a rationality constraint on manner on explaining something to someone, for in requiring the explainer to shift the question in an explaining episode, in effect it requires that he acknowledge the explainee's reason. It will be recalled that according to condition (e) of Hypothesis Five the tutor in an explaining episode must try to answer not only the underlying question of the episode but at least one subsidiary question which on his view is necessary or effective or at least helpful in removing the basis of the state the tutee is in. This seems to be the very sort of thing the rationality constraint on manner requires of teaching. Indeed, if we conceive of teaching along the lines in which Bromberger conceives of explaining, that is, in terms of episodes each involving some question, the rationality theory of teaching can be understood as maintaining that for an episode to be a teaching episode, there must not only be an underlying question to be answered but there must also be one or more subsidiary questions and they must be taken seriously.

There are problems with a question-answering approach to teaching, problems which do not arise when this approach is taken to explaining something to someone. For one thing we must construe the notions of an answer and of giving an answer very broadly so as to include pointing, showing, demonstrating, and the like. Only if we do this can we plausibly construe the teaching of skills (*teaching how*), for example, in question-answer terms. "How do you tie a shoe?" can be considered to be the underlying question of some *teaching how* episode only if we allow as an answer to the question such things as a demonstration of tying a shoe, a series of commands, shoves, and pushes. Indeed, even if we restrict ourselves to teaching for the acquisition of beliefs (*teaching that*), we must take a broad view of what can constitute an answer. "Why did the Pilgrims settle in the New World?" is a candidate for underlying question in a *teaching that* episode, but again we must allow as an answer all sorts of things, for example, movies and maps. But apart from this problem, it is still not entirely clear whether every legitimate teaching episode can be characterized as having an underlying question. I have in mind, for example, the teaching of attitudes, propensities, and the like (*teaching to*). It is far from obvious what the underlying question is when you are teaching someone to be a conservationist or to be sensitive to others.

For the present purpose, however, these problems need not detain us. Our interest in a question-answering approach to teaching is not so much to illuminate teaching—although it may in the long run do this—as to illuminate the way the rationality constraint on manner governs explaining something to someone. Consider therefore a teaching episode where there is no problem about determining its underlying question. Our Pilgrim example will do. We can construe rationality theorists, then, as maintaining something about the "structure" of that episode: it must have an underlying question (UQ), an answer to that question (AUQ), at least one subsidiary question (SQ), and answers to the subsidiary questions (ASQ). For example:

(UQ)   Why did the Pilgrims settle in the New World?
(AUQ)   They wanted to worship as they pleased and were not allowed to do so in England.
(SQ₁)   Why didn't they settle in Holland or Spain or France?
(ASQ₁) They tried Holland but became dissatisfied and they could not worship as they pleased in France or Spain.
(SQ₂)   Did they really feel so strongly about freedom of religion that they were willing to risk their lives for it?
(ASQ₂) Yes they did, but don't forget that they may not have

realized what an enormous risk they were taking—
that the hardships would be so great and that so many
would die in the first year.

Our discussion of the rationality constraint on manner in the
last section should make it clear that this account of the "structure" of a teaching episode is neither an account of the *actual* discourse in the episode nor of the *division* of discourse between
teacher and pupil. Rationality theorists are not, despite their talk
about questioning and justifying, saying that the pupil must ask
and the teacher must answer. As I have interpreted the rationality
theory, moreover, the constraint on manner is to be taken dispositionally. A subsidiary question and an answer to it, then, are not
strictly speaking required in a teaching episode; rather they are required if the appropriate occasion arises.

I will argue in Chapter 6 that explaining something to someone
does involve a particular *division* of discourse as well as a particular *kind* of discourse and that in this respect it diverges radically
from teaching. I should point out here that explaining diverges
from teaching also in that the rationality constraint on manner
governs explaining more strictly than it governs teaching. A dispositional interpretation of the constraint, which seems the proper
one in relation to teaching, is not suitable in relation to explaining:
there can be a teaching episode without a shift in question provided
there would be a shift were the appropriate occasion to arise, but
there can be no explaining episode without a shift in question. A
nondispositional interpretation of the constraint on manner is
needed when it governs explaining. If teaching is closely connected
with acknowledging the other's reason, how much more so is explaining.

Consider now the rationality constraint on learning. We have
stated all along that one who is explaining something to someone is
trying to get someone to understand something. To try to do this
is not simply to try to get someone to acquire beliefs. Understanding does involve belief, but it surely involves more than this. For
example, someone who understands why the engine seized up must
do more than believe that it was due to an oil leak. At the very

least this belief must have backing. The continuous-series model discussed earlier may be construed as requiring that the backing for this belief be of a very special nature, namely the tracing or ability to trace a continuous series of events between seizure and oil leak. As we have seen, this requirement is too restrictive. On the other hand, it does not seem that any sort of backing at all will fill the bill. Having an argument from authority, for example, "The mechanic, who is very competent and reliable, said the seizure was due to an oil leak," does not warrant our saying that the person *understands* why the engine seized up.

Understanding and knowing diverge in at least this respect: someone who has an argument from authority can, other things being equal, qualify as knowing something, for example, why the engine seized up; he will not, however, qualify as understanding that thing, for example, why the engine seized up. To understand, for example, why the engine seized up, he must have backing of a certain sort. It need not involve a continuous series, although it may. Rather, it must be the sort of backing which rationality theorists have in mind in relation to teaching, that is, backing from within the relevant subject matter.[24] In the engine-seizure case this could consist of some theory, a continuous series of events, or perhaps something else entirely. We may describe explaining something to someone, then, as being governed by a rationality constraint on learning.

As in the case of teaching, the rationality constraint on learning is best viewed as governing the activity of explaining something to someone as a whole, that is, in relation to its underlying question. We have seen that the explainer must try to answer subsidiary questions in the course of answering the question underlying each explaining episode. But it is not the case that he must aim at understanding in relation to these questions as well as in relation to the underlying question. In connection with these questions, beliefs backed up by appeals to authority are permissible. Thus, although we are conceiving of explaining in terms of question shifting, we are conceiving of it as aiming at understanding only in relation to the underlying question of an explaining episode. The overall aim of an explaining episode is understanding, whereas the aim in rela-

[24] See Scheffler, *Conditions of Knowledge*, pp. 67ff.

tion to the subsidiary questions—the instruction of Bromberger's condition (e)—can be much more modest.

This discussion brings us back to the issue of the adequacy of Hypothesis Four (and also Hypothesis Five) as a set of conditions such that any episode meeting all of them is an explaining episode. Implicit in Bromberger's analysis of explaining something to someone is that the tutor is trying to get his tutee to know the right answer underlying the particular episode. But this view of the explainer's task is inadequate for two reasons. First, given some right answers to a question, it is possible for a tutor to try to get his tutee to know the right answer without caring at all whether he is able to connect the right answer to the underlying question. Consider, for example, the question "Why did the engine seize up?" and the right answer "There was a leak in the oil reservoir." A tutor could try to get his tutee to know that there was a leak in the oil reservoir—that is, believe truly that there was a leak and have adequate evidence for this belief—hence know the right answer, without ever worrying about whether the tutee recognized that the seizure was due to the leak. The conditions of Hypothesis Four (and Five) would be fulfilled, but the tutor would not have explained to his tutee *why the engine seized up*.

It is possible to defend Hypothesis Four (and Five) from this attack on the grounds that an answer such as "There was a leak in the oil reservoir" is elliptical for "The engine seized up because there was a leak in the oil reservoir." Given a nonelliptical answer, it will be argued, Hypothesis Four (and Five) does not fall short in the way just suggested. This is a fair answer to my objection, but a nonelliptical construal of the notion of a right answer will not in the long run save Hypothesis Four (or Five). Suppose we grant that the tutor's task, given the underlying question "Why did the engine seize up?", is to get his tutee to know the answer "The engine seized up because there was a leak in the oil reservoir." To know this, the tutee must believe truly that the engine seized up because there was a leak in the oil reservoir and must have adequate evidence or the like for this belief.[25] An appeal to authority could constitute such evidence, but if this were the sort

[25] See Scheffler, *Conditions of Knowledge;* Roderick Chisholm, *Perceiving: A Philosophical Study* (Cornell University Press, Ithaca, N.Y., 1957).

of backing the tutor wanted his tutee to have he would not have been trying to get his tutee to understand why the engine seized up.

Hypothesis Four (and Five) is compatible with an episode which is not governed by the rationality constraint on learning, hence is not an explaining episode. Bromberger's tutor may be described as trying to get his tutee to know W, where "W" indicates a position occupied by an indirect question. But to know W, for example, why the engine seized up, is not necessarily to understand W. Yet it is understanding W and not simply knowing W that is the aim of explaining something to someone. Indeed, since understanding W is the aim of every explaining episode, explaining something to someone is governed by a rationality constraint on learning which is not to be construed dispositionally.

Once again explaining may be said to acknowledge the pupil's rationality in a stronger way than teaching does. I do not think that either Hypothesis Four or the continuous-series model brings out adequately the fact that rationality, in the form of reason giving and reason having, plays a central role in explaining something to someone. It is left to a theory of teaching to do this. But if explaining involves acknowledging the explainee's rationality, it does not only involve this. It involves, besides the things pointed to by the rationality theory of teaching, Hypothesis Four, and the continuous-series model, a particular use of language. For more on this point, let us turn to a quite different theory of teaching.

Chapter 6

EXPLAINING AS A
USE OF LANGUAGE

What I am calling the linguistic theory of teaching has many versions. The one I have chosen for discussion here is Kingsley Price's.[1] I will examine Price's account of teaching in the first section of this chapter, and in the second section I will reinterpret it as a theory of explaining something to someone. Only after we get clear on the role of language in explaining will I attempt to bring together our findings about explaining based on our study of two theories of teaching, Bromberger's Hypothesis Four and Dray's continuous-series model.

[1] See "On 'Having an Education,' " *Harvard Educational Review,* 28:320–337, 1958. Page references in the text of this chapter will be to this essay.

1 A Linguistic Theory of Teaching

Price may be characterized as an "extreme" linguistic theorist in contrast to a "moderate" such as B. Othanel Smith.[2] Smith is much more cautious than Price in the role he assigns to language in teaching, and for this reason alone his theory provides a better account of teaching than Price's does. But the very extremity of Price's version is, at least from our standpoint, a virtue. If more moderate versions of the linguistic theory provide more balanced accounts of teaching, they do not provide as much insight into explaining something to someone as does Price's version.

There are, of course, some similarities between Price's linguistic theory of teaching and the rationality theory. Both view teaching as something that one can engage in, that takes time, that can be improved upon with practice; both view it as involving a relation between two people; both view it as goal-directed or goal-oriented. But the two theories differ on what they take the key to teaching to be: for Price it is a certain use of language by teacher and pupil; for the rationality theory it is the acknowledgement of the pupil's rationality by the teacher.

According to Price, teaching involves four uses of sentences: an assertive use, a clarificatory use, an explanatory use, a supervisory use (p. 326). However, teaching does not only involve these four uses of language; the teacher does any number of things to promote his aim—understanding that and understanding how—but these things vary from one situation to another, and their place in teaching is to supplement the four uses of sentences (p. 327). Yet although teaching in general involves these four uses of language, in any particular situation one or another use may dominate. Indeed, from Price's remark that to teach the shape of the earth involves using the sentence "the earth is an oblate spheroid" in *at*

[2] "A Concept of Teaching," in B. Othanel Smith and Robert H. Ennis (eds.), *Language and Concepts in Education* (Rand McNally, Chicago, 1961), pp. 86–101. There is some reason also to consider Gilbert Ryle a linguistic theorist; *The Concept of Mind* (Hutchinson, London, 1949), pp. 309–314.

least an assertive way (p. 326), one may infer that in particular cases teaching need only involve the assertive use of sentences. But if so, then what exactly is Price saying about teaching? He is *not* holding that

> (1) In every case of teaching, sentences are used in all four ways.

He is, rather, holding that

> (2) In every case of teaching, sentences are used in at least an assertive way.

It is most important to note that Price distinguishes between an active and an acquiescent use of sentences: communication involves active uses of sentences by a speaker and corresponding acquiescent uses by a listener. Thus, for example, a sentence is not used in merely an assertive way, but rather in an active or else an acquiescent assertive way. Since teaching involves communication between teacher and pupil, it is not surprising that Price insists that when sentences are used in that activity they are used in an active or acquiescent way. He goes further than this, however, and claims that teaching involves the passive use of sentences by the pupil:

> The word "teaching" stands for a certain use of sentences along with the activities which supplement it. The use is assertive, clarificatory, explanatory, and supervisory; and active on the part of the speaker who teaches, but correspondingly acquiescent on the part of the hearer who learns (p. 327).

Teaching succeeds, he continues, "where the student's use of sentences corresponds in an acquiescent way to that to which the teacher puts them" (p. 327).

Price's theory has been shown to be woefully inadequate.[3] First, the aim it ascribes to teaching, namely the promotion of understanding that and understanding how, is too narrow, for it

[3] By Israel Scheffler, "Comment," *Harvard Educational Review*, 28:337–339, 1958.

rules out from the scope of teaching attempts to develop character traits such as honesty, punctuality, etc., which do not necessarily involve the acquisition of understanding but rather involve the acquisition of habits and propensities. Second, the manner of proceeding it requires of the teacher, namely that sentences be used in an active assertive way by him, is too narrow, for it rules out from the scope of teaching many methods used by good teachers, including all attempts to get the pupil to figure things out for himself. Third, the criterion it sets for successful teaching, namely that the pupil's use of sentences corresponds in an acquiescent way to the teacher's, is too narrow in that it rules out cases where the pupil, instead of parroting the teacher's views, disagrees intelligently with them.

Suppose, however, that instead of taking the theory to be a theory of teaching, as Price to be sure intended it, we take it to be a theory of explaining something to someone. Can the same objections be made to it? The first objection, namely that the theory rules out attempts to develop certain propensities and tendencies, is no longer valid, for the realm or scope of explaining something to someone is not as broad as that of teaching. We can explain to someone that such and such is the case, we can explain to someone how to do something, but we cannot explain to someone to be honest, to be punctual, to obey rules. Thus the goal of explaining something to someone cannot be the acquisition of propensities or tendencies or what is sometimes referred to as patterns of action. The goal of promoting understanding that and understanding how, although too narrow to apply to teaching, is sufficiently broad to apply to explaining something to someone.

Although explaining something to someone diverges from teaching in that it does not aim at the development of patterns of action and the like, one might conclude from the fact that we speak of *explaining that* and *explaining how to* that explaining something to someone is like teaching insofar as teaching aims at the acquisition of beliefs and skills. However when someone, A, explains to someone, B, how to do something, A is not necessarily trying to get B to acquire a skill or capacity: A wants B to understand how to do the thing but this is to say that A wants B to acquire certain beliefs or knowledge about the skill, and not necessarily the skill itself. To understand how to do something is not necessarily to be able to do that thing. Consider the difference between A's explaining to B how to ride a bicycle and A's teaching B how to ride a bicycle. In the latter case A wants B to learn how to ride, that is he wants him to acquire a skill, to be able to ride. In the former case A's concern is not that B be able to ride a bicycle but that B believe or know certain things about how to ride a bicycle, that is, certain principles of bicycle riding.

Explaining how seems to be a special case of *explaining that,* while the *understanding how* it tries to promote can be considered a special case of *understanding that.* In this respect *explaining how* takes its place alongside of *explaining why, explaining where, explaining what;* linguistic form should not be allowed to obscure this. The scope of explaining something to someone, then, is relatively narrow as compared to the scope of teaching. Whereas teaching can rightly be said to deal with "the whole child" in that it aims at equipping him with skills and norms as well as beliefs, explaining something to someone is limited in aim to promoting understanding. Indeed, in comparison to teaching it may be said to be quite intellectualistic. I stress this here because Price's theory of teaching is open to criticism for being overly intellectualistic. One who has an education, Price says, believes what he has been taught. But surely although one who has been successfully taught how to do something has learned how to do it and presumably knows how to do it, the notion of believing what he has been taught is not relevant.[4] Believing is relevant, however, if the activity in question is *explaining how to* rather than *teaching how to.* Thus again, a valid objection to Price's theory of teaching loses its force when the theory is viewed instead as applying to explaining something to someone.

Another major objection to Price's theory of teaching concerns his criterion of success, namely that the pupil's use of sentences must correspond in an acquiscent way to the teacher's. Whether or not this objection to the theory disappears when the theory is viewed as an account of explaining something to someone depends

[4] *Ibid.,* p. 339.

on how this criterion of success is interpreted. If we take the student's corresponding acquiescent use of sentences to be a parroting of the teacher's views, then this criterion is no more appropriate for explaining something to someone than it is for teaching.

But suppose we take the notion of the student's corresponding acquiescent use of sentences to refer not to his parroting of the teacher's views but to his believing and accepting what the teacher says. Then Price's criterion of success, although it does not do full justice to explaining something to someone, does capture an important aspect of success in that activity. For when A explains something to B, A expects or intends that B accept the substantive content of the explanation offered him. Understanding is the desired outcome, but it is the understanding that A is trying to promote and not any old understanding. If teaching is sometimes counted successful when the student rejects the teacher's views and substitutes his own, explaining something to someone is not. Price's criterion in this respect is appropriate for the latter activity although not the former.

2 *A Linguistic Theory of Explaining*

Consider now the most interesting part of Price's theory, namely his view of the manner in which teaching must proceed. It should be clear that (2) above does not adequately capture his thesis. He maintains at least:

(3) In every case of teaching, sentences are used by the teacher in at least an active, assertive way.

Now it is my own view that A can teach B something although A does not use sentences at all, let alone use them in an active, assertive way. Consider a silent demonstration, for example, of a dance step, a scientific experiment, a technique of painting. Given certain contexts, such a demonstration could qualify as a teaching episode. But even if this is denied and it is held that one who is teaching must use language, indeed must use language actively, it is surely not the case that one must use language in an assertive$_S$ way. One can restrict oneself to asking questions or to issuing commands and exclamations. Other things being equal, for example, that learning is being striven for and the pupil's rationality acknowledged, this may qualify as teaching.

I realize that some people would claim on the basis of a teacher's silence or nonassertive use of language that teaching is not taking place: education, maybe; teaching, no. But these people, it should be pointed out, identify teaching with what is normally considered to be one *sort* or *way* of teaching—the sort Jerome Bruner seems to have in mind when he speaks of teaching in the "expository mode" and others seem to have in mind when they speak of "instruction." [5] Given this "lecture method" conception of teaching, any number of things normally called teaching would not qualify as such, and the particular gap between teaching and explaining something to someone to which I am pointing in this section would be well on the way to disappearing. But it should be stressed that this view of teaching is not the ordinary one. Bruner *contrasts* a mode or method of teaching in which the teacher is the expositor and the student the listener with a mode in which these roles are shared or even reversed. And we are all accustomed to contrasting the lecture method of teaching with such things as the case method, the Socratic method, the seminar method.

The question remains whether A can explain something to B if A does not use sentences in an active, assertive way. This depends on what an active, assertive use of sentences involves. If A is truly explaining something to B, he must give B an explanation$_D$. If he doesn't give B an explanation$_D$ but instead, for example, tries to get B to figure things out for himself, A may (or may not) be indulging in excellent pedagogy, but he is not explaining this

[5] Jerome S. Bruner, "The Act of Discovery," in *On Knowing* (Harvard University Press, Cambridge, 1962), p. 83; R. F. Dearden, "Instruction and Learning by Discovery," in R. S. Peters (ed.), *The Concept of Education* (Humanities Press, New York, 1967), pp. 135–155. See also B. Paul Komisar, "Teaching: Act and Enterprise," *Studies in Philosophy and Education*, 6:187–188, 1968.

particular thing to B. In explaining something to someone, there is no analogue to the "discovery method" of teaching. If we adopt Price's terminology, to give B an explanation$_D$ is to use sentences in a certain way, for an explanation$_D$ of something for someone is a statement or set of statements. It is, in the first place, to use sentences in an *active* way, provided that "active" is construed broadly enough to include writing as well as speaking. Price himself seems to view his notions of an active and an acquiescent use of language as applying to a speaker and a listener, respectively (p. 325), but I see no reason why they should not be conceived of as applying also to a writer and a reader, respectively.

On first sight it would appear that explaining something to someone does not involve the assertive use of sentences by the explainer—or at least does not require that use. It will be recalled that Price speaks of an explanatory use of sentences, and it is reasonable to assume that in explaining something to someone, the explanatory use is involved. Price does say that a given sentence may at one and the same time be used for many different purposes (p. 325), so that the assertive use is not necessarily excluded by the explanatory use. According to Price, however, one use is usually more important than the others, and the one which dominates is revealed by the context in which the sentence is uttered. It would surely seem that in the context of the activity of explaining something to someone, if anywhere, the primary use to which sentences were put would be explanatory; sentences could be used in an assertive way, but this way would be relatively unimportant. If this is really the case, then thesis (3) does not hold true for explaining something to someone: sentences although used in an active way by the explainer would not have to be used in an assertive way.

There is, however, an ambiguity in Price's notion of an assertive use of sentences, and only in one sense of that notion can we correctly say that in explaining something to someone the assertive use of sentences is at best secondary. Price characterizes the assertive use as the employment of sentences to assert facts (p. 324). But this characterization tends to blur two quite separate points: (a) that some sentences state something about something;

(b) that some sentences when uttered are used for the purpose of reporting or describing things.[6] If in distinguishing various uses of sentences Price is referring to the user's purpose or object in making a statement, then he is justified in differentiating an assertive use from his other uses; indeed, it makes sense to say that in the context of explaining something to someone the explanatory use is dominant and the other uses, including the assertive use, are secondary. For given that someone is explaining something to someone, his general object or purpose is not merely to say something or report something or get something on the record as it would be if he were telling someone something or informing him of something; rather it is to explain something. In this sense of "assertive use," which I will henceforth refer to as *assertive$_P$ use*, where the subscript "P" is intended to remind the reader that the user's *purpose* is at issue, thesis (3) does not hold true for explaining something to someone.

On the other hand, when someone is engaged in explaining something to someone, the sentences he uses must state or assert something *about* something. Consider someone who uses sentences in an active way but none of whose sentences state anything about anything, for example, they are all questions. Again we have a situation in which A may (or may not) be using an excellent pedagogical technique, but is not *explaining* to B. The "Socratic method," like the "discovery method" with which it is often linked, has no analogue in explaining something to someone. If A only asks questions, he may indeed be trying to get B to understand something or know the right answer, but he will not be explaining to B unless the sentences *he* uses state or assert things *about* whatever it is he is explaining to B.

If in speaking of an assertive use of sentences Price is referring to the fact that when some sentences are used they assert or state things about the world and what have you, then it is a mistake to contrast this "use" with his other three uses. This feature of certain sentences is independent of the speaker's general object in

---

[6] G. J. Warnock, for one, in his discussion of the statement or assertion "That's true," makes clear just how important it is to keep these points distinct; "A Problem about Truth," in George Pitcher (ed.), *Truth* (Prentice-Hall, Englewood Cliffs, N.J., 1964), pp. 54–67.

using the sentences; indeed, he may often achieve his general object, be it reporting or supervising or clarifying or explaining, *just because* the sentences he uses assert things about something or other.[7] In particular, when a person is explaining something to someone—when, to use Price's terminology, he is using sentences in an explanatory way—the sentences he uses must assert something about the issue in question. In this sense of "assertive use," which I will henceforth refer to as *assertive$_S$ use,* where the subscript "S" is intended to remind the reader that the sentences involved *s*tate something about something, thesis (3) does seem to hold true for explaining something to someone. One who explains something to someone must use sentences which assert things and must himself be the one who does the uttering or writing of the sentences.

It should be noted that in claiming that the sentences used in explaining something to someone are used in an active, assertive$_S$ way, I have made no references to facts, although Price characterizes sentences used in an assertive way as sentences used to assert facts. If assertive$_S$ sentences—or, if you wish, the statements made by means of assertive$_S$ sentences—assert facts, then they must be true. But as we argued in connection with Bromberger's Hypothesis Four, to require of the explainer that the statements made must be true is quite unreasonable. If thesis (3) is to hold true for explaining something to someone, the notion of the assertive$_S$ use of sentences must be construed broadly enough to accommodate both those false statements which the explainer takes to be true and the ones he takes to be false but uses for sound pedagogical reasons.

If assertive$_S$ sentences are interpreted as asserting *facts,* another difficulty mentioned in connection with Hypothesis Four arises in applying thesis (3) to explaining something to someone. For facts, at least in the sense of "fact" in which facts are contrasted with value judgments, need not enter into explaining something to someone. A can explain to B why the schools ought to be desegregated, and although facts may be relevant generally to the issue of

---

[7] "We seem to find, in the case of 'That's true,' a (noncolloquial) agreement-indicating role *because of* what is meant by the words and done by one who utters them." *Ibid.,* pp. 62–63, author's italics.

school desegregation, in a particular context A may think it necessary to assert the relevant moral principles rather than the facts. Unless the notion of a fact is construed very broadly so as to include particular value judgments, moral principles, and for that matter also general laws and theories, it is not helpful in illuminating the activity of explaining something to someone.

Provided then that (i) the notion of the active use of sentences is taken to include writing as well as speaking; and (ii) the notion of the assertive use of sentences is (a) restricted to the assertive$_S$ use and (b) taken to include certain false as well as true statements, and value judgments, theoretical statements, and the like, Price's thesis (3) holds for explaining something to someone. In every case of explaining something to someone, sentences are used by the explainer in at least an active, assertive$_S$ way.

This finding casts doubt on the adequacy of Hypothesis Four —and for that matter on Hypothesis Five as well—as a set of conditions such that any episode meeting all of them is an explaining episode. It will be recalled that condition (d) of Hypothesis Four requires that the tutor *present* the relevant facts to the tutee. But we have just seen that to explain something to someone the tutor must himself *state* or *assert* the facts. This requirement is stronger than the requirement of presenting them. A tutor could present the facts to his tutee simply by *pointing*. Thus, for example, given the question 'Why is the air of our city polluted?", a tutor could present the facts to his tutee by taking his tutee on a field trip and pointing to the offending smokestacks and automobile exhaust. Such a lesson would, in some contexts at least, meet condition (d) of Hypothesis Four, but it would not constitute an explaining episode.

Condition (e) in Hypothesis Four requires that instruction be given, and it might be argued that the imagined field trip fulfills condition (e) rather than condition (d). To be sure, such a field trip might in some contexts fulfill condition (e) rather than condition (d), but it need not. The field trip could serve the function of presenting the facts the tutee must learn to know the right answer to the question "Why is the air of our city polluted?", while the instruction required by condition (e) consisted in something else, for example, in showing a documentary film designed to fill in some needed theoretical background. The film itself might present facts but they would not in the context envisioned be the ones the tutee must learn to know the right answer to the underlying question. Moreover, even if the film presented the facts the tutee must learn to know the right answer, the problem raised initially would remain. Facts presented in a film shown by a tutor are not facts stated by him. For the tutor to have explained something to his tutee, he must do the linguistic work himself. In this respect explaining something to someone *is* like telling, although in other respects it is not.

Consider now the following situation: A tutor states the facts he thinks the tutee must learn to know the right answer to the question, but he does so in a random or irrelevant order; for example, he states them in alphabetical order or he writes down the facts on slips of paper, mixes these up in a hat, closes his eyes, pulls out one at a time, and reads them. I take it that this would not constitute an explaining episode. In leaving it to the tutee to organize the facts he states, to make sense of them, to relate them to the question underlying the episode, the tutor abdicates his responsibility as explainer. As explainer the tutor must not only state the relevant facts; he must relate them to one another and to the underlying question. *He* must do the explaining. Again we see that explaining something to someone diverges drastically from the so-called "discovery method" of teaching.

In sum, if someone is truly explaining something to someone, he must give that person an explanation$_D$. If he lets his tutee do the work, for example, figure out the answer for himself or figure out how the facts presented combine to yield the answer, he may be teaching but he is not explaining. Similarly, he cannot let books or films or programs answer the underlying question for him and still be explaining. This is not to say that a tutor cannot use books, films, and programs to provide the instruction required by condition (e), that is, to answer subsidiary questions; it is simply to say that he must state the facts mentioned in (d) and he must organize them or pattern them for the tutee.

With respect to the use of language, explaining something to someone differs from tutoring as well as from teaching. Explaining can enter into both activities but is not to be confused with either one. A particular use of language—what we have called the assertive$_S$ use—which is essential for something to be an explaining episode is compatible with teaching and tutoring but essential to neither. A particular division of discourse between the two parties to the activity—the active use of sentences by A and the passive use by B—is also essential for something to be an explaining episode but not for teaching or tutoring. Finally, if something is to constitute an explaining episode, language must be used in such a way that the relevant facts or fact substitutes are organized or patterned for B. This is true of neither teaching nor tutoring.

3 Conditions of Explaining Something to Someone

The moral to be drawn from our discussion of Price's theory is that there is a linguistic condition on explaining something to someone: A has explained something to B only if A has used language in a particular way, namely actively and assertively$_S$. This condition relates to manner, that is, to the way explaining proceeds. It serves, moreover, to differentiate explaining from such endeavors as teaching, tutoring, and showing, none of which requires a particular use of language. On the other hand, this linguistic condition does not in itself enable us to distinguish between explaining something to someone and telling; nor does it enable us to distinguish between explaining and informing someone of something or reporting something to someone, all of which require an active, assertive$_S$ use of sentences.

When we consider the matter of A's intent or purpose, however, we have no difficulty in separating explaining from those activities with which it shares the linguistic condition under discussion here. I have pointed out that in one sense of the phrase "assertive use," namely the sense in which the user's purpose is at issue —the assertive$_P$ use as opposed to the assertive$_S$ use—language is not used assertively in explaining something to someone. Given Price's list of purposes for which language can be used, we would have to say that the language used actively and assertively$_S$ in an explaining episode is used for an explanatory purpose. In the present context, however, this is not a very illuminating way of putting it. We are better off saying, as we have said all along, that the explainer's purpose is to create understanding. For A to have explained something to B, in other words, A must have intended or wanted or been trying to get B to understand that thing.

There is, then, an understanding condition on explaining something to someone as well as a linguistic condition. We discussed this understanding condition in Chapter 5 for the rationality constraint on learning, which according to rationality theorists governs teaching and which according to our own view governs explaining —requires, in effect, that the explainer try to get his explainee to understand. We will, moreover, have occasion to say more about this condition in the next chapters. We need here, therefore, do no more than remark on its force. This understanding condition serves to distinguish explaining from such things as telling, informing, and describing.[8] It serves another function, too, that of placing what might be called practical, or better still pedagogical, constraints on the way the explainer proceeds. If A is trying to get B to understand something, certain ways of proceeding will normally be more appropriate than others. These may of course vary depending on the nature of A and the information available to him, the nature of B and the nature of the thing being explained. Nonetheless, given some particular explainer, explainee, and thing to be understood, it will normally not be the case that every way of proceeding is equally good.

As we saw in Chapter 5, explaining, like teaching, involves a twofold acknowledgement of the explainee's rationality. Suppose A is trying to get B to understand why the engine seized up. A hypnotizes B and says, "When you awake you will understand why the engine seized up, when you awake you will understand why the engine seized up. . . . It's due to an oil leak, it's due to an oil leak. . . . When the oil leaks out the piston gets overheated, when the oil leaks out the piston gets overheated. . . ." A has not

---

[8] A may nonetheless have given B an explanation$_D$. More on this in the next section of this chapter.

in this case explained to B why the engine seized up, no matter how effective he has been at creating understanding, for although he may be said to have acknowledged B's rationality with respect to the goal or outcome of his activity in that he was trying to get B to understand something, he has not acknowledged B's rationality in relation to his manner of proceeding. There is a rationality condition relating to the manner of explaining distinct from the understanding (or rationality) condition which relates to the goal of that activity or, if you will, the purposes of those who engage in it.

As our discussion in Chapter 4 of Bromberger's Hypothesis Four should have made clear, there is also a truth condition on explaining something to someone: A has explained something to B only if A has told B the truth—or at least tried to tell B the truth—unless, of course, A has good reason for doing otherwise. This truth condition on explaining is, I should add, independent of the three conditions so far mentioned. Along with the linguistic condition and the rationality condition, it relates to the manner in which explaining proceeds. It is distinct from the linguistic condition for, as I have interpreted the notion of an assertive$_s$ use of language, using language actively and assertively$_s$ yet not telling the truth or even trying to tell the truth is quite possible. A uses language actively and assertively$_s$ when he says or writes things about things regardless of the truth of what he says or writes; A explains something to B only if he says things about things and only if what he says is true, or at least on his view is true, other things being equal. A truth condition is distinct, too, from the rationality condition relating to manner. A can acknowledge B's reason in the sense at issue, namely in the sense of giving B reasons and allowing B to exercise his own reason and judgment at every point along the way, yet fail to tell or even try to tell the truth. Truth is one thing; giving reasons, answering questions, allowing someone to exercise his judgment is something else again: explaining something to someone, like teaching, but unlike telling, requires both.

Now all of this might be granted yet it might be argued that since explaining must meet an understanding condition the issue of

truth is taken care of; that formulating a truth condition in relation to manner is redundant. This position is plausible for, as we
will see in the next chapter, there is a truth condition on understanding. However, it does not follow from the fact that A is
trying to get B to understand something (given a truth condition
on understanding) that A must tell or try to tell B the truth. A
could, for example, lie to B or at least misrepresent the facts to B
in the hope that B would detect the lie or misrepresentation and go
on to figure out the truth for himself, thereby gaining understanding. Such a strategy might, indeed, be considered a fruitful one to
pursue in teaching. If A were to follow it, however, he would not
be explaining to B, whatever his success in getting B to understand.

Suppose now that A wants B to understand something, uses
language actively and assertively$_S$, speaks only the truth, and
throughout acknowledges B's rationality. Suppose, however, that A
speaks in French, that B does not understand French, and that A
knows that B does not understand French. Perhaps there are some
contexts in which this would constitute an explaining episode; normally, however, we would say in a case like this that A has not explained whatever he was trying to explain to B. In discussing the
understanding condition on explaining, we suggested that it exerts
pedagogical constraints on the way the explainer proceeds. It might
be argued, therefore, that if A is trying to get B to understand something, he will speak in a language—or for that matter at a level—
that B can comprehend. But this is true, I submit, only if we assume that A is rational. A rational person will do what is appropriate, or at least what on his view is appropriate, other
things being equal, to achieve his goal. A person who is not rational may not do what is appropriate.

We may view the requirement that the explainer be rational—a
requirement built into Hypothesis Four, it will be recalled—as another condition on explaining something to someone. To distinguish it from the condition requiring the explainer to acknowledge
the explainee's reason in the course of proceeding, let us call the
former the rationality$_E$ condition on explaining and the latter the

rationality$_P$ condition on explaining.[9] The rationality$_P$ condition bears on the explainer's attitude and behavior toward the explainee, not on his efficiency or the effectiveness of his methods. It rules out ways of proceeding no matter how effective if they prevent the explainee from exercising his reason. The rationality$_E$ condition, on the other hand, has to do with the relation between the explainer's means and his ends. It requires him to choose means which are necessary for or conducive to, or at least are on his view necessary for or conducive to, achieving his ends. Thus the rationality$_E$ condition ignores, so to speak, the explainer's treatment of his explainee except as it bears on achieving an end result, while the rationality$_P$ condition ignores the problem of whether means are suited to ends except as some means prevents or allows for the acknowledgement of the explainee's rationality.

One more condition on explaining something to someone needs to be mentioned. There is, as our discussion of Dray's continuous-series model brought out, a question-shifting condition on explaining: A has explained something to B only if A has answered what, following Bromberger's approach to explanation, I have called the underlying question of an explaining episode and at least one subsidiary question. Thus a mechanic who meets the five conditions summarized above but who simply says "It's due to an oil leak" has *not* explained to his assistant why the engine seized up. He has answered the question "Why did the engine seize up?" and perhaps has given his assistant an explanation$_D$ of why it seized up. But unless he does some filling in, that is to say, unless he shifts the question to, for example, "Why did the leak lead to the seizure?" or "How could there possibly have been a leak?" and answers the new question, he would not qualify as having explained to his assistant why the engine seized up.

Six conditions of explaining something to someone can, then, be abstracted from our discussion of that activity: (1) a *linguistic condition;* (2) an *understanding condition;* (3) a *rationality$_P$ condition;* (4) a *truth condition;* (5) a *rationality$_E$ condition;*

[9] See Chap. 5, sec. 1, for a discussion of the distinction between rationality$_E$ and rationality$_P$.

(6) a *question-shifting condition*. These conditions of explaining something to someone have logical status: they are necessary conditions of explaining; each one must be met if someone is to be described truly as having explained something to someone.[10]

4 Explanations of Something for Someone

Consider now Hypothesis Six. Whether or not it constitutes a set of sufficient conditions of explaining something to someone I do not know. It does, however, incorporate the necessary conditions of explaining something to someone just set forth. It is, therefore, an improvement over Hypothesis Five, itself an improvement over Hypothesis Four:

HYPOTHESIS SIX

The essential characteristics of explaining episodes are the following:

(a) the underlying question is sound, i.e., admits of a right answer or the tutor believes, or at least assumes, that the underlying question is sound, i.e., admits of a right answer;

(b) the tutor is rational and understands W at the time of the episode, or thinks, or at least assumes, he understands W at the time of the episode;[11]

(c) during the episode the tutor knows, or believes, or at least assumes that at the beginning of the episode the tutee was in some rational predicament with regard to the underlying question;

(d) in the course of the episode the tutor states the right answer or what he believes or at least assumes to be the right answer, to the underlying question, or that part of

---

[10] These six necessary conditions of explaining could equally well have been formulated as general, constraining principles governing explaining (see Chap. 5): as constraining principles having logical force.

[11] "W" here occupies a position taken up by an indirect question whose corresponding direct question underlies the episode.

the right answer, or what he takes to be the right answer, that in his opinion the tutee must learn in order to understand W,

or for good pedagogical reasons he states what he knows, or believes, or at least assumes is not the right answer to the underlying question, but is in his opinion sufficiently related to the right answer so that it will not prevent the tutee from understanding W at some later date;

(e) in the course of the episode the tutor also provides or attempts to provide the tutee with answers to such subsidiary questions as he (the tutor) thinks necessary or effective or at least helpful for removing the basis of the predicament he deems the tutee to be in;

(f) in the course of the episode the tutor encourages or allows the tutee to exercise, or at least does nothing to prevent the tutee from exercising, his reason and judgment with respect to the underlying and subsidiary questions and the answers to them given the tutee by tutor;

(g) at the end of the episode the tutor has organized for the tutee and stated to him the answers mentioned in (c) and in (e).

According to Bromberger, to have explained something$_R$ is to have become able to explain it as a result of one's own endeavors and ingenuity.[12] This is not to say that if A has explained$_R$ W, then A has fulfilled the role of tutor in the sort of episode described by Hypothesis Six. There is always a gap between being able to do something and doing it, so that to say that A is able to explain W to B is not to say that A has explained, is explaining, or will ever explain W to B. This view of the connection between explaining$_R$ something and explaining something to someone, then, maintains a gap between the two notions and for this it is to be commended. One wonders, however, whether the gap has not been

[12] Sylvain Bromberger, "An Approach to Explanation," in R. J. Butler (ed.), *Analytical Philosophy,* 2d ser. (Blackwell, Oxford, 1965), p. 101. Actually Bromberger discusses statements of the form "A explained W." I am taking this discussion to be a discussion of what I have called explaining$_R$ something.

made too narrow. What does it take to be competent to act as a tutor in an explaining episode? If we believe Hypothesis Six, it takes things which there is no reason to suppose will have been acquired simply by virtue of someone's having explained something$_R$.

Bromberger sees the connection he does between explaining$_R$ something and explaining something to someone because he requires one who has explained W to B to know the answer to the underlying question Q and takes one who has explained$_R$ W to know the answer to Q. But this, I think, is a mistake. One who explains W to B is trying to get B to *understand* W and not merely to know the answer to Q; but then, he must himself *understand* W and not merely know the answer to Q [see condition (b) of Hypothesis Six]. One who has explained$_R$ W, on the other hand, need not have come to understand W. To have explained$_R$ W one must have come up with an explanation$_F$ of a certain sort; to understand W, even to know the answer to Q, one must have certain beliefs and have adequate backing for them; [13] there is no guarantee, however, that one who comes up with an explanation$_F$ of W has the relevant beliefs or the required sort of backing. A person can have explained$_R$ W unwittingly, he can have hit on the right answer to Q yet not realize that it is the right answer to Q: in these and other cases he may be said to have the information which could yield the understanding yet not have the understanding or knowledge required of a tutor in an explaining episode.

But suppose that one who has explained$_R$ W does know the answer to Q, indeed does understand W, simply by virtue of his having explained$_R$ W. He then has one sort of competence needed for explaining. There is no guarantee, however, that he has another sort which is equally necessary. One who explains W to B has the job of bringing B from the state or predicament B is in, or is thought to be in with regard to Q, to the state of understanding W; that is to say, one who explains W to B must shift the question [see condition (e) of Hypothesis Six] or, if you prefer, provide instruction, fill the gap. Competence in this—in diagnosing B's state and acting on the diagnosis toward the end of creating understanding—is required of the tutor in an explaining episode.

[13] This point will be discussed further in Chap. 7.

Although such competence is not something which can only be acquired through instruction in pedagogy, it is surely not something which is necessarily acquired by one who has explained$_R$.

Bromberger's account of the connection between explaining$_R$ something and explaining something to someone brings out well the fact that the explainer of W must have the answer to Q and that explaining$_R$ W is one way to get that answer. But this account is nonetheless misleading. It misleads because it makes too light of the similarities between explaining something to someone and teaching, and too much of the similarities between explaining something to someone and telling. Competence in one's subject matter is all one needs for telling someone W; indeed, it is more than one needs. For teaching someone W, however, one cannot get along with just this: one needs competence in getting subject matter across to somebody. For explaining one also needs more than competence in one's subject matter.

In Chapter 2 I described the connection between explaining$_R$ something and explaining something to someone by saying that one who has explained$_R$ something may be viewed as a producer of raw materials for one who is explaining something to someone. Another way of putting this is to say that the explainer$_R$ comes up by his own efforts with answers the explainer$_T$ needs to do his job. The advantage of viewing the explainer$_R$ in this way—as a provider of raw materials to the explainer$_T$ rather than as one able to explain—should be obvious. A provider of raw materials is in no better position to use those materials than anyone else: if special competence is needed in order to use them—and in the case of explaining it is—there is no reason to suppose that the provider qua provider has it.

Someone can have explained$_R$ something without being able to explain it to someone, let alone having explained it to someone. Moreover, a given person, A, can have explained something to someone without having explained$_R$ it himself. Can A have explained something to someone, however, if *no one* has ever explained$_R$ it? Let us bracket this question for the present and turn instead to the relationship between explaining something to someone and explanation$_D$ of something for someone.

Can someone have explained something to someone without having given that person an explanation$_D$? This question has already been answered. In arguing that one objection to Price's linguistic theory of teaching—namely that it does not allow the pupil to figure out things for himself—disappears when the theory is viewed in relation to explaining something to someone, I pointed out that if someone explains something to someone, he gives that person an explanation$_D$. The linguistic and truth conditions set forth above are intended to capture this aspect of explaining. Conditions (d) and (e) of Hypothesis Six are also intended to capture it.

There can be no explaining something to someone without an explanation$_D$ of something for someone. There can, however, be an explanation$_D$ of something for someone without explaining something to someone.[14] A set of statements may constitute an explanation of something for someone quite accidentally. For example, one who has just explained$_R$ W could enter his explanation$_F$ of W in his diary, never intending that anyone see it. He would not have explained W to anyone, yet it is conceivable that someone could happen upon the diary and, on the basis of the explanation$_F$ of W contained therein, understand W. The explanation$_F$ of W in the diary would constitute an explanation$_D$ of W for that person, yet no one would have explained W to him; indeed, the explanation$_F$ of W could have been an explanation$_D$ for him even if there had *never* been an explaining episode with W as the underlying question. Explanations$_D$ can be given in the course of activities which are not explaining—in the course of telling or reporting, for example—and can also be found quite apart from activity contexts.

In Chapter 2 I stressed the close connection between explanations$_D$ of something for someone and explaining something to someone. It will be recalled that the subscript "D" was used to remind the reader that these explanations were part of someone's discourse, the implication being that the someone was the explainer$_T$. It is true that the discourse of the explainer$_T$, or some part thereof, constitutes an explanation$_D$, but it is not the case that the

[14] For a different view of this matter, see Bromberger, *op. cit.,* p. 104.

explainer is the *only* one whose discourse can constitute an explanation$_D$. We must distinguish between two classes of explanations$_D$ of something for someone: those which are *intended* for the person and those which are *not intended* for the person. The explanation$_D$ the explainer$_T$ gives his explainee is intended to do the job of creating understanding, and it is intended to be appropriate for him, but in fact it may not be appropriate for him and may not do the job it is supposed to do. One can have explained W to B, hence given B an explanation$_D$ of W, yet not have succeeded in getting B to understand W.[15] Those explanations$_D$ which are given when explaining is successful [16] can be said to be *for* someone in a twofold sense: for him in that they are *intended* for him and for him in that they *do the job* (create understanding) for him. We must recognize, however, that there can be explanations which do the job for someone, that is to say, give him understanding, yet are not intended for him.

Recall now the comment Dray's mechanic made to his assistant: "It's due to an oil leak." We have made it clear that the mechanic was not explaining to his assistant why the engine seized up although he did tell him why. Did he, nonetheless, give his assistant an explanation$_D$ of the seizure? Supposing that "It's due to an oil leak" enabled the assistant to understand why the engine seized up, must we not say that this was an explanation$_D$ *for him?* I think we must. And the present analysis allows us to say this, for it admits instances of explanations$_D$ in nonexplaining contexts. Indeed, this case of an explanation$_D$ without explaining differs from our diary example in that the explanation$_D$ given the mechanic's assistant was in a sense intended for him. We see, then, that there can be explanations$_D$ both suitable for and intended for someone apart from explaining contexts; indeed, we see that someone can *give* someone an explanation$_D$ of something without at the same time explaining that thing to him.

But wait. "It's due to an oil leak" contains no shift in question.

[15] For example, B may not be in the predicament the explainer takes him to be in and the explainer may shift the question in a direction which is not in fact helpful in relation to B's predicament.

[16] In the course of what Bromberger calls *proper* explaining episodes; *op. cit.*, p. 101.

Can it, after all, be an explanation$_D$ of something for someone? I have argued that shifting the question is essential to explaining something to someone. Are we to say that it is essential to explaining, but not to explanations$_D$? Yes we are, for it seems quite clear that in the context envisioned and countless others like it there can be explanations$_D$ without there being some shift in question. This is not to say that the explanations$_D$ one encounters in explaining episodes need not contain some shift in question. These explanations$_D$ are a subclass, if you like, of explanations$_D$ of something for someone in that they must answer some shift in question as well as answering the question underlying the episode. Explanations$_D$ occurring in nonexplaining contexts can of course answer some shift in question but they need not, just as they can be intended for someone but they need not be. Explanations$_D$ in explaining contexts, on the other hand, must be intended for someone and must answer some shift in question.

For a statement or set of statements to constitute an explanation$_D$ of something for someone, it must not only speak, as it were, *to* someone, it must speak *about* something, namely the explanandum event. Moreover, it cannot say anything at all about the explanandum event. In any given context certain statements may fail to qualify as an explanation$_D$ of something for someone not because they are inappropriate for him—although they might fail to qualify on this score—but because they do not provide the right sort of account of the explanandum event. What sort of account of an explanandum event E is the *right* sort? I do not intend to answer this question in detail here; indeed, the question is, in effect, the one that I am on principle bypassing in this essay. For our purposes it is sufficient to point out that an explanation$_S$ of E provides the right sort of account of E. We do not, of course, want to require that an explanation$_D$ of something E for someone be a carbon copy of an explanation$_S$ of E. Yet we can insist that if some statement or set of statements is to qualify as an explanation$_D$ of E it must bear some sort of relationship to some explanation$_S$ of E.

There can be an explanation$_S$ of something without there being a corresponding explanation$_D$ of that thing for someone; this much follows from the context-free nature of the notion of an explanation$_S$ of something. But there cannot be an explanation$_D$ of something for someone if there is no corresponding explanation$_S$ of that thing. For a statement or set of statements to be said to constitute an explanation$_D$ of something for someone, there must be a corresponding explanation$_S$ of that thing. This is not to say that one who gives an explanation$_D$ of something for someone must have at his fingertips an explanation$_S$ of that thing, nor that he must supply it if challenged. There must *be* such an explanation$_S$ but it need not be *known* at all, let alone known by the one whose discourse constitutes the corresponding explanation$_D$.

What I am saying is that a statement or set of statements X is an explanation$_D$ of something for someone only if there is an explanation$_S$ of E. Something must be added to this thesis, of course, for it is clearly not the case that, given that there is an explanation$_S$ of E, any set of statements appropriate for B will constitute an explanation$_D$ of E for B. The statements X must bear some relation to an explanation$_S$ of E if they are to be considered an explanation$_D$ of E for B. I do not propose to spell out the relation here; indeed, I do not even know whether it can be spelled out in any general way. The relation is one of transformability: the statements X must be transformable into an explanation$_S$ of E if they are to constitute an explanation$_D$ of E for B. The problem, of course, is to determine which sorts of transformations (from an explanation$_S$ to an explanation$_D$) are legitimate and which are not. I am assuming, I think with good reason, that in context there will normally be no great difficulty in deciding whether a given statement or set of statements qualifies as a legitimate transformation of some explanation$_S$. The problem as I see it lies in finding some general rules or principles of transformation.

The thesis I am propounding here concerning the relation between explanations$_D$ of something for someone and explanations$_S$ of something is in an important respect like the thesis Morton White has set forth concerning the relation between explanatory statements and what he calls explanatory deductive arguments. In his book *Foundations of Historical Knowledge* White presents a version of the regularity theory of historical explanation which he calls existential regularism. On his view a singular explanatory statement, that is, one of the form "A is a contributory cause of C," is true if and only if there is an explanatory deductive argument containing A as a premise and C as its conclusion.[17] My thesis is existential in the same way White's is: I am saying that something is an explanation$_D$ only if *there is* an explanatory argument of a certain sort. But it should be emphasized that mine is not a regularist thesis whereas White's is. I am purposely remaining neutral on the question of the conditions which an explanation$_S$ of something must meet; White, on the other hand, takes a stand on the nature of these conditions.[18]

Another obvious difference between the present thesis and White's is that he is talking about necessary and sufficient conditions for something while I am simply talking about necessary conditions. A less obvious but very important difference between the two theses is that they are concerned with different notions of explanation. In the course of his discussion of explanatory statements White shows no concern at all for what might be called the pedagogical dimension of explanation. Statements of a certain form are true if and only if there is an argument of a certain sort, and such statements, if true, are presumably explanatory statements. Never mind their suitability or lack thereof *for someone*. White is not disinterested in historical practice: historians give statements of this sort, he claims, and they rightly consider the statements explanatory. Indeed, in his book he is concerned to reconcile this aspect of historical practice with the regularity theory of explanation, and he makes use of the distinction between explanatory statements and explanatory arguments for this end. Yet his interest in practice must not be confused with an interest in "who says it to whom."

White's singular explanatory statements seem to me to fall into our category of explanations$_F$ of something by someone. His explanatory statements are not the only things that fit into this category—they are causal statements and not every explanation$_F$ is a causal explanation$_F$—but they may, I think, be interpreted as con-

[17] Morton White, *Foundations of Historical Knowledge* (Harper & Row, New York, 1965), p. 60.
[18] *Ibid.*, chaps. II, III.

stituting a subclass of explanations$_F$ of something by someone. But then, the notion of explanation he is analyzing—his analysandum —is not the one we have been discussing. To be sure, there may in fact be instances of explanation$_F$ which serve as explanations$_D$ in that they "do the job" for someone—are appropriate for him, get him to understand. An analysis of the notion of an explanation$_D$ of something for someone, however, cannot leave the pedagogical dimension of such statements up to fate: granting for the moment White's existential regularism, it should be clear that it is not enough in the case of explanations$_D$ that an explanatory argument of a certain sort exists, for this requirement at best ensures that the right sort of account of E is provided; something over and above this is needed to ensure that the account also be suitable for B.

As I interpret White's notion of an explanatory statement, it is an explanation$_F$ of something by someone, not an explanation$_D$ of something for someone. Suppose now we change our analysandum so that we, too, are concerned with explanations$_F$ of something by someone. The connection between these explanations and explanations$_S$ of something is similar to the connection between explanations$_D$ of something for someone and explanations$_S$ of something: a statement or set of statements X is an explanation of something E by someone A only if there is an explanation$_S$ of E and X is transformable into that explanation of E. What differentiates explanations$_F$ from explanations$_D$ is not the relation they bear to explanations$_S$ but the range and nature of legitimate transformations in the two cases and, of course, the contexts in which they occur.

Now that we have shifted our own analysandum to coincide, more or less,[19] with White's, the question remains whether the analysans in the two theses are not totally different. White's requirements that there must be an explanatory deductive argument of a certain sort is stronger than my requirement that there must be an explanation$_S$ of something. But I think it fair to view his notion of an explanatory deductive argument as a semantic notion of explanation. That is to say, an explanatory deductive argument can be viewed as an explanation$_S$ of something—an explanation$_S$

---

[19] In view of the fact that his explanatory statements are causal, our analysandum coincides less, not more, with White's.

meeting certain requirements. There are, then, some important differences between the present account of explanation notions and White's, but there are also some interesting similarities. So far as I can see, the distinctions White has drawn between explanation notions are quite compatible with the fivefold distinction drawn in this essay. His focus, however, is on the regularity theory, while mine has been primarily on explaining something to someone and the explanations$_D$ contained therein.

If there can be no explanation$_D$ of E for B unless there is an explanation$_S$ of E, then there can be no explaining E to B unless there is an explanation$_S$ of E, for explaining episodes include explanations$_D$. But what of those episodes in which the explainer takes the underlying question to be sound when in fact it is not sound? Hypothesis Six allows for such, for example, for A to explain to B why the engine seized up when in fact it did not seize up. Yet an unsound question admits of no right answer; that is to say, there can be no explanation$_S$ of why the engine seized up if in fact it did not seize up. There would seem, then, to be cases of explaining without some corresponding explanation$_S$ unless, of course, we change our mind about Hypothesis Six and decide it is too liberal after all. The tendency of our discussion of explaining something to someone has been to liberalize the conditions placed on it by others. Must we now tighten the reins?

I think not. We need simply adjust our account of the relation between explaining something to someone and explanations$_D$ of something for someone. We said that there can be no explaining something to someone without an explanation$_D$ for that person. We must now amend this view as follows: there can be no explaining something to someone without an explanation$_D$ for that person or *what on the explainer's view* is an explanation$_D$ for that person. This account preserves the connection between explanations$_D$ and explanations$_S$ just presented but weakens a bit the connection between explaining and explanations$_D$ given above. I do not see that this does any real harm; indeed, it appears to be very much within the spirit of Hypothesis Six, for, like that hypothesis, it makes explaining something to someone primarily a matter of the explainer's view of his subject matter and his explainee.

In sum, then, we find explanations$_D$, or what are taken to be explanations$_D$, to be required for explaining episodes and explanations$_S$ to be required for explanations$_D$. Since I have paid relatively little attention here to explaining$_R$ something and explanations$_F$ of something by someone, I suggest in a more tentative spirit that explanations$_S$ are required by explanations$_F$ and explanations$_F$ are required by explaining$_R$. The question remaining is that of the connection between explanations$_D$ and explaining something to someone on the one hand and explanations$_F$ and explaining$_R$ something on the other hand. I have said that explaining$_R$ provides raw materials for explaining something to someone. It should now be clear that it provides them, in particular, for the explanations$_D$ given in explaining episodes. But is it the only provider of such materials? Can A explain X to B only if *someone* has explained$_R$ X? I fear we will have to leave this question unanswered here. The issue is complicated and to decide it we would have to delve not only into the nature of explaining$_R$ but also into the nature of explanation$_F$. Such an investigation would lead us too far afield and is best left for another occasion.

Part Three

UNDERSTANDING

Chapter 7

UNDERSTANDING
AS SEEING
CONNECTIONS

Let us look more closely now at the notion of understanding to see if we can get clear on exactly what the goal of explaining something to someone is. We will begin by distinguishing two quite different notions of understanding. Once we establish the relationship between these two notions and the relationship of each one to explaining something to someone, we will be in a better position to discuss that sort of understanding aimed at by explaining something to someone.

1   Understanding Something and Being Understanding

In any discussion of understanding it is important to recognize that there is a difference between understanding something and being understanding toward someone.[1] To say that someone is un-

---

[1] For an interesting account of various uses of "understand," see May Brodbeck, "Meaning and Action," *Philosophy of Science,* 30:309–324,

derstanding toward someone, or that he is being understanding, is to say that he is taking a certain attitude toward someone. I will call this *being understanding* and will use the subscript "A" when referring to it to remind the reader that it is an *a*ttitude. I will not attempt here to give a general analysis of this attitude. It is sufficient for our purposes to point out that being understanding$_A$ toward someone involves looking or at least trying to look at things through the other person's eyes and being sympathetic toward him. If someone takes this attitude consistently in a wide range of situations, we refer to him as an understanding$_A$ person. But whether someone takes this attitude only on occasion or whether it permeates his behavior to such an extent that it can be called a general trait of character, one thing is certain: this sort of understanding is not what the activity of explaining something to someone necessarily aims at.

Indeed, being understanding$_A$ cannot be the general aim of explaining something to someone. An attitude can be the thing the explainer explains to his explainee but, as we have already seen, explaining does not aim—at least not directly and in general—at the acquisition of such things as attitudes. This is not to say that the explainer might not on particular occasions intend that his explainee acquire some attitude, for example, that he be understanding$_A$, nor is it to say that an explainee might not acquire some attitude as a result of something having been explained to him regardless of the explainer's intentions. The point being made here is simply that one can explain something to someone without intending that he acquire some attitude, hence without intending that he be understanding$_A$.

The understanding which explaining aims at is properly described neither as an attitude nor as a character trait. This understanding bears a kinship to knowing and believing and has nothing to do with sympathy or empathy or identification, all of which are closely connected with being understanding$_A$. It is this sort of un-

1963. And for an illuminating discussion of understanding something, being understanding, and empathy, see Michael Martin, "Understanding and Participant Observation in Cultural and Social Anthropology," in R. Cohen and M. Wartofsky (eds.), *Boston Studies in the Philosophy of Science*, vol. IV (Humanities Press, New York, 1969), pp. 201–228.

derstanding people have in mind when they call "understand" a cognitive verb. I will speak of it here as *understanding something* and will use the subscript "C" when referring to it to remind the reader of its cognitive affinities. Understanding something$_C$ and the understanding attitude just discussed are independent of one another. A person can understand$_C$ someone's behavior yet not be understanding$_A$ toward him at all; and conversely, a person can be understanding$_A$ toward someone yet fail to understand$_C$ his behavior.

It may be the case that where people and their actions are the things being explained to someone, understanding$_C$ will be more easily attained if the explainee takes an understanding attitude. But then again this may not be the case, or at least this may not always be the case but may depend on the sort of people and the sort of actions being explained and on the sort of person the explainee is. In any event, supposing that the explainee's being understanding$_A$ toward someone helped him understand$_C$ that person's actions and supposing that the explainer, knowing this, therefore tried in the course of an explaining episode to get the explainee to be understanding$_A$ toward that person, it still would not follow that getting the explainee to be understanding$_A$ was the goal of explaining something to someone, or that understanding$_C$ something and being understanding$_A$ toward someone were connected logically.

Just as being understanding$_A$ may lead a person to understand$_C$ something, so understanding$_C$ may lead a person to be understanding$_A$. Thus, for example, if an explainer can get his explainee to be understanding$_A$ toward some historical character, the explainee may become motivated to find out all about that character, and his understanding$_C$ of that character's actions may thereby be facilitated. And on the other hand, if an explainer can get his explainee to understand$_C$ some initially unsympathetic historical figure, the explainee may find himself being more understanding$_A$ toward that figure than he had ever expected he could be. There is no guarantee, however, that understanding$_C$ will bring about understanding$_A$ any more than there is a guarantee that understanding$_A$ will lead to understanding$_C$. Again we must stress that even if an explainer hopes and has reason to expect that his explainee will upon the completion of an explaining episode achieve understanding$_A$, his explaining will have been successful so long as the explainee attains the proper sort of understanding$_C$. An explainer may hope for results over and beyond the minimum set by his activity, but it does not follow that such results, even if achieved, are what he must be aiming at if he is to qualify as engaging in that activity.

If explaining something to someone necessarily aims at understanding$_C$, it does not necessarily result in understanding$_C$ any more than teaching necessarily results in learning. There can be explaining something to someone without understanding$_C$ thereby being attained. We may note also that understanding$_C$ can be attained although no explaining has taken place. Just as one can learn something without having been taught it, so there are many ways to acquire understanding$_C$ besides being a party to an explaining episode. That we are discussing understanding$_C$ as the goal of explaining something to someone ought not to obscure the fact that there are many ways to achieve understanding$_C$. The educator who views his job—or at least one of his jobs—as the promotion of understanding$_C$ in his students ought not to suppose that his classroom role is therefore that of explainer. It is an open question whether explaining is the best way to produce understanding$_C$ in a given situation, even though explaining by definition aims at just this.

The task before us is to shed some light on the notion of understanding$_C$. We will approach our task via a notion that crops up time and again in talk about understanding$_C$; namely, the notion of seeing connections. We will on the one hand explore the sorts of *connections* that can be seen and the sorts of *things* these connections can hold between if there is to be understanding$_C$, and we will on the other hand try to get clearer than we now are on what it is to *see* connections. Our discussion of understanding$_C$ will begin with a brief examination of Gilbert Ryle's account of it. I have selected Ryle's views for special attention for several reasons: his negative thesis about understanding$_C$ is correct and is not only worth stressing in its own right, but is particularly relevant to an interpretation of understanding$_C$ in terms of the notion of seeing connections; his positive thesis, although in my view mistaken, foreshadows important formulations by contemporary philosophers of the doctrine that human actions require a special sort of understanding and is also very relevant to the claims of many educators that a particular sort of competence is necessary if one is to understand$_C$ a certain class of things.

2 *Competence in Performance*

One thing is certain: feelings and flashes of insight are neither a guarantee that someone has understood something nor essential for someone's understanding something.[2] A person may feel perfectly sure he understands, for example, why the engine seized up, yet be mistaken about why it seized up and hence be mistaken that he understands why it seized up; on the other hand, he may understand why it seized up without experiencing a flash of insight or feeling of certainty. As Gilbert Ryle has said:

> Even if you claimed that you had experienced a flash or click of comprehension and had actually done so, you would still withdraw your other claim to have understood the argument, if you found that you could not paraphrase it, illustrate, expand or recast it; and you would allow someone else to have understood it who could meet all examination-questions about it, but reported no click of comprehension.[3]

According to Ryle "it is part of the *meaning* of 'you understood it' that you could have done so and so and would have done it, if such and such, and the *test* of whether you understood it is a range of performances satisfying the apodoses of these general hypothetical statements" (p. 170, author's italics). Since Ryle does not say what the *rest* of the meaning of "you understood it" is, it is diffi-

[2] From now on the discussion will focus on understanding something, and to facilitate reading we will henceforth do without the identifying subscript "C." In those cases where being understanding is at issue, the subscript "A" will still be used.

[3] *The Concept of Mind* (Hutchinson, London, 1949), pp. 170–171. Page references in the text of this chapter will be to this book.

cult to evaluate his partially dispositional account of the term. There is no doubt, however, that the *test* of understanding lies in performances. Subjective-sounding phrases such as "catching on," "getting the point," and "seeing the connection" are used in relation to the verb "understand," but these should not be taken to indicate that we judge whether or not a person has understood something on the basis of either an examination of his "ghostly" mental operations or his introspective self-reports.

One who understands, like one who appreciates or follows, is a spectator, while one who executes, like one who makes or invents, is a performer (pp. 54–55). Nonetheless Ryle calls understanding a part of *knowing how:* execution and understanding "are merely different exercises of knowledge of the tricks of the same trade" (p. 55). "The words 'understanding' and 'following' designate certain of those exercises of your knowledge *how* [to tie a clove hitch], which you execute without having, for example, any string in your hand" (p. 55). Understanding or appreciating a performance does not involve the same degree of competence as the ability to execute it, but "The knowledge that is required for understanding intelligent performances of a specific kind is some degree of competence in performances of that kind. The competent critic of prose-style, experimental technique, or embroidery, must at least know how to write, experiment or sew" (p. 54). To understand an argument, for example, is to be able to put it in one's own words, translate it into French, invent appropriate concrete illustrations, stand up to cross-questioning, draw further consequences correctly, etc. No single "nuclear performance" determines whether a person has understood an argument; on the other hand, although we cannot specify how many or what tests must be met, a finite set of well-designed tests is enough in any given case (p. 171).

This analysis of understanding something is open to serious criticism. There is no doubt that Ryle brings to light one important way in which we understand performances and that his discussion of the ways in which we test for understanding is enlightening. Yet one must question his requirement that "some degree of competence in performances of that kind" is necessary. To be sure, understanding a performance requires *some* competence but this need not be competence in *executing* the skill in question. If a fan is to understand a baseball game he must know *something* about baseball but he does not have to be able to *play* baseball.

Furthermore Ryle limits his discussion of the notion of understanding something to performances. We speak, however, of understanding events, concepts, rules, people, stories, etc. In these cases the analysis of understanding in terms of a spectator as opposed to an agent and in terms of competence in performance seems inappropriate. A garage mechanic understands the engine seizure when he discovers that there is a leak in the oil reservoir. The notion of performance and the spectator-agent distinction are inapplicable here and in a great many other instances: the seizure is not a performance except in a whimsical sense; it is impossible for us to have competence in seizing up since this happens to engines, not people; there is no spectator-agent distinction to be made, for we do not execute seizures nor need we be a spectator of a given seizure in order to understand it.

In cases where performances are to be understood, although a person may apply the same rules and criteria to them which the agent follows, he need not. An anthropologist may understand the performance of a ritual in terms of its function in the society, a historian may understand it in terms of its origins, a choreographer may understand it in terms of its patterns of movement, a psychologist may understand it in terms of the responses made to various stimuli. Understanding a performance in terms of the rules governing the performer, therefore, is one among many ways in which performances can be understood.[4]

In a sense, we can say with Ryle that understanding something involves *knowing how,* for one who understands something can

[4] It might be admitted that a performance can be understood in a variety of ways yet argued that knowing the rules governing the performer is a necessary condition for *any* way of understanding. If knowing the rules involves being able to perform in accordance with them, then this claim is simply not tenable. On can understand baseball yet not be able to play it. If knowing the rules is a matter of *knowledge that,* even if the claim is tenable, Ryle's thesis is not reinstated, for on this interpretation of "knowing the rules" one who knew them would not necessarily have the same sort of competence as the performer.

answer certain questions or perform certain operations; for example, one who understands why the engine seized up knows how to answer the question "What has the oil leak got to do with the engine seizure?" or to draw a diagram. But this is merely to say that there are objective tests for understanding and that internal clicks and flashes are irrelevant; it is not to say that the notion of understanding applies only to performances or that understanding performances involves being able to do what the performers do, albeit in an amateurish way.

Like the verb "to explain," the verb "to understand" is sometimes followed by an indirect question and sometimes not. Thus we say that the assistant mechanic understands why the engine seized up but also that he understands the engine seizure; that the critic understands how the work of art hangs together, but also that he understands the work of art. Now in those cases where someone is said to understand something but no indirect question is specified, it would seem that one or more such questions could be supplied without doing violence to the initial attribution of understanding. It is a mistake to suppose, however, that when a person is said to understand a particular object, for example, the Civil War, or a class of objects, for example, historical events, there is one and only one indirect question which will apply in all contexts. In effect, Ryle makes just this mistake regarding performances. To understand a performance, for example, a baseball game, on his view is to understand how to perform the given activity, for example, how to play baseball.[5] But what about all the other questions that can be asked about performances the indirect forms of which can legitimately follow the verb "understand"? Ryle overlooks the fact that one can understand what function a performance serves, one can understand why the performance occurred, one can understand what the performance really is, and so on and on.

Recognizing that the verb "understand" takes a variety of indirect questions is perhaps the first step toward wisdom. We see then that different sorts of understanding can be had of one and the

[5] If I am right about this, then Ryle actually makes two mistakes, for understanding how to do something does not necessarily involve being able or knowing how to do it. See my discussion of Price's linguistic theory of teaching, Chap. 6, sec. 1, on this point.

same thing or class of things. Consider Dray's engine seizure. We have all along been assuming that to understand it is to understand why it occurred. But one could understand it by understanding, for example, how it could possibly have happened. It might of course be argued that one sort of understanding of the engine seizure would be *better* or *deeper* than another. This may be so, but it does not affect the point at issue, namely that given any object of understanding, more than one indirect question may be applicable to it. It is this fact about understanding that suggests the dangers in maintaining, as philosophers are so often tempted to do, that a particular sort of competence or set of beliefs is required for understanding.

To be sure, in a given context some particular indirect question may have privileged status. That is to say, it may be the case that relative to some particular context one is only said to understand a thing X if one understands X in terms of a particular indirect question, for example, "what function X serves" or "why X occurred" or "how X works." Thus, for example, a student in a sociology course may be said to understand a given institution, for example, the public school, only if he understands what function it serves in society; an apprentice watchmaker may be said to understand a watch only if he understands what makes it tick; and a child at his first baseball game may be said to understand the game only if he understands how to play it.

It is sometimes held that the various theoretical disciplines can be distinguished in terms of the questions they ask and purport to answer about phenomena. It is surely not the case that for every discipline there is one and only one characteristic question; some disciplines characteristically ask more than one question about phenomena, for example, sociologists ask "What is its structure?" as well as "What is its function?" Nor is it the case that the questions which are associated with a discipline are necessarily unique to that discipline; disciplines can share questions, for example, both biologists and sociologists ask "What is its structure?" and "What is its function?" Yet the theoretical disciplines can be viewed as asking and trying to answer certain characteristic questions, and it seems fair to say that in order to gain the sort of understanding associated with one of those disciplines, one will indeed have to understand things in terms of certain indirect questions and not others.

Still, no discipline has sole rights over the phenomena it studies. Disciplines share phenomena just as they share questions, vocabulary, and other things.[6] Thus, even if some particular question did have privileged status relative to some discipline so that understanding within the framework of that discipline would have to be in terms of the corresponding indirect question, it would still not be the case that the question had privileged status in some absolute sense. Outside the framework of that discipline the phenomenon at issue could be understood in terms of some other indirect question. Similarly, where some practical purpose or special interest rather than some discipline and its attendant theories makes one sort of indirect question the privileged one if understanding is to be achieved, this privileged status is still a relative matter. For one can change one's purposes and interests just as one can get outside a discipline and its theories, and once one does change, some other indirect question may be appropriate to understanding the very same phenomenon.

3   Internal and External Understanding

Perhaps the most notable characteristic of understanding is its open-endedness. We speak of a person's understanding of a given thing X as partial, the implication being that our own understanding of X is complete. Yet one cannot help wondering whether a person's understanding of a given thing can ever be complete in an absolute sense. One's understanding of X can perhaps be complete relative to a given theory of X or to some practical interest in X or to some standard of competence set by educators. When we call someone else's understanding of X partial, presumably we have that theory or interest or standard in mind. But there are always new ways to view phenomena and other questions that could be

[6] See Israel Scheffler, "Is Education a Discipline?" in Scheffler (ed.), *Philosophy and Education,* 2d ed. (Allyn and Bacon, Boston, 1966), pp. 64–77.

asked about them. The indirect-question approach to understanding is, I think, one good way of getting at the open-ended character of understanding, but it is not the only way. I want in this section to take a rather different approach to understanding in order to bring out this very same feature.

It is often said that understanding involves seeing connections or relationships. I think it does, and indeed, my discussion of the continuous-series model of explanation in Chapter 3 was based in part on this assumption. Recall the case of the engine seizure. In the context envisioned by Dray, to understand the seizure is to understand why the engine seized up. To understand this it is not enough simply to know that there was a leak in the oil reservoir; indeed, as I argued in connection with Hypotheses Four and Five, it is not even enough to know that the engine seizure was due to a leak in the oil reservoir. To understand why the engine seized up, one must *see the connection* between leak and seizure: but it may not occur to one who simply knows that there was a leak that the leak had anything to do with the seizure; and even if it does occur to him—for example, if he knows that the seizure was due to a leak—he still may not see the connection between leak and seizure.

The case of the engine seizure brings out clearly, I think, the crucial—indeed the essential—role that connection seeing plays in understanding. It should be stressed that although the seizure case is a case of understanding why something happened, understanding seems to involve seeing connections whatever the indirect question may be. If someone is to understand how possibly something could have happened or what the significance of something was or what function something serves, he must see some connection between things. The sort of connections to be seen will differ, of course, depending on the sort of understanding—for example, understanding why, how possibly, what—at issue and depending on the sort of thing being understood. In the last section of this chapter we will discuss the notion of *seeing* connections, for an approach toward understanding via this notion is not without pitfalls. Let us first, however, explore the sorts of connections that can enter into understanding and the sorts of things these connections can hold between.

There are in general two different sorts of connections that may be involved in understanding, depending on the way the thing to be understood, X, is treated. On the one hand, X may be treated as a whole, a unity, and may be connected or related to something else, something apart from it; let us call connections or relations of this sort *external*. On the other hand, X may be taken in isolation—that is to say, without relating it to other things—treated as a composite, and parts or aspects of it may be connected or related; let us call connections or relations of this sort *internal*. A work of art is often treated in this latter way where understanding is concerned: it is taken by itself, parts or elements are singled out for attention, and relationships are sought. All sorts of events appear to be treated in the former way: an event is taken as a unity; is related to another event, for example, to an event thought to be the cause; and a relationship between the two distinct entities is pointed to, for example, a causal relationship.

Let us call the sort of understanding that takes something X as a unity and relates it to something else *external understanding,* and let us call the sort of understanding that takes X as a composite, singles out parts or aspects of X, and discovers relationships *internal understanding*.[7] It should be readily apparent that whether a given thing is treated as a unity (that is, as a simple whole) or as a composite (that is, as a complex whole) depends on one's interests and purposes and point of view. Thus, it does not follow from the fact that one has external understanding of an engine seizure and internal understanding of a novel that one could not also have internal understanding of that engine seizure and external understanding of that novel. One could, for example, connect the novel up with other novels, with the novelist's life, or with the social conditions of the times, and other things being equal, one could

[7] Alfred North Whitehead, for one, distinguishes two modes of understanding: internal understanding and external understanding. See *Modes of Thought* (Capricorn Books, New York, 1958), p. 63. Whitehead's distinction, however, is not quite the same as the one I am drawing here. On Whitehead's account the internal mode conceives of the thing to be understood, X, as an outcome, while the external mode conceives of X as a causal factor. On the present account of external understanding, X may be conceived of as an outcome, as a causal factor, or as neither. On the present account of internal understanding, the question of X's relation to other things does not arise.

have understanding of it. One could view the engine seizure in isolation and, other things being equal, understand it by singling out parts and, for example, seeing how they interact.

It should also be readily apparent that although two people may both have internal understanding of a given thing X, their understanding may be very different. We never understand a thing per se; rather we understand it under some description. Thus, for example, we may describe the same "chunk of reality" as a war, a civil war, or a revolution. Given different descriptions of some "chunk of reality," then, there is room for variation in people's understanding, for what is taken as a part or element of X may vary according to the way X is described, so that under different initial descriptions X may be taken to have different parts. For example, if X is described as a war, battles may be singled out as its parts; if it is described as a revolution, social relationships and class behavior may be singled out as its parts. If we want to be precise in talking about understanding something, then, we must describe it not simply by the form "A understands X," where "A" indicates a position occupied by an expression through which a person or persons are mentioned and where "X" indicates a position occupied by an expression through which some thing or things are mentioned, but by the form "A understands X under D" where "D" indicates a position taken up by a description of the thing to be understood.

It should not be thought, however, that for any given description, D, of a given thing, X, there is one and only one set of parts or elements of X. There is no reason why X under D cannot be broken down into quite different sets of parts. Thus, if something is described as a sonata its parts may be taken to be its several movements, but other parts could be singled out, for example, its rhythm, melody, harmony, texture. Nor is it the case that there is one and only one description which holds for X given some set of parts. It is possible for X under different descriptions to have the same parts since the parts of X do not uniquely determine its description. It seems, then, that if we are to judge whether two people vary in their internal understanding of X, we must know not only what their initial description of X is but also what parts p_1, p_2, p_3, . . ., p_n of X they single out relative to that description.

To say that someone has internal understanding of something, then, is in effect elliptical for saying that he understands it under a particular description as having a particular set of parts or aspects.

The issue is more complex than this, however, for we must take into account the fact that when the parts of a thing are singled out for attention, different sorts of relationships can be seen. When people talk about their understanding, or lack thereof, of the human body or some other organism, they are often referring to their grasp of the contribution the various parts of the organism make to the whole. The connection between each part and the whole is at issue here, not the connection among the parts. But one could single out for attention connections or relations among the parts of some whole, and this sort of connection could, in turn, take many different forms. For example, the relationships might be temporal, spatial, causal, logical; they might be linear in that each part was related to one other, or organic in that each part was related to every other, or they might be something less than organic but more than linear.[8]

The connection or relationship must be there to be seen if there is to be understanding. The sense of "see" at stake when I say that understanding involves seeing connections, although not to be confused with literal seeing, is not to be taken as a form of imagining, fancying, visualizing, picturing.[9] Since there is no reason to suppose that the parts of a given thing stand in all possible relationships to each other and to the whole, there are built-in limits to the variations that can occur in people's internal understanding of a given thing. On the other hand, since it may be the case that the parts of a given thing are in fact related in more than one way— the movements of a sonata, for example, may be related temporally and tonally—we cannot in general infer from the fact that certain parts $p_1, p_2, p_3, \ldots, p_k$ of X under D have been singled out for attention that a particular sort of relationship R will be seen.

[8] See Maurice Mandelbaum, "A Note on History as Narrative," *History and Theory*, 6:413–419, 1967, for an interesting discussion of the role of linear and nonlinear relationships in historiography.
[9] Jonas F. Soltis, *Seeing, Knowing and Believing* (G. Allen & Unwin, London, 1966), gives a systematic and illuminating analysis of the notion of seeing.

If many factors combine to afford the possibility of wide variation in people's internal understanding of a given thing X, the factors combine also to afford variation in their external understanding of X. Quite naturally, given different initial descriptions of X,
people's external understanding of X will be different. But even
given the same initial description of X, it is possible to connect X
to different things and to see different connections between X and
these things. Thus it is possible for two people to differ in their external understanding$_C$ of X although they agree in their initial description of X.

Consider, for example, an event such as the Civil War. It can
be understood externally in terms of its causes and also in terms of
its consequences. Moreover, it can be understood in terms of things
which stand to it as neither cause nor effect. Thus to understand
how the Civil War could possibly have happened or what it really
was, one must relate it to something apart from it which is neither
cause nor effect.[10] A given thing bears all sorts of relationships to
things outside it and although it is surely not the case that every
sort of relationship, if perceived, yields understanding in every context, I am not at all sure that any sort can in general be ruled out
as yielding understanding in some context. External understanding
of a given thing X under a given description D may vary then, to
the extent that the sort of relation perceived between X and something outside of it, Y, varies.

But this is not all. For one thing, it is possible for X to bear
the same relationship to different things; the Civil War, for example, can be seen in relation to different causes and also to different
effects. Thus it matters in determining whether or not two people
have the same external understanding of X not only what sort of
relationship is perceived, but exactly what is seen as being related
in that way to X. It is not the case that one can in general infer

[10] The how-possibly case may be simply a matter of relating X to something else whose presence made it not impossible for X to occur; the
what-it-really-is case may be simply a matter of classifying X as something else. For an account of explanation in relation to these sorts of
cases, see William Dray, *Laws and Explanation in History* (Oxford University Press, London, 1957), chap. 6; William Dray, " 'Explaining What'
in History," in Patrick Gardiner (ed.), *Theories of History* (Free Press,
New York, 1959), pp. 403–408.

from the sort of relation at issue to the specific thing being related to X. Moreover, X is never related to Y per se, but rather to Y under some description. If two people perceived a relationship between X and Y, but viewed Y under different descriptions, their external understanding of X would differ. To say that someone has external understanding of something, then, is in effect to say that he understands something under some description as bearing some relation to something else which is itself under some description.

One of the most common forms of external understanding involves classifying X in some illuminating way. For example, we may gain understanding of a painting if it is classified as an impressionist work; of someone's behavior if it is classified as neurotic; of a civil disturbance if it is classified as a demonstration. In these and all other cases of what may be called *understanding by classifying,* what is involved is really a *re*classification or *re*description of X. As we have already seen, X is never understood per se, but always under some initial description. Thus, in effect, whatever sort of understanding one may have of X, classification is involved. What characterizes understanding by classifying is not, then, the act of classification—this is always a component of understanding something—but rather the act of changing the classification of X, of relating X to some different class of things.

When X under description D is redescribed as D_1, the legitimacy or adequacy of D_1 depends on X's having certain features or properties. It may seem, then, as if focusing on the parts of X is after all involved in this sort of external understanding. The role played by the parts of X in understanding by classifying is quite different, however, from the role they play in internal understanding. In understanding by classifying, one's primary interest is in the way X fits in with other things and not in the parts of X as such at all. The redescription or classification does rest on them, and they may have to be invoked in justifying that classification; furthermore, the classification itself may well bring to our attention parts of X hitherto unnoticed. But in understanding by classifying, our interest is in the relation of X under D to things under D_1 and to whatever these things may in turn be related, and not in the parts of X under D and the pattern they make.

No limits can be set in advance on the ways in which a given thing X can legitimately be redescribed. Of course it is not the case that every true redescription of X will yield understanding of X in every context. If a person knows nothing about the impressionist movement, it will be of no avail to redescribe something he knows to be a painting as an impressionist work. Understanding is a context-bound affair, for there is always someone who must do the understanding. Thus it is a mistake to suppose that a given classification or redescription of X will necessarily yield understanding: it may or may not, depending on the person involved— his experience, his knowledge, his competences, his purposes, and so on. On the other hand, I doubt very much that any legitimate classification or redescription of X can be ruled out a priori as yielding understanding in *some* context. To be sure there are classifications which in most contexts seem to be singularly unilluminating, and it is very tempting to conclude, therefore, that they are incapable of yielding understanding. Yet I suspect that in every such case some context could arise in which the classification would turn out to be illuminating.[11]

4 Analysis and Placing Things in Context

We noted earlier that the verb "understand" takes a variety of indirect questions. It would be convenient if we could map these various questions onto our distinction between internal and external understanding, but I do not think this is possible. To be sure, given a particular context, if we are told that someone understands, for example, why something happened or how something works or what something is, we will be able to assign that understanding to one or another category with some confidence. We will not, however, be able to make absolute assignments of all questions to categories; that is to say, we will not be able to assign every

[11] Refer to Carl G. Hempel, "Aspects of Scientific Explanation," in *Aspects of Scientific Explanation and Other Essays in the Philosophy of Science* (Free Press, New York, 1965), pp. 453–457, for what I take to be a rather different stand on this question. Hempel's discussion of illuminating and unilluminating classifications ignores questions of context, however.

question a priori to one and only one way of understanding. For one thing, some questions are ambiguous. Thus questions of the form "Why did he do such and such?" may be asking for the agent's reasons for his action or for the causes of it. In such cases it is possible that one sense of the indirect question corresponds to one way of understanding but the other does not.

There is a further difficulty confronting one who wishes to correlate once and for all every indirect question with internal or external understanding: different interpretations can be given of a thing and of what is and is not a part of it. For example, at first glance it surely seems that when Dray finally does understand why his engine seized up, the understanding he has of the engine seizure is external understanding. For he seems to be taking the thing to be understood, the engine seizure, as a whole and relating it to things outside it, namely the series of events beginning with the oil leak which led up to it. There is some indication, however, that Dray actually conceives of the thing to be understood, X, as encompassing those things we took to be distinct from it: the leak and the events in the continuous series. Thus, for example, he sometimes seems to conceive of X not as an engine seizure but as an engine seizure after an oil leak. On this latter view of X the events in the continuous series between oil leak and engine seizure are all part of X as, of course, is the leak itself.

In Chapter 3 we noted Dray's singular lack of concern for the problem of explanation which regularity theorists take to be central, namely the problem of justifying the claim that one thing rather than another led to or caused or resulted in something else. At that point in our discussion we were content with assuming simply that Dray's interest lay primarily in the pragmatic dimension of explanation. In view of the present discussion we may wonder whether Dray's conception of historical events is not such that the problem with which regularity theorists struggle disappears or at least *seems* to disappear.[12] If he takes the causes or conditions leading up to an event to be *part* of that event, then they have, in

[12] It could be argued that the problem does not really disappear but arises at another level, namely that of choosing one description of the event rather than another.

effect, been singled out as relevant in advance and there is no need to show that they are related to the event. An interpretation of the continuous-series model as conceiving of the understanding of events as internal understanding is consistent, then, not only with many of Dray's remarks but also with his overall approach to the nonpragmatic dimension of exploration. But if such an interpretation is plausible, then I think we must conclude that the prospects for the general program of correlating indirect questions with internal or external understanding are not good, for at the very least, we must assume that indirect questions of the form "why such and such happened" could be assigned to either category depending on the way one construes what happened.

This is not to say, however, that the distinction drawn here between internal and external understanding has no value. If it is granted that a given thing can be understood internally or externally, then the claim one so often hears, that one particular sort of competence or knowledge is necessary if that thing is to be understood at all, seems simply to be mistaken. Of course, if it could be shown that a given thing X could not be connected with something else, Y, then external understanding of X would not be possible; and similarly, if it could be shown that X had *no* parts or aspects, then internal understanding of X would not be possible. But I do not see how either of these things could be shown. To be sure, the state of our knowledge about X might be such that one or another sort of understanding of X would be considered relatively superficial or uninteresting in most contexts. But proponents of the "special competence" view of understanding typically argue from the nature of X itself, not from the nature of our present knowledge about X, to the need for a particular sort of competence or knowledge. Moreover, they present it as a view about understanding and not as a view about deep or interesting understanding.

Our distinction between internal and external understanding can also help us clarify two rather general assumptions about understanding: (1) to understand something you must place it in some larger context or framework; (2) to understand something you must analyze it. The first of these can be interpreted as a claim about external understanding and the second as a claim about internal understanding. In each case, however, it is difficult to determine the exact claim being made, for the notion of analysis can be construed in two ways and so can the notion of placing something in some context or framework.

On one (the weaker) sense of "analysis"—the sense in which analysis is contrasted with synthesis—to analyze something is simply to break it into its parts; on another (the stronger) sense of the term, however—the sense in which analysis is contrasted with, for example, mere description—to analyze something involves a good deal more than this, for example, criticism or evaluation in depth. It is not altogether clear which sense of "analysis" is at stake in the claim that to understand something you must analyze it. If the weaker sense is at stake, then presumably internal understanding without any specification of the details is being made requisite for understanding something; if the stronger sense is at stake, then presumably some special form of internal understanding is being made requisite. Yet in light of our discussion of internal and external understanding, it does not seem either that any sort of internal understanding at all or that some particular sort of internal understanding is necessary if one is to understand something, for one always has the option of understanding the thing externally.

We can isolate a weaker and stronger sense of "placing something in a framework or context" too. Any time we see a connection between one thing and another, for example, between an event and a cause or an event and its effects, I suppose we may say that we have placed it in some larger context or framework. But we sometimes have in mind something more specific, for example, classifying the thing as a case of something else or showing the thing to be a part of a larger whole. If the first (the weaker) sense is at stake, then presumably external understanding without any specification of the details is being made requisite for understanding something; if the second (the stronger) sense is at stake, then presumably one particular form of external understanding—I have called it understanding by classifying—is being made requisite. But again it does not seem that one must have some sort of external understanding of a thing in order to understand it, let alone that one must have one particular sort of external understanding of it in order to understand it.

As we have seen, a given thing can be understood in two quite different ways: by looking around or beyond it, so to speak, or by looking into it. In one sense of "analysis" and in one sense of "placing a thing in some context or framework," then, we can say that to understand something X one must either analyze X or place X in some context or framework. But one need not do both in order to understand X; nor must one do either. This is not, of course, to say that a person might not be better off if he had both internal and external understanding of X. Indeed he might be. Nor is it to say that in certain circumstances one sort of understanding might not be much more valuable than another. Indeed it might. These issues, however, take us beyond the present purpose, which is simply to point up the open-endedness of understanding and to stress the great variation there can be in people's understanding of any given thing.

5   Seeing Connections

Before we turn to a discussion of what some take to be a special case of understanding, namely the understanding of human actions, a few remarks are in order about our use of the verb "to see" in connection with understanding. Needless to say, in this context "see" must not be taken as involving a perceptual claim. The connections at stake are not the sorts of things that can be seen in the way that trees and tables can be; moreover, even if they were, we surely would not want to say that understanding necessarily involves visual perception or visual discrimination.[13] On the other hand, we must guard against reinstating Ryle's ghost in the machine: it is all too easy to suppose that if "see" is not used in reference to physical sense experience, it must be used to indicate some nonphysical or ghostly sense experience, for example, flashes of insight or clicks of comprehension.

It is well known that the verb "to see" can be used to make epis-

[13] Soltis, *op. cit.*, chap. 4, establishes a basic, simple, literal sense of "seeing" in which visual discrimination is essential.

temological claims—that is to say, claims of knowledge or belief.[14] I suggest that seeing talk in relation to understanding be interpreted along these lines. But how? Can we, for example, interpret it solely in terms of belief? I think not. Part of the force of saying that someone *sees* a connection between two things is that the connection in question is there to be seen. In this respect seeing a connection is no different from seeing a tree or a table: the world must cooperate in both cases. If the tree or table is not there, one has not seen it no matter how certain he is that he has; if the connection is not there—that is to say, if there is no connection of the sort in question between the things at issue—one has not seen it no matter how certain he is that he has. At the very least, then, the notion of seeing connections has to be interpreted in terms of true belief.

But true belief is not enough. Someone A may believe that two things X and Y bear connection C to one another, and X and Y may in fact bear connection C to one another, yet A may or may not *see* the connection between X and Y. This, I take it, was the point Dray was trying to make when he said that "It's due to an oil leak" may or may not be an explanation of the engine seizure depending on who says it to whom. I may believe that the engine seizure was due to the oil leak because my mechanic said so, and indeed, it may be true that it was due to an oil leak. Yet I really haven't the foggiest notion what the leak has to do with the seizure; *I* don't see the connection although my mechanic does and I am more than willing to take his word for it that there is one. But then, not only is true belief not enough, an interpretation in terms of *knowledge that* is not enough either. For if my mechanic, known to me for his reliability, assures me that the seizure was due to an oil leak, and it was due to an oil leak, I know that the seizure was due to an oil leak although I do not necessarily *see* the connection between leak and seizure.

Seeing is something each person has to do for himself. No one can do your seeing for you. Others can point things out to you, give you relevant information, enlarge your conceptual repertoire, and all the rest, but in the last analysis you have to come through

[14] See *ibid.;* Arthur W. Collins, "The Epistemological Status of the Concept of Perception," *The Philosophical Review,* 76:436–459, 1967.

and do the actual job—the seeing—yourself. This element is missing from an interpretation of the notion of seeing connections in terms of *knowledge that*. Moreover, seeing something involves confrontation with that thing. Now of course we do not want to say that to see a connection one must "visually" confront the connection in the way that one must a tree if one is to see the tree. I need not be and need not have ever been in the presence of the engine seizure in order to see the connection between leak and seizure. I must, however, have confronted the relevant information about leak and seizure. It is intellectual, not visual, confrontation that seems to be a crucial element of understanding, an element missing from a *knowledge-that* interpretation of the notion of seeing connections.

A caution is in order here. I do not mean by this that one must have dug up the relevant facts and theory for oneself; that seeing connections, hence understanding, is incompatible with being told. To say that someone understands something is not to take a position on the *way* the relevant information was acquired any more than it is to take a position on when it was acquired. It is, however, to say that there was some sort of *active* engagement with the information no matter how the information may have been acquired.

There is nothing to prevent someone who has been presented with all the relevant information organized in the appropriate way from seeing connections and achieving understanding of a given thing; however, someone who has undergone this experience—for example, someone who has been an explainee in an explaining episode—will not see connections and achieve understanding unless he in one way or another works through the information presented him on his own. In the last chapter I pointed out that there is no analogue in explaining something to someone to the so-called discovery method of teaching. It would be a grave mistake, however, to assume that because explaining must meet a linguistic condition and therefore precludes use of the discovery method as it is usually conceived, the explainee must play only a passive role in an explaining episode. To be sure, the explainee, unlike the explainer, *can* be passive throughout an episode, but this is simply to say that there can be explaining without understanding. To be successful, the explainee must come to understand, and to come to understand, he himself must work with the relevant material. It should not be thought that his having been a party to an explaining episode prevents him from doing this.

Those concerned with improving the quality of education deplore the amount of rote learning which takes place in the schools; they implore teachers to teach for understanding. There is a tendency for these critics to assume that rote learning necessarily goes hand in hand and only hand in hand with an active, assertive$_S$ use of language by the teacher (telling, lecturing, explaining, etc.) while understanding just as inevitably accompanies and only accompanies an active, assertive$_S$ use of language by the pupil (discovery learning, Socratic teaching, inductive teaching, etc.). But this neat pairing of teaching method or approach and learning outcome simply will not do. The kernel of truth in this view is that understanding requires active engagement with information whereas rote learning does not. It is a mistake, however, to assume that an active, assertive$_S$ use of language by the teacher precludes an active confrontation with the relevant material by the pupil. As I have already suggested, it is necessary to distinguish the question of how the relevant information is acquired from the question of what the student does with it when he has it. There may indeed be good reasons for the teacher to refrain from taking the role of explainer in the classroom, but it must not be thought that one of these reasons is that by explaining to his pupils he necessarily keeps them from understanding.

Our discussion in Chapter 5 of the rationality constraint on learning suggests another interpretation of the notion of seeing connections, one that I think incorporates this element of confrontation or active engagement with the relevant information. It will be recalled that rationality theorists argue that teaching aims not simply at the acquisition of beliefs or even at the acquisition of beliefs with backing. Rather they argue that the backing must be of a special sort, namely from within the relevant subject matter, and must be *had* in a special sense, namely in the sense of recognizing that the backing *is* backing.[15] We may apply this view to the no-

---

[15] See, for example, Israel Scheffler, *Conditions of Knowledge* (Scott, Foresman, Glenville, Ill., 1965), chap. 3.

tion of seeing connections as follows: to say that A sees a connection C between X and Y is at least to say that (1) A believes that X and Y bear connection C; (2) X and Y bear connection C; (3) A has a case from within the relevant subject matter for his belief that X and Y bear connection C; (4) A recognizes the case he has for the belief mentioned in (3) *as* a case for that belief. This interpretation has the virtue of ruling out appeals to authority without restricting unduly the sort of case one can have.[16] It also takes into account the element of activity we have just been discussing. We may call this a *modified-knowledge-that* interpretation of the notion of seeing connections. I have said it is more adequate than the other interpretations considered here. Whether this interpretation is adequate enough is another matter. I doubt very much that it is as it stands, yet it does point in what seems to me to be the proper direction.[17] If mistaken in detail it nonetheless suggests in broad outline a way of construing the notion of seeing connections without reviving Ryle's ghost.

I conclude, then, that seeing connections is a matter of having knowledge of a certain sort, if not exactly the sort described here. As we now know, the connections that can be seen if one is to understand something are various, and so are the things to be connected. Thus even if seeing connections is a matter of knowledge of a certain sort, as I am urging, the particular content of people's understanding of a thing can vary greatly. But understanding is not simply a matter of seeing connections between things: one must, I suppose, at the very least see the things to be connected as well as the connections between them if one is to understand. How is this use of the verb "to see" to be interpreted? This seeing would also seem to be a matter of knowledge of a certain sort. Indeed, it may even be the case that whatever understanding consists in over and above seeing connections, that too is a matter of knowledge. We must, however, leave this question open.

[16] As the continuous-series model does, for example.
[17] See R. S. Downie, "Knowing and Understanding," *Mind,* 71:237–240, 1962, for the view that understanding belongs to the *knowing-that* family, as well as for a critique somewhat like the one presented above of Ryle's theory of understanding.

Chapter 8

THE DOCTRINE
OF *VERSTEHEN*

The longstanding doctrine that a special kind of understanding—empathic understanding—is required in the field of human behavior has been given new life in recent years. Traditionally, this doctrine has been part of the general thesis that the natural and social sciences differ fundamentally because of their different subject matter. Roughly, the claim is that to understand human beings and their actions we must put ourselves in their position, for example, think their thoughts, feel their feelings. We are able to do this because we too are human; that is to say, we understand others on an analogy with ourselves. This doctrine, usually called the theory of *Verstehen,* has found wide support among philosophers, social scientists, and historians.[1] In the past it has been

[1] See, for example, Wilhelm Dilthey, in H. P. Rickman (ed.), *Meaning in History* (G. Allen & Unwin, London, 1961); Heinrich Rickert, *Science and History: A Critique of Positivistic Epistemology* (George Reisman,

expressed in vague, metaphorical language and supported by metaphysical arguments. Contemporary philosophers have tried to strip it of these trappings while preserving the core of the doctrine.

The standard criticism of the *Verstehen* doctrine has been that empathic understanding is nothing more than a useful heuristic device for thinking up explanations; it is in no sense required for understanding human behavior. Empathic understanding, it is objected, does not guarantee that the explanation of behavior so obtained is sound; nor is it necessary for obtaining sound explanations of behavior.[2] In effect the critics of the doctrine have maintained that empathic understanding belongs to the context of discovery rather than to the context of validation and that proponents of the *Verstehen* doctrine have failed to distinguish these two contexts adequately.[3] Some have gone so far as to assert that the method of empathy is available to anyone; that it is not the affair of the social scientist and historian exclusively since physicists can use it in studying atoms.[4] But even when it is granted that empathy is exclusively the affair of social scientists, the criticism that its status is that of a heuristic device hits home, at least with modern *Verstehen* theorists. In reformulating the doctrine their concern is not simply to state it in the relatively precise language of contemporary philosophy but to give the doctrine "logical force."

Since one of the things educators most want students to come to understand is human behavior, we would do well to examine the *Verstehen* doctrine here. Because modern formulations purport to have discarded the objectionable features of the traditional formulation while preserving the sense of the doctrine, we will confine our

---

trans.) (Van Nostrand, Princeton, N.J., 1962); Max Weber, *On the Methodology of the Social Sciences* (F. A. Shils & H. A. Finch, trans.) (Free Press, Glencoe, Ill., 1949).

[2] See, for example, Carl G. Hempel, "The Function of General Laws in History," in Hempel, *Aspects of Scientific Explanation and Other Essays in the Philosophy of Science* (Free Press, New York, 1965), pp. 239–240.

[3] For a discussion of the two contexts, see Richard Rudner, *Philosophy of Social Science* (Prentice-Hall, Englewood Cliffs, N.J., 1966), pp. 5–7. See pp. 71–73 for Rudner's discussion of *Verstehen*.

[4] For example, Karl R. Popper, *The Poverty of Historicism* (Beacon Press, Boston, 1957), p. 138.

attention to these. It is not possible in one chapter, however, to isolate and examine closely every formulation or even every important formulation of the doctrine. For the modern or, as I will call it, the *neo-Verstehen* position has attracted a number of able supporters, for example, William Dray, W. B. Gallie, and Peter Winch, each presenting a somewhat different account than the next.[5] My procedure, therefore, will be to formulate and discuss in some detail one account of the theory. I select Dray's for three reasons: it is more or less representative of the views of neo-*Verstehen* theorists; it is relatively easy to get clear on; it has been the subject of much philosophical discussion yet it has not been assessed in the way it will be here, namely as a theory of understanding human actions.[6] Much of what I have to say about Dray's version of the doctrine will apply to other versions as well. But the reader ought not on the basis of the present discussion to jump to hasty conclusions about the views of other neo-*Verstehen* theorists: careful study of a particular version of the doctrine on its own merits is necessary before that version is embraced or rejected.

My procedure will be to set forth and clarify Dray's position and then to criticize it, first as a general theory of understanding human actions and next as a theory of historical understanding of human actions. I shall, in other words, be considering Dray's version of the *Verstehen* doctrine in its own right. In effect, Dray takes the standard criticism of the doctrine as given; rather than try to defend traditional formulations of the doctrine against the

---

[5] William Dray, *Laws and Explanation in History* (Oxford University Press, London, 1957). Page references in the text of this chapter will be to this book. W. B. Gallie, *Philosophy and the Historical Understanding* (Schocken Books, New York, 1964); Peter Winch, *The Idea of a Social Science* (Humanities Press, New York, 1958). See also William Dray, "The Historical Explanation of Actions Reconsidered," in Sidney Hook (ed.), *Philosophy and History* (New York University Press, New York, 1963), pp. 105–135; and Dray, *Philosophy of History* (Prentice-Hall, Englewood Cliffs, N.J., 1964), chap. 2.

[6] Dray's account of human actions has been discussed and criticized primarily as a theory of explanation. See, for example, Carl G. Hempel, "Aspects of Scientific Explanation," in Hempel, *op. cit.*, sec. 10; Hempel, "Reasons and Covering Laws in Historical Explanation," in Hook (ed.), *op. cit.*, pp. 143–163; and the other essays in the Hook volume, including Dray's own essays, in which Dray's views are discussed.

criticism, he seeks a formulation which will get around it. For the present purpose I too shall take it as given, but I want to make it clear that my discussion of Dray leaves open the question of whether or not the standard criticism does in fact do justice to traditional formulations of the *Verstehen* doctrine.

1   Rational Explanation and the Agent's Point of View

Traditionally, *Verstehen* theorists have held that laws and causal explanations are inappropriate to the understanding of human actions. Dray adopts a modified form of this thesis: he does not deny that human actions fall under law, but he argues that even if they do, "discovery of the law would still not enable us to understand them in the sense proper to this special subject-matter." [7] Causal explanation looks at phenomena from the outside, but human actions, according to Dray, can only be understood from "the actor's point of view."

"When we ask for the explanation of an action," says Dray, "what we very often want is a reconstruction of the agent's *calculation* of means to be adopted toward his chosen end in the light of the circumstances in which he found himself" (p. 122). This does not mean that every action is performed with a plan consciously preformulated; Dray points out that the historian may have to *construct,* rather than reconstruct, a calculation:

> But such an admission need not affect the main point; for in so far as we say an action is purposive at all, no matter at what level of conscious deliberation, there is a calculation which could be constructed for it: the one the agent would have gone through if he had had time, if he had not seen what to do in a flash, if he had been called upon to account for what he did after the event, &c. And it is by eliciting some such calculation that we explain the action (p. 123).

Explanations of this sort are called "rational" since they display the point or rationale of what was done. There is an element of

[7] Dray, *Laws and Explanation in History,* p. 118.

appraisal in them, moreover, for they show in what way an action was appropriate; that is to say, they show an action as the thing to have done under the circumstances. The notions of explanation and justification therefore overlap in rational explanations. Reasons for acting have generality, of course, but this generality is the generality of principles of action rather than empirical laws. These principles state the thing to do in certain circumstances, not the thing that everyone does. Dray believes there is a standing presumption in favor of giving a rational explanation of an action: "rational and nonrational explanations are alternatives—alternatives sought in a certain order. We give reasons if we can, and turn to empirical laws if we must" (p. 138).[8]

"Only by putting yourself in the agent's position can you *understand* why he did what he did" (p. 128). Thus formulated by Dray, the doctrine of *Verstehen* does not merely give methodological advice; such advice would be worded, "Only by putting yourself in the agent's position can you *find out* why he did what he did." Rather, it sets forth certain conditions which must be satisfied before a historian is prepared to say, "Now I have the explanation." By the phrase "putting yourself in the agent's position," Dray means "giving an explanation from the agent's point of view," that is, giving a rational explanation. In other words, the doctrine of *Verstehen* as formulated by Dray consists in the claim that rational explanations alone allow us to understand human actions. This is not to say that every rational explanation is correct or self-evidently true merely by virtue of its form; rational explanations have "an inductive, empirical side" and are built up from the evidence. But rational structure is necessary for understanding human actions; hence the doctrine is interpreted as a logical one.

The doctrine of *Verstehen* is often interpreted as a theory of explanation:

(1) There can be no causal explanations of human actions.

Dray, however, formulates it as a theory of understanding:

[8] See Dray, "The Historical Explanation of Actions Reconsidered," pp. 115–116, for some clarification of this position.

(2) Only by putting yourself in the agent's position can you understand his action.[9]

Notice that (2) leaves open the possibility of causal explanation of human actions; on (2) these explanations would simply not yield understanding. This in itself is unobjectionable, for it is quite true that there can be explanations of a thing without there being understanding of that thing. In the first place there can be explanations$_S$ of a thing, and if there are, it does not follow that there will be understanding. But even apart from the context-free notion of explanation there can be explanation without understanding: explanations$_D$ of something for someone may fail to produce understanding and so may explanations$_F$ of something by someone.

To put oneself in the agent's position, according to Dray, is to give a "rational" explanation of his action; it is to show the point of the action, to construct the agent's calculation. It seems quite clear, however, that at least in the ordinary sense of the phrase, one can put oneself in an agent's position without giving or being able to give a rational explanation of his action. Moreover, one can give a rational explanation, that is, construct an agent's calculation, without putting oneself in his position. It seems advisable for purposes of analysis, therefore, to distinguish between the notions of rational explanation and putting yourself in the agent's position. If we do this, Dray's formulation of the *Verstehen* doctrine can be given two separate interpretations:

(2.1) Only by putting yourself in the agent's position can you understand his action.

(2.2) Only by giving (or being given) a rational explanation can you understand his action.

[9] Actually Dray says, "Only by putting yourself in the agent's position can you understand *why he did what he did*" (italics added). This is a narrower thesis than (2), for it leaves open the possibility of understanding, for example, *what he did* or *how he possibly could have done what he did* without taking the actor's point of view. Because it is narrower, this version of the doctrine of *Verstehen* is exempt from some, but by no means all, of the criticisms of (2) which follow. It is exempt at a price, however, for it allows for the sort of understanding of actions which *Verstehen* theorists traditionally oppose. I will proceed, therefore, as if (2) captures the intent of *Verstehen* theorists, Dray included.

Dray presumably holds both (2.1) and (2.2), but it is possible to subscribe to one without subscribing to the other.[10]

2   A Theory of
Understanding Actions

There is no doubt that one good way to understand an action is in terms of a rational explanation of it. To revert back to the discussion of the preceding chapter, this sort of understanding would be a form of internal understanding. The action itself would be taken in isolation, so to speak, and looked into. Such elements or parts of the action as the agent's goal, his beliefs about means, and his beliefs about his circumstances would be singled out for attention. These elements or parts of the action would be related to one another in the way that the parts of a plan or calculation are related. So far so good. The only question to raise about (2.2) is whether this is the *only* way to understand an action.

Let us grant all the things *Verstehen* theorists want us to grant about human behavior: that it is rule-governed, that it is meaningful, that it has a point. It does not follow that we can *only* have internal understanding of actions or that the *only* internal understanding we can have involves the singling out of the aforementioned elements and relationships. Actions, like everything else in the world, bear connections or relationships with things outside them, and I see no reason at all for supposing that at least some of these relationships could not in certain contexts be illuminating. As a matter of fact we do at times consider it to be illuminating to be shown the connection between an action and some antecedent event, for example, a childhood experience, or some standing condition, for example, a state of society, and we also consider it illuminating on occasion to be shown that an action fits into a larger context, for example, a historical trend, or falls under some interesting and surprising category.

The *Verstehen* doctrine as formulated in (2.2) in effect claims

[10] For example, Patrick Gardiner, *The Nature of Historical Explanation* (Oxford University Press, London, 1952), part IV, appears to be maintaining (2.1) or something very much like it, but not (2.2).

that external understanding is inapplicable to human actions.[11] Arguments for this position, however, are few and far between. Thesis (1), that there can be no causal explanations of human actions, may be thought to supply support for (2.2). Yet we may grant *Verstehen* theorists the truth of (1) without granting that external understanding of human actions is impossible. For even if there can be no causal explanations of actions, external understanding is not thereby ruled out. On the one hand, actions can still be classified as something else, can still be related to their effects, can still be related to noncausal antecedent conditions, and so on. Moreover, thesis (1) does not maintain that actions have no causes at all, but only that no causal explanations can be given for actions.[12] But then actions can even be related to causes on (1).

It is important to remember that the denial of (2.2) does not commit one to the thesis that external understanding of actions is *complete* understanding. This thesis is surely false. But to say that there can be external understanding of actions is not to say that there can only be such understanding or that such understanding is sufficient or that it is the best sort. To deny (2.2) is to make the very modest claim that external understanding of actions is possible. It is for this reason that one may grant the truth of (1) if one wishes—one may even go further and grant that actions have no causes—while denying that (2.2) is true. For neither causal explanation nor even the existence of causes is necessary for external understanding. External understanding can take many different forms and even if one form is ruled out a priori, others remain available. If someone should argue that the external understanding of actions will be partial understanding since one form cannot be attained, we need only remind him that this is no matter for we are not talking about complete understanding. If he argues that rational explanation might yield further or perhaps better understanding of the same action, we can only reply that this is no matter either.

A second argument that might be adduced in support of (2.2)

[11] As we will see, it also in effect claims that many forms of internal understanding are inapplicable.

[12] It is important, I think, to distinguish between the notion of a causal explanation of an action and the notion of a cause of an action.

is that to have external understanding of an action is to take the spectator's point of view and that one must take the agent's point of view if one is to understand an action. Let us for the moment grant *Verstehen* theorists their distinction between the agent's and spectator's point of view. We may then ask why it is we must take the one point of view toward actions rather than the other. We are sometimes told that we are in a privileged position relative to human actions (as opposed to stones and stars) because we ourselves are agents. But supposing this is true, it does not follow from the fact that we *can* take the agent's point of view in connection with actions but not other things, that we *must* take it. What follows is that actions, unlike other things, are open to a double viewpoint. If so, and if to have external understanding is to take the spectator's point of view, then external understanding of an action would not by itself be complete understanding. But, of course, neither would the understanding specified by (2.2) be complete understanding.

It is normally taken for granted that our understanding of a thing will increase if we look at it in different ways. There is no reason why actions should be an exception to this dictum. Indeed, one would suppose that just because we ourselves are agents it would be illuminating to get some other perspective on human actions. The *Verstehen* doctrine is disturbing in its implication that human actions are forever exempt from scrutiny except from one particular viewpoint. To say that we are in a privileged position with regard to actions as opposed to stones is one thing; to hold, as the doctrine does, that *actions* are in a privileged position with regard to us is something else. If we could not take a spectator's point of view toward actions, actions would be doubly different from stones and stars. But *Verstehen* theorists who argue in this way do not deny that we *can* take the spectator's point of view toward actions, just as we can toward stones and stars. They simply deny that such a point of view can yield understanding, and this, it seems to me, is simply arbitrary.

Now a *Verstehen* theorist might be willing to grant that our common humanity does not in itself require us to take the agent's point of view toward an action. He might hold, however, that taking the agent's point of view is required by the very nature of an action. Actions, after all, are goal-directed; they involve intentions or purposes; they are done for reasons.[13] How can we understand them, he will say, if we do not take these factors into account? We can, he will tell us, focus our attention on other factors and in doing so perhaps gain understanding. But such understanding would not be of *actions;* it would be of *behavior.* Yet supposing our *Verstehen* theorist's account of the nature or defining characteristics of actions is correct, is it really the case that we must focus on these if we are to understand actions? To be sure, if a thing has certain defining characteristics we will be able to understand the thing in terms of those characteristics. It is far from obvious, however, that we *must* understand a thing in terms of its defining characteristics. "Bird" can be defined as "a feathered biped" but we can understand birds in all sorts of ways, some of which have nothing to do with feathers.

The notion that an action is an action when viewed from one standpoint but not from another is questionable. Should we say also that a desk is a desk only when viewed, say, from the front; that when viewed from the side or above, it is a material object not a desk? To be sure, from some vantage points we may not in fact *recognize* a desk as a desk, and from others we may not be able to *decide* whether it is a desk no matter how hard we try. Similarly, we may not in every case recognize an action as an action, and in some cases we may not be able to decide whether it is an action. But the point at issue is not one of recognition or correct labeling but one of understanding. If we recall that we understand a thing under some description and that alternative descriptions are always possible, we will have to acknowledge that it sometimes makes good sense to say of someone that what he is understanding is not an action but mere behavior; it makes good sense on those occasions when he initially describes in behavioral terms what we might initially describe in action terms. But given that someone initially describes a thing *as an action* and goes on to

[13] For an account of the notion of action, see, among others, Charles Taylor, *The Explanation of Behaviour* (Humanities Press, New York, 1964).

seek understanding of it in terms of things other than the agent's purpose, plan, etc., I can see no reason for denying that the thing he is understanding is an action.

There is a difference of course between saying that if one takes the spectator's point of view he will not understand actions but only behavior, and saying that if one takes this point of view he will not understand actions *as* actions. The latter claim is a relatively weak one: it allows us to understand actions from the spectator's point of view, and it simply rules out one sort of understanding of actions. I will argue presently that to understand an action in terms of what Dray calls a rational explanation is not necessarily to understand it from the agent's point of view. But this is a minor point and if we overlook it and assume that to give the agent's plan, reasons, etc., is to take his point of view, the claim that if one takes the spectator's point of view he will not understand actions *as* actions does seem to be correct. For what does it mean to say that an action is understood *as* an action except that it is understood in terms of the things by virtue of which it *is* an action? And surely some of the things by virtue of which an action is an action are the agent's purpose, reasons, and so on.

The question remains of how much we have granted our *Verstehen* supporter when we have granted him this claim about understanding actions *as* actions. One is inclined to say that we have granted him very little since, in having admitted that actions *can* be understood from the spectator's point of view, he has given up thesis (2.1) and, on his view if not ours, (2.2). Our *Verstehen* supporter may not, however, be content with this rather minor triumph but may attribute special status to understanding actions *as* actions. He might argue, for example, that this is the *right* way to understand actions, the way we *ought* to understand them. But surely there is no one right way to understand actions or anything else: the right or appropriate way will vary according to our interests and purposes; what is right for one context may not be for another. Our *Verstehen* theorist is in a bind. His best argument is his weakest, for once he allows that we can understand actions if we take the spectator's point of view, it is difficult to see how he can then be warranted in telling us to refrain from so understanding them.

Now it might be argued that the *Verstehen* doctrine, at least on some formulations, does not deny absolutely that the spectator's point of view can yield understanding, but holds merely that understanding acquired from this viewpoint "presupposes" or is "parasitical" upon understanding acquired from the agent's viewpoint. Perhaps so. Indeed, in attributing to Dray the position that the possibility of such understanding is ruled out completely, I may be doing him an injustice. Be this as it may, this more moderate position seems to be in much the same boat as the less moderate one. To be sure, we are now allowed to look at actions from a double viewpoint, but we are still denied all hope of understanding if we do not take the agent's viewpoint. The agent's viewpoint, if not now the only legitimate one, is still the privileged one. But is it really the case that one who sees an action as a resultant of various social forces must also give a rational explanation or put himself in the agent's position if he is to understand it? That one who looks to child-rearing patterns in an effort to understand an action is doomed to failure unless he also puts himself in the agent's position or gives a rational explanation? So far as I can see, this position, albeit a moderate one, is still an arbitrary one.

If (2.2) is to be condemned for being unduly restrictive, (2.1) must be condemned on the same grounds, for it, too, rules out external understanding. Indeed, it also rules out various forms of internal understanding although it is perhaps not as restrictive in this respect as is (2.2). We have just recalled that a thing is never understood per se, but rather under some description, and that alternative descriptions can be given for any particular thing. Now the *Verstehen* doctrine, as represented by theses (2.1) and (2.2), requires not only that actions be understood internally but that they be understood under a particular initial description, namely the one the agent himself would give, Thus, for example, if an agent himself describes what he is doing as restoring the glory of Spain, we must understand his action under this description rather than, say, under the description "massacring innocent Basques."

Otherwise we could scarcely give his rationale for his action as (2.2) requires or put ourselves in his position as (2.1) requires.

Theses (2.1) and (2.2) restrict the sort of internal understanding we can have of actions, then, in that they limit the sort of initial description under which we can understand them. Now as we have seen, the initial description D, given a thing X, does not uniquely determine the parts of X to be singled out for attention. However, (2.2), in making a rational explanation necessary, in effect specifies these parts: the agent's goal, his beliefs about means, his beliefs about his circumstances, and so on. It therefore rules out the possibility of internal understanding of an action under the description the agent would give but involving the singling out of nonrational elements of the action, for example, the agent's feelings, his emotions, his crazy impulses. In this respect (2.1) is more liberal: to single out for attention the agent's feelings and the like is compatible with taking his position. But (2.1) is by no means liberal enough, for it presumably would rule out a priori someone's selecting as the parts of the action features of the situation the agent himself fails to see, for example, the agent's unconscious motives.

Actually, the distinction which Dray and many others draw between the point of view of the agent and the point of view of the spectator is in many ways misleading. The impression is usually given that the spectator's point of view is unitary when actually the spectators of an action can be a varied lot, each one having quite different understanding of the action. Some spectators might single out external relationships for attention, others might single out internal relationships. Thus it is not even possible to construe the spectator's point of view as that which yields external understanding. The impression given by Dray, moreover, is that to single out the agent's plan is to take his point of view. By Dray's own admission, however, the agent need not himself have consciously formulated a plan; a rational explanation can be a construction, not a reconstruction. But then, his notion of the agent's point of view does not involve taking the real agent's point of view at all. Indeed, in some cases at least there would be no difference between the point of view of Dray's agent and the point of view of a particular sort of spectator.

In this connection it is interesting to recall that Ryle conceives of one who understands as being a spectator. Accordingly, he puts into the spectator's position the typical, nontechnical audience of a performance, for example, the sports fan. One suspects that Dray's agent, at least where the giving of rational explanations is concerned, is very close to Ryle's nontechnical spectator: one follows the game, the other follows the plan. Ryle ignores the fact that there can be other sorts of spectators, those who take a technical or theoretical point of view, and that they can understand in a host of other ways. It is this technically or theoretically minded spectator that Dray wants to bar from all possibility of understanding human actions, hence his drawing of the line at the agent's point of view. It would seem, however, that distinctions need to be made within the spectator's point of view and that Dray himself has allowed one sort of spectator to understand performances.

To put oneself in the agent's position, the requirement of (2.1), is, presumably, to take the agent's point of view. Dray could be interpreted, then, as holding that understanding an action requires taking both the agent's point of view and the point of view of one particular sort of spectator, namely the sort who tries to construct the plan. Yet this leaves out of the picture a great variety of spectator viewpoints, each able to illuminate actions in its own way.

3 A Theory of Being Understanding toward Actions

Now perhaps it is the case that to be understanding$_A$ toward someone's action we must put ourselves in his position, take his point of view. Even if it is not, this supposition has a plausible ring to it. This in turn suggests that we may have been misinterpreting the *Verstehen* doctrine. We have been consistently construing (2.1) and (2.2) as theses about understanding something but perhaps the *Verstehen* theory is a theory of being understanding$_A$. *Verstehen* theorists tend to worry about whether we can understand the actions of extraordinary persons in unfamiliar situations.[14] The standard reply is that we can and do in fact understand such actions for we have at our disposal theoretical knowledge, for example, depth psychology. But it is true that we may not be able to be understanding$_A$ toward the actions of such people, and this may be what *Verstehen* theorists are driving at.

If the *Verstehen* doctrine is construed as a theory of being understanding$_A$, thesis (2) may be interpreted as follows:

(2.3) Only by putting yourself in the agent's position can you be understanding$_A$ toward his action.

(2.4) Only by giving (or being given) a rational explanation can you be understanding$_A$ toward his action.

Being understanding$_A$ is often interpreted as involving looking at a situation through a person's eyes, and this seems simply to be another way of saying that it involves putting yourself in that person's position. (2.3), then, appears to be true. But to be understanding$_A$ it is not necessary that one succeed in seeing a situation as the person sees it, that one succeed in putting oneself in his position. If one tries to see it as the person does and *thinks* he sees it as the person sees it, if one *tries* to put oneself in the person's position and *thinks* he has done so, then he is understanding$_A$ toward the person. Thesis (2.3), then, is false if it is construed as requiring that one succeed in putting himself in the agent's position. Understanding$_A$, as I think it is commonly interpreted, requires less than this.

Whatever the case may be with respect to (2.3), one can be understanding$_A$ toward an action without giving or being given a rational explanation of it. Being understanding$_A$ is an attitude, and not a particularly intellectual one. One who is understanding$_A$ toward an action may give or be able to give a rational expla-

---

[14] Dray, *Laws and Explanations in History*, p. 126, n. C, expresses a worry of this sort in cases in which we find the agent's principles "uncommonly wrong-headed"; Gardiner, *op. cit.*, who is a critic of some forms of the *Verstehen* doctrine but to my mind an advocate of another form of it, also discusses this question.

nation of it, but he certainly can be understanding$_A$ without this intellectual competence. Thus (2.4) is false.

Now suppose for the sake of argument that (2.3) is true. What does the claim that the doctrine of *Verstehen* has logical force then amount to? Empathic understanding, interpreted as putting yourself in the agent's position, would be necessary for being understanding$_A$ toward actions, but it would not be necessary for understanding actions. We could say, then, that the doctrine has logical force in relation to being understanding$_A$ toward actions although not in relation to understanding actions. But we would then have to go on to ask what role being understanding$_A$ itself plays in connection with human actions. For if the *Verstehen* doctrine amounts only to the claim that to be understanding$_A$ toward someone's action you must put yourself in his position, it verges on triviality unless there is reason to believe that being understanding$_A$ is itself in some sort of privileged position vis-à-vis human actions.[15]

Understanding$_A$ is an attitude that *can* be taken toward agents and their actions, but it does not *have* to be taken; people are free to be understanding$_A$ or not. It does no good to argue that this attitude is uniquely applicable to agents and their actions, for even if it is, and some might question whether it is, malice and prejudice and spite are equally uniquely applicable to agents and their actions. If being understanding$_A$ toward an agent and his actions were necessary in order to understand the action, a claim of privileged status for this attitude could perhaps be made. But there is no reason at all to suppose that to understand an action one must be understanding$_A$ toward it. Our discussion of theses (2.1) and (2.2) as well as our earlier discussion of understanding something should make this clear. Actions can be understood externally as well as internally, under the agent's own description and under other descriptions: in a word, they can be understood in a host of ways, for some of which, at least, being understanding$_A$ toward the agent and his action would be quite irrelevant.

[15] Let me reiterate that I am assuming, for the sake of argument, that for someone A to be understanding$_A$ toward someone B, A must put himself in B's position. If this is not, in fact, the case—and I think it is not—the case against thesis (2.3) is just that much stronger.

To be sure, being understanding$_A$ toward an agent and his action might in some cases help one understand the action: it might help one discover the agent's plan or calculation or it might help one discover other sorts of information which would enable one to understand the action in other ways. But to say this is, in effect, to deny logical force—except in the trivial sense already mentioned —to the *Verstehen* doctrine; indeed, it is to give the doctrine the very sort of status that neo-*Verstehen* theorists want to deny it has. Moreover, it should be pointed out that although being understanding$_A$ surely can be a help on many occasions, it can on other occasions be a barrier to understanding an action—or at least to certain ways or forms of understanding. An agent may see some things in his situation very clearly but other things not at all. Certain aspects of an action might well be lost to view by one who puts himself in the agent's position. As a methodological device, then, being understanding$_A$ has its uses but also its dangers and possible abuses.

The logical force of the *Verstehen* doctrine could, I suppose, be preserved by the simple expedient of denying that any sort of understanding except being understanding$_A$ is relevant where human actions are concerned. But to deny that actions can be understood is surely absurd. What about those peculiar actions of unfamiliar agents in strange situations? We say we understand them and we cannot possibly have in mind being understanding$_A$ toward them, for in these cases we probably could not be understanding$_A$. What we mean, of course, is that we understand them. Our theoretical knowledge, not our capacity for empathy, makes this possible. What about those occasions where, although we are understanding$_A$ toward a person and his actions, we find his actions bewildering because we cannot figure out what makes the person tick? It is surely fair to say that our bewilderment is due to lack of understanding, the presumption of course being that such understanding is possible. To deny the possibility of understanding in relation to human actions is a desperate move. If this is the cost of adhering to the *Verstehen* doctrine one can only say so much the worse for the doctrine.

4 A Theory of Historical Understanding

So far I have interpreted the doctrine of *Verstehen* as applying quite generally to the understanding of actions. It may be the case, however, that the doctrine is intended to apply only to the understanding of actions in a specific context. Proponents of the doctrine may be willing to grant, in other words, that not only actions can be explained without empathic understanding, but that actions can be understood without empathic understanding. The claim of these proponents may be the relatively weak one that empathic understanding is necessary only for one sort of understanding.

Many supporters of the *Verstehen* doctrine would object to this weakened version of it on the grounds that the doctrine has "logical force" in relation to the understanding of actions in general. Dray's primary concern, however, is with historical explanation and understanding, and he does at times seem to be upholding a more limited version of the doctrine.[16] Dray's version of the doctrine, when limited to historical understanding, can be formulated as follows:

(3) Only by putting yourself in the agent's position can you have historical understanding of his action.

For reasons set forth earlier, (3) can be broken into four distinct theses:

(3.1) Only by putting yourself in the agent's position can you have historical understanding of his action.

(3.2) Only by giving (being given) a rational explanation can you have historical understanding of his action.

(3.3) In historical contexts only by putting oneself in the agent's position can you be understanding$_A$ toward his action.

---

[16] Gallie, *op. cit.*, also seems to be formulating a theory of *historical* understanding; Winch, *op. cit.*, does not limit his version of the *Verstehen* doctrine to the historical context, however.

(3.4) In historical contexts only by giving (being given) a rational explanation can you be understanding_A toward his action.

Let us consider theses (3.1) and (3.2). There is no doubt that in certain contexts certain ways of understanding things have preferred status. Thus the anthropologist seeks to understand things in terms of their structure and function, while the lawyer is forever searching for precedents. In the one case preferred status seems to be conferred by scientific, or quasi-scientific, theory; in the other case preferred status seems to be conferred simply by tradition. The historical context would seem to be more like the legal one than the anthropological one: there is no scientific theory conferring preferred status either on rational explanation or on the agent's point of view, but perhaps this status is conferred by long-established practice. To determine whether or not it is, hence whether or not (3.1) and (3.2) are true, requires, then, an extensive examination of historical practice, for the claims of (3.1) and (3.2) are ultimately factual ones: to determine their truth we must study the conditions under which historians and readers of history say "I understand."

Now it may be argued that the theory of *Verstehen,* although not scientific, is epistemological and that as such it does confer preferred status on putting oneself in the agent's position and on the act's rationale. It is true that insofar as the theory is an attempt to clarify the notion of understanding it is, or at least is intended to be, epistemological. But proponents of (3.1) and (3.2) cannot appeal to this epistemological theory in order to justify giving preferred status to empathy as a way of understanding actions without begging the question. It is this theory whose validity is at issue. An appeal to it, therefore, does nothing to increase the warrant for the view that in the historical context actions must be understood in the way specified by (3.1) and (3.2). Similarly, if the validity of Freudian theory were questioned, justifying understanding dreams in relation to their latent meaning by appealing to that theory would not suffice.

How is one to study the conditions under which historians and readers of history do in fact say "I understand"? One way is to observe historians carefully, note when they say "Now I understand" or something equivalent, and see what conditions obtain. Another way is to examine historical writing and see whether the conditions specified by (3.1) and (3.2) are fulfilled there. For we may assume that if putting yourself in the agent's position and giving or being given a rational explanation are necessary conditions of historical understanding, the historian's writing will reflect this. After all, by means of his writing he hopes to enable his readers to understand. It is reasonable to assume that he wants *them* to gain *historical* understanding, not just any old kind of understanding, and that he will do what is necessary to achieve this.

We cannot undertake an investigation of this sort here, but the reader is urged to launch his own tests of (3.1) and (3.2). On the face of it, it seems easier to test (3.2) than to test (3.1). In the case of (3.2) all that is needed is to make an "objective" observation, that is, see whether a historian does in fact give rational explanations of actions. But in the case of (3.1), how is one to know whether he has in fact put himself in the agent's position? And supposing this to be no problem, we must note that since readers vary in their ability to put themselves in another's position, a given work may fulfill (3.1) relative to some readers but not relative to others.

Thesis (3.2) is not quite so easily tested as one might suppose, however. How much of the agent's calculation must be presented if an explanation$_D$ for the reader is to qualify as a rational explanation$_D$? Is it sufficient for the historian to refer to one aim of the agent or give one reason, or is more than this required? Yet perhaps this is not so great a problem as it seems. One must expect to find borderline cases as well as easily decidable ones.

A more serious problem of testing arises because (3.2) and, for that matter, (3.1) are not theses about historical understanding in general but rather about historical understanding of actions.[17]

---

[17] That is to say, they are not theses about historical understanding in general unless their proponents hold that actions alone are the historian's proper subject matter. R. G. Collingwood, for one, appears to take this position; see *The Idea of History* (Oxford University Press, New York,

Where actions are not at issue in a historical work, then, we seem not to have a testing ground for (3.1) and (3.2).[18] Presumably historical understanding of nonactions could be provided by the work, and this would not have to involve putting oneself in the agent's position or giving a rational explanation. Indeed, the continuous-series model discussed in Chapter 3 can be viewed as providing an account of just this sort of historical understanding. It will be recalled that our interest in it was as a general theory of explaining something to someone and that we took it to be talking about understanding regardless of context. However, Dray intended his model to provide an account of historical explanation, and, were we to construe it thusly, the understanding it talks about would indeed be historical understanding.

Whether or not the continuous-series model provides an adequate account of explaining and understanding in history cannot be decided here. More needs to be said here about testing the *Verstehen* doctrine of historical understanding in the face of historical works which seem not to deal with actions. When we find the historian discussing the revival of commerce, the ascendancy of towns, the rise of a merchant class, we are tempted to say unequivocally that he is not dealing with actions at all and that such works constitute no rebuttal to theses (3.1) and (3.2). But let us recall once again that things are always understood under some description and that, for any object of understanding, alternative descriptions are available. We have no guarantee that what the historian has described as "the revival of commerce" or as "the rise of the merchant class" could not have been described by him in such a way that we would take him to be talking about actions; that what one historian has described as "the landlords abolished or modified serfdom" could not have been described by another as a nonaction, for example, as "serfdom changed or disappeared." The point is that whether or not something qualifies as an action de-

1956), part V. Dray, however, seems to reject Collingwood's stand on this matter; see *Philosophy of History*, p. 13.
[18] Except insofar as the nonfulfillment of (3.1) or (3.2) in the case of a nonaction could be said to constitute confirmation of (3.1) or (3.2). In this connection see Israel Scheffler's discussion of the paradoxes of confirmation, *The Anatomy of Inquiry* (Knopf, New York, 1963), part III.

pends on the description given of it and that in some cases, at least, both action and nonaction descriptions can legitimately be given. Consciously or not the historian chooses the description under which we are to understand a given thing X. If he chooses a non-action description what are we to say about theses (3.1) and (3.2)?

If no action description were available for a given thing X, then I should think it would be correct to conclude that failure to put oneself in the agent's position and to give a rational explanation did not count against (3.1) and (3.2). Were such a description available, however, I am not so sure that such failures could justifiably be ignored. In the last section we interpreted (2.1) and (2.2) as requiring that the initial description under which X was understood be the description the agent himself would give of X. Now in those cases in which the historian gives a nonaction description of X although an action description is available, he is most likely, although perhaps not necessarily, failing to describe X as the agent himself would describe it. But then, accounts of the disappearance of serfdom, the rise of commerce, and the like would most likely constitute counterexamples to (3.1) and (3.2).

Of course we can reject this interpretation of (2.1) and (2.2), hence of (3.1) and (3.2). We can refuse to look behind the historian's initial description and say that if he gives a nonaction description of X, that is all that matters: for all intents and purposes X is not an action and (3.1) and (3.2) are unaffected by the historian's failure to put one in the agent's position and to give a rational explanation of X. This interpretation will serve to ward off numerous potential counterexamples to (3.1) and (3.2), but it will do so at a price. The *Verstehen* doctrine will on this construal be hypothetical. In effect it will say: if the historian views something as an action, he can only have historical understanding if he does such and such. Since it will not require him to view things as actions even if the agents did so view them, it will be compatible with his taking standpoints the agents never dreamed of.

The question is not whether such a doctrine is correct or praiseworthy but whether it is what *Verstehen* theorists subscribe to. I have my doubts on this score. For one thing, *Verstehen* theorists normally talk as if historians deal primarily, if not exclusively, with actions. Yet on this interpretation I think we would find that although some historical works are filled with action descriptions, in others action descriptions appear infrequently if at all. Moreover, on this interpretation the *Verstehen* doctrine allows the historian in describing human behavior to use technical and theoretical concepts. But this surely is at odds with the program of which the doctrine is a part, namely that of drawing a sharp line between history and the sciences.[19] If *Verstehen* theorists were to accept this hypothetical version of (3.1) and (3.2), they would be well on the way to abandoning the "core" they claim to preserve of traditional formulations of the doctrine.

Let us assume now that the problems we have been discussing in connection with testing (3.1) and (3.2) against historical writing are resolved. One caution is still in order. Theses (3.1) and (3.2) specify necessary, not sufficient, conditions for historical understanding. Thus, on the one hand we cannot assume that because these theses are met by a work, that work actually provides historical understanding; and on the other hand we cannot assume that because a work does not provide historical understanding, these theses have not been met. We originally put the test of (3.1) and (3.2) in terms of discovering the conditions under which a historian or reader of history says "Now I understand." There is nothing wrong with this as long as we keep in mind that (3.1) and (3.2) do not purport to give us all the conditions under which he says this, and that his failure to say this cannot itself be held against (3.1) and (3.2).

What about theses (3.3) and (3.4)? Like (3.1) and (3.2),

---

[19] See Morton White, *Foundations of Historical Knowledge* (Harper & Row, New York, 1965), p. 184, for a brief account of some methodological implications of the position he calls moralism, a position which bears a close resemblance to the *Verstehen* doctrine as formulated here in (3.2). It should be noted in this connection that White is perhaps more generous toward moralism than I am being toward the *Verstehen* doctrine. He points out that historians explain things other than actions (he is interested in moralism as a doctrine of explanation, not understanding), but does not hold nonaction descriptions of the historian's subject matter against moralism as I am suggesting they should be held against the *Verstehen* doctrine.

they might be true even though their more general counterparts, (2.3) and (2.4), are not. Presumably they can be tested against historical practice in the same manner as (3.1) and (3.2), the only difference being that the concern would now be with the conditions under which the historian and the reader of history say "I am understanding$_A$." But there is one question that must be asked about (3.3) and (3.4), a question which does not arise in connection with (3.1) and (3.2): Supposing (3.3) and (3.4) are true, what significance does the *Verstehen* doctrine have as a theory of historical understanding$_A$? We argued in the last section that being understanding$_A$ is not in a privileged position vis-à-vis human actions: it is an attitude which one can take but one need not take; it is an attitude which may help one achieve understanding but then again may not. Can it be shown that the historical context is special, that in this context being understanding$_A$ does play a role sufficiently important to bear out the claims of the *Verstehen* theorists?

Must historians and students of history be understanding$_A$ toward people and their actions even though the rest of us need not be?[20] Are they, like some professionals, for example, social workers, required by their occupational status to take a certain attitude toward their "clients"?[21] There is no doubt that historians can and as a matter of fact sometimes do take an understanding$_A$ attitude toward historical figures. The question at issue, however, is whether there is something special about it. Must they be understanding$_A$ if they are not to forfeit the title "historian"? If it is simply that being understanding$_A$ helps them in their work, that is, helps them to achieve historical understanding, the old criticism that the *Verstehen* doctrine merely gives methodological advice will be deserved. If, however, historians cannot stand at a distance from the agents and actions they are discussing and take a detached

---

[20] It should be emphasized that someone, A, who is not understanding$_A$ toward someone, B, is not necessarily hostile toward B; A might, for example, have no feelings at all about B.

[21] See Annette Garrette, *Interviewing: Its Principles and Methods* (Family Service Association of America, New York, 1942), part 1, for an account of the attitude social workers are expected to take toward their clients.

attitude, if they cannot be critical and even disapproving, etc., the claim of "logical force" may be borne out. We cannot possibly settle this issue here. What is needed once again is a study of historical practice.

Dray and his fellow *Verstehen* theorists should be pleased to find us asking for studies of historical practice, for he and his colleagues pride themselves on sticking fairly close to what the historian actually does and they criticize their opponents for imposing their own preconceived ideas on historical practice instead of taking historical practice at face value. I myself am far from convinced, however, that a study of historical practice will yield the results Dray apparently expects. As everyone knows, but as those philosophers and historians who write about history tend to forget, history is immensely various. I would expect to find theses (3.1) to (3.4) gaining confirmation from some historical practice—although not all four theses from the same bits of practice—and not gaining it from other practice. That is to say, I would expect these results provided that the investigation ranged over the whole of historical practice.

It is all too easy to stack the evidence in favor of these theses by ruling out—as bad, perhaps, or as parasitic or as nonprimary or as nonstandard—all sorts of practice which, if included in the sample, would tend to refute theses (3.1) to (3.4). Unless there is some independent criterion for ruling out a particular sort of practice as historical practice, advocates of the *Verstehen* doctrine as it is represented by these theses must rest content with an investigation which studies a wide-ranging sample of historical practice. Such a sample may, of course, make it difficult for theses (3.1) to (3.4) to survive their confrontation with the real world, but such is the fate of theses of this sort. Had theses (3.1) to (3.4) been claiming merely that putting oneself in the agent's position, etc., was *one* way to understand actions historically, they would, needless to say, have an easier time of it when confronted by the facts of practice. But then, of course, the doctrine of *Verstehen* would lose much of its interest, for surely it is the very lack of modesty of its various claims that on the one hand endangers its truth but on the other hand makes it worthy of discussion and extended investigation.

Educators ought also to be interested in the sort of investigation of theses (3.1) to (3.4) advocated here. For if they are true, it would seem that the study of history might have educational value over and beyond that which is usually attributed to it. This is not to say that an analysis of historical practice dictates educational practice. It does not. Yet it is surely the case that the clearer we are about the nature of historical practice—and any other practice, for that matter—the clearer we can be about what benefits can accrue from the study of it. If we do not care whether our students can put themselves in another's position, the truth of (3.1) to (3.4) is immaterial to us as educators. I will argue in the next chapter, however, that we should care about this. To be sure, if we do want our students to be able to put themselves in another's position and if (3.1) to (3.4) are true, it does not follow that our students must study history: there is always more than one way to achieve an educational objective. Nor, of course, does it follow that if (3.1) to (3.4) are not true, there is no reason to study history. Yet it is important that educators be aware of the various ways to achieve a given objective and of the various objectives which can be achieved by the study of a given practice.

Part Four

EXPLAINING AND UNDERSTANDING IN EDUCATION

Chapter 9

EXPLAINING
AS METHOD
AND GOAL

I would like to inquire now into some of the roles which explanation plays in education. Various claims, some of them rather extreme, have been made for explanation: explaining has been called *the* major methodological technique available to the teacher;[1] getting students to arrive at explanations and the grounds for making them on their own has been said to be *the* function of education;[2] the study of explanatory languages has been said to be *the* focus of a university education.[3] These and other claims are difficult to evaluate for two reasons: first because

[1] Reginald D. Archambault, "Teaching and Explanation," *Proceedings of the Philosophy of Education Society,* 21st Annual Meeting, 1965, p. 20.
[2] *Ibid.,* p. 24.
[3] Michael Oakeshott, "The Study of 'Politics' in a University," *Rationalism in Politics* (Methuen, London, 1962), p. 327; reprinted in Jane R. Martin (ed.), *Readings in the Philosophy of Education: A Study of Curriculum* (Allyn and Bacon, Boston, 1970).

it is not always clear from the context exactly which notion or notions of explanation are at issue; second because the role attributed to explanation is not always clear. In view of these difficulties our discussion of explanation will proceed somewhat independently of these claims. I will, however, comment on them when it seems appropriate.

1   Teaching by Explaining
Something to Someone

The first thing to get clear on in connection with the role of explaining something to someone in teaching and education is whether it is possible for one who is teaching to engage in explaining. We have seen that explaining and teaching, although alike in certain respects, are distinct activities just as telling and teaching are. But of course this in itself does not prevent the teacher from explaining any more than it prevents him from telling. All sorts of things which are not themselves teaching enter into teaching. Thus, for example, a teacher asks questions, gives demonstrations, lectures, evaluates, motivates, and so on and on. None of these is itself teaching; indeed, it would be strange if these were. To suppose that the parts of an activity must themselves be instances of that activity is no more reasonable than to suppose that the parts of an army must themselves be an army or that the parts of a house must themselves be a house.

The fact that an activity is distinct from teaching does not mean that someone who engages in it cannot be teaching. He can be, provided that the activity is compatible with teaching. That is to say, he can be, provided that engaging in the activity does not prevent him from satisfying the various general constraining principles having logical status which govern teaching.[4] If, for example, an activity were such that it was impossible for one who en-

---

[4] Two of these were discussed at length in Chap. 5. It should not be thought, however, that teaching is governed by those two alone. It should be noted that if the activity prevented him from satisfying other sorts of general constraining principles, for example, social or moral ones, he could still be teaching, albeit badly, antisocially, immorally.

gaged in it to acknowledge his pupil's rationality, we would have to conclude that it could not enter into teaching. Whether the things rationality theorists want to rule out of teaching, for example, indoctrination, propaganda, brainwashing, hypnosis, do in fact make it impossible for the rationality constraint on manner or learning or, perhaps, other constraints we have not discussed, to be fulfilled is an important question and is not one to be answered hastily. Fortunately, we need do no more than raise it here, since our own interest is in the compatibility of explaining and teaching. There is nothing so far as I can see to suggest that one who was explaining something to someone would be prevented from meeting the conditions of teaching.

One necessary condition of explaining something to someone does require comment here, however, for although it does not make explaining incompatible with teaching, it does make it incompatible with certain methods or ways of teaching. I have in mind of course the linguistic condition on explaining something to someone.[5] If the explainer must use sentences in an active, assertive$_8$ way, then it is not possible for the teacher both to explain something to his pupil and to have his pupil figure that thing out for himself; nor is it possible for him to have his pupil find that thing out for himself from a book, a film, or the like. In deciding if explaining is *the* methodological technique available to the teacher, then, this linguistic limitation on explaining is of crucial importance. Logically speaking, there is nothing that prevents the teacher from explaining things to his pupils, but it should be remembered that explaining is one option among many open to the teacher and that the teacher must take into account the costs of explaining as well as the benefits.

Another factor to take into account in determining the role of explaining in teaching is the relatively narrow range or scope of explaining as opposed to teaching. There is no *explaining to* in the sense in which there is *teaching to,* that is, in the sense of trying to get people to acquire active propensities, tendencies, habits, and the like. Nor is there *explaining how* in the sense in which there is *teaching how,* that is, in the sense of trying to get people to acquire

[5] For a discussion of this condition, see Chap. 6.

skills, facilities, and the like. One who explains to someone how to do something, for example, how to play the guitar, will give all sorts of information about how to do it, for example, about how to hold the instrument and how to pluck the strings, and perhaps will show how; but his aim will be that the person have an intellectual grasp of it rather than that he be able to do it.

A very narrow view of teaching and, indeed, of education emerges if explaining something to someone is assigned too central a role in teaching. Explaining something to someone is a good deal more limited than teaching, both with respect to range or scope and with respect to manner. Whereas the teacher can aim at the acquisition of skills, propensities, etc., and, when *teaching that,* can proceed by stating the "facts" himself or by having the pupil acquire them from some other source, the explainer can only *explain that* and must himself state the "facts." To view the teacher as primarily an explainer would seem to have the effect of ruling out of teaching, and hence perhaps out of a pupil's education, important goals and valuable methods.

Yet we must not be too quick to assume that because explaining does not itself aim at equipping someone with skills, propensities, and the like, it cannot enter into *teaching how* and *teaching to.* Explaining can enter into both sorts of teaching. For example, in the course of teaching some skill, the teacher may explain why a particular method is the best one to use in performing a certain action; in the course of teaching someone to act according to some norm, he may explain why that particular norm ought to be followed. Moreover, although explaining something to someone is incompatible with getting that person to figure the thing out for himself, we should not assume that explaining cannot enter into teaching where the intent is to get the pupil to figure something out for himself. If the teacher wants his pupil to figure something out for himself, for example, why the engine seized up, he cannot explain to him why the engine seized up, but he can explain other things to him—things, for example, which will help him figure out why the engine seized up. Analogously, if he wants his pupil to find out something for himself from a book or film, he cannot explain that thing to him, but he can explain all sorts of other related things to him.

All of this suggests that in talking about explaining in teaching it is necessary to specify carefully exactly what it is that is being taught and what it is that is being explained. Someone can teach his pupil the causes of the American Revolution by explaining to him the causes of the American Revolution; or he can teach his pupil the causes of the American Revolution by having him read primary sources and having him determine the causes for himself, in which case he will not be explaining to the pupil the causes of the American Revolution although he may be explaining other things to the pupil, for example, why historians have tended to discount the first hypothesis the pupil proposed.

It will be recalled that in Chapter 5 I suggested that teaching episodes be viewed as having some underlying question and also some subsidiary questions. Insofar as answering either sort of question is a matter of transmitting beliefs—as opposed to skills, propensities, and the like—explaining may be used in relation to it. Thus, explaining can be the method or technique used in relation to the underlying question of any *teaching-that* episode but it can also be the method or technique used in relation to the subsidiary question of some *teaching-how* and *teaching-to* episodes as well as some *teaching-that* episodes. It is well to distinguish, then, two methodological roles for explaining something to someone in teaching: in one role it would be the method or means of answering the underlying question of a teaching episode; in another role it would be the method or means of answering subsidiary questions.

Once these two methodological roles for explaining are distinguished, we are better able to evaluate claims about the importance of explaining in teaching. We see first of all that, given episodes with certain goals, for example, the acquisition of some skill or propensity, explaining cannot be the method used relative to the underlying question; that is to say, it cannot be unless we adopt a view of the learning of skills and the acquisition of propensities which reduces them to the acquisition of beliefs or knowledge. This sort of view of *learning how* and *learning to* is quite untenable, however.[6] We see also that given episodes with another sort

[6] On this point, see Gilbert Ryle, *The Concept of Mind* (Hutchinson, London, 1949), chap. 2; Israel Scheffler, *The Language of Education* (Charles C Thomas, Springfield, Ill., 1960), chap. 5. See also Marcus

of goal, for example, the acquisition of beliefs, explaining can be the method or technique used relative to the underlying question, but that its merits in this role have to be measured against the merits of other approaches and ought not to be taken for granted.

The picture changes, however, once we take into account the role explaining can play in relation to the subsidiary questions of teaching episodes, for explaining now becomes applicable to *teaching how* and *teaching to* as well as to *teaching that* which proceeds without explaining the underlying question Q to the pupil. Of course in this role too there will be techniques or methods in competition with explaining; thus, it does not follow from the fact that a teacher tries to get his pupil to figure out W for himself that he must explain W_1 to him, for he could have him find out W_1 in some other way, for example, from a textbook. Yet there is no doubt that the potential value of explaining in teaching increases significantly when both roles are taken into account.

In discussing explaining as a method to be used in relation to the subsidiary questions of a teaching episode, one is reminded of the role W. B. Gallie assigns to explanation in history.[7] Gallie has argued that works of history are best understood as stories: that is to say, they are primarily narrative in form, and a narrative is, in effect, a story. Historical narratives contain nonnarrative elements, notably explanations, but the historian's primary business is the writing of narrative. Explanations are supplied to enable the historian to get on with his narrative; they are in the nature of intrusions—intrusions which are necessary so that the progress of the narrative is not blocked. Explanations in history enable the reader to follow the narrative when he has gotten stuck or confused or bewildered. Like the explanations for which a spectator asks his fellow spectators at a game, they are not what he came for although he may need them from time to time if he is to follow the thing he came for.

Brown, "The Importance of a Theory of Knowing for a Theory of Learning," in B. Paul Komisar and C. B. J. Macmillan (eds.), *Psychological Concepts in Education* (Rand McNally, Chicago, 1967), pp. 167–192; B. Paul Komisar, "More on the Concept of Learning," in *ibid.*, pp. 211–223.

[7] *Philosophy and the Historical Understanding* (Schocken Books, New York, 1964), chap. 5.

Whatever one's assessment of this view of the function of explanation in history, Gallie's account does, I think, have something important to say about explanation in teaching. For when explaining enters into teaching in relation to the subsidiary questions of teaching episodes, it is not the teacher's primary business but is introduced in order to enable him to get on with that business. In a sense it *is* an intrusion. Yet it is a beneficial, even a necessary, intrusion for it serves to fill in gaps between the pupil's knowledge about the topic at hand—or at least what the teacher takes to be the pupil's knowledge—and the information or knowledge the teacher is trying to get across.

Gallie speaks of explanation in history as serving a "corrective purpose"—as being intended to get the reader who is stuck back on the track.[8] This way of putting it is a bit narrow, however. One corrects someone who is wrong or mistaken or in error. But neither the reader of history nor the pupil need be wrong in order to benefit from some explaining. Suppose a reader or pupil is in what Bromberger has called a b-predicament with regard to the question Q: he cannot conceive of the answer to Q. Suppose, moreover, that he cannot because he lacks the requisite theoretical background. This reader or pupil does not necessarily need to be corrected. He may be stuck, but he is not necessarily *off* the track in the sense of being *on* some wrong track. He needs some subsidiary questions answered if the historian or teacher is to be able to get on with his primary business—in the one case writing a narrative (at least according to Gallie) and in the other case getting him to learn W. But he may need these answered not so that his mistakes can be corrected but so that gaps in his knowledge or beliefs can be filled in.

Given a teaching episode in which explaining enters relative to some subsidiary questions, then, the purpose of explaining can be "corrective" but it need not be. It can be intended to "fill in" where correction is not at issue. This broader conception of the function of explaining in relation to the subsidiary questions of a teaching episode suggests that although explaining is not in these cases the teacher's primary business, it is nonetheless important business of his. Indeed, this conception suggests that explaining

[8] *Ibid.,* p. 110.

plays too important a part in teaching to be likened to the explaining or explanations$_D$ one spectator gives another at a game.

Gallie is right: the explanations$_D$ for which a spectator asks his fellow spectators at a game are not what he came for; a spectator at a game is not there in order to explain things to his fellows. A teacher *is* there, however, to answer or at least be prepared to answer, if the occasion should arise, some subsidiary questions. If we take as given that he answers these questions by explaining, as we are doing in this discussion, we find that he *is* there, among other reasons, to explain to his pupil and that his pupil *is* there, among other reasons, for his teacher's explanations$_D$. The spectator of a game is a spectator of a game whether or not he explains things to his fellows. The teacher need not himself explain to his fellows but he must take account of the gaps in their knowledge and, other things being equal, try to do something about them.

I say the teacher need not explain because, as I have already noted, explaining is one means among many at his disposal even in relation to subsidiary questions, and it is an open question whether it is the best means. Nonetheless some might object in principle to explaining in teaching, even in this "filling-in" role, on the grounds that it requires an active teacher. Education, they might argue, would be a good deal better off if students, not teachers, were the active ones in teaching episodes. No doubt teachers often do talk too much. No doubt they often do work they should be getting their students to do. Yet it must be remembered that explaining, in requiring an active teacher, does not deny an active role to the student. And it should also be remembered that explaining is not simply telling. Advocates of active learners—learners who engage in inquiry, discovery, and the like—do not, I fear, distinguish sufficiently between explaining something to someone and telling. Were they to maintain this distinction, some of the objections to explaining in this "filling-in" role might well dissolve.

Whereas some might object to the teacher's explaining things to his pupil on the grounds that the pupil would be better off figuring out the answers to underlying *and* subsidiary questions himself, others might want to argue that explaining is an essential part of teaching. I have taken the position here that explaining *can* enter into teaching, not that it *must*. Is this position too weak? Is it, perhaps, impossible to teach without doing some explaining? The rationality theory of teaching would seem to lend support to this stronger position, for according to one rationality theorist, the object of the teaching conversation, essential to instruction which in turn is central to teaching that, "is to give reasons, weigh evidence, justify, *explain,* conclude and so forth." [9] And according to another, teaching has a special connection with rational *explanation* and dialogue.[10] Surely, these remarks suggest that explaining something to someone is not merely compatible with teaching but a necessary part of it.

Appearances notwithstanding, I do not think this strong view of the connection between teaching and explaining is tenable. In Chapter 5 I accepted a modified version of the rationality theory of teaching. That version requires that reasons be given—or at least be given should the appropriate occasion arise—and the giving of reasons may, to be sure, be viewed as the giving of explanations. But the theory does not require the teacher to explain to his pupil. For one thing, the teacher need not be the one to give reasons; the pupil may be the one who gives them. Thus, the teacher need not give explanations$_D$ to his pupil; the pupil can figure out the reasons himself, that is, he can come up with explanations$_F$ instead of the teacher's having to give explanations$_D$. Moreover, there is nothing in the rationality theory to suggest that the teacher must go so far as to *explain to* his pupil. The suggestion is rather that he must give him explanations$_D$. But explanations$_D$, as we saw in Chapter 6, are detachable from explaining. There can be explanations$_D$ without explaining. Thus, even if it is thought that the teacher must be the one to give explanations$_D$, it does not follow that explaining something to someone is essential to teaching.

The rationality theory may not be the only source of support for the view that the teacher must explain to his pupils or else he will not be teaching. Yet I myself find it difficult to construct a

[9] Thomas F. Green, "A Topology of the Teaching Concept," *Studies in Philosophy and Education,* 4:288, 1966, italics added.
[10] Israel Scheffler, *Conditions of Knowledge* (Scott, Foresman, Glenville, Ill., 1965), p. 11.

more plausible argument than the one from acknowledging the pupil's reason. And this argument seems to me to be inadequate. Teaching, despite its links with reason and rationality and its differences from indoctrinating, brainwashing, and the like, is a wide-open activity. There simply is no one method that has to be used, no one "subactivity" the teacher must engage in, no one way of proceeding he must adopt. This does not mean that explaining something to someone may not in fact play a terribly important role in teaching. Nor does it mean that it ought not to play such a role. It does, however, mean that whether to explain something to one's pupils or not is a practical decision to be made by one who is teaching. And this, I think, is as it should be.

2 Explaining as an Educational Objective

We can safely conclude that explaining is *a* major methodological technique available to the teacher, if not *the* such technique. But if this is so, then at least one sort of education, namely teacher education, should take explaining something to someone as part of *its* content: prospective teachers should learn how to explain things to others. Actually, explaining is an activity in which people of all sorts and of all ages engage. A doctor may have to explain to his patient why he must take 1½ pills a day rather than 9 pills every six days; a lawyer may have to explain to his client why the case must be built on more than the client's word; an electrician may have to explain to a homeowner why it is advisable to change the loading on his circuits. And so on and on with "vocational" or "professional" explaining. When we add to this the explaining that a parent must normally engage in, that public servants need to engage in, and that students in their examinations are made to engage in, we begin to wonder why so little attention is paid to explaining as something to be learned.

Explaining would seem to be a qualified curriculum candidate. Of course there are many such candidates and there is no reason to suppose that in all cases explaining would or should win out over its competitors for inclusion in the curriculum. Yet it is a bona fide candidate, and I for one cannot help thinking that it has been too long ignored. Indeed, people not only need to *learn how to explain,* they need also to *learn to explain.* One gets the feeling that the occasions on which explaining is needed, or at least would be desirable, far outrun both people's ability and propensity to explain. It is the unusual doctor or electrician or politician who makes the effort or takes the time or sees the need to explain something to someone, and this is a shame.

The failure or refusal to explain when an appropriate occasion arises may be due simply to practical considerations, for example, the time it takes or the difficulty of getting a layman to understand. Yet the difficulty may not be so great as imagined, especially for one who has learned how to proceed, and the time lost may be made up in the long run when the explainee, because of his understanding, avoids making some costly mistake. More than this is at stake, however. Sooner or later in our dealings with doctors, electricians, and politicians, and in their dealings with us, the time comes when we must decide what course of action ought to be taken. In situations of this sort what R. S. Peters has called the "norm of respect for persons" applies.[11] To be sure, failure or refusal to explain does not necessarily entail failure to meet this norm—the norm could be met in other ways. Yet in many situations explaining may be the most appropriate way of meeting it and one can even imagine situations in which a failure to explain would in itself constitute a failure to meet the norm.

Peters' statement of what we mean when we say that someone shows lack of respect for persons is worth quoting here:

> The implication is that he does not treat others seriously as agents or as determiners of their own destiny, and that he disregards their feelings and view of the world. He either refuses to let them be in a situation where their intentions, decisions, appraisals, and choices can operate effectively, or he purposely interferes with or nullifies their capacity for self-direction. He ensures that for them the question "What ought

11 *Ethics and Education* (G. Allen & Unwin, London, 1966), chap. VIII (chap. 7 of the American edition, Scott, Foresman, Glenview, Illinois, 1967).

I to do?" either scarcely arises or serves as a cork on a tide of events whose drift derives from elsewhere. He denies them the dignity which is the due of a self-determining agent, who is capable of valuation and choice, and who has a point of view of his own about his own future and interests.[12]

We have all been treated in the sort of way Peters describes on occasions when all that was needed to ensure that the norm of respect for persons was fulfilled was that an explaining episode take place. One who explains something to someone must acknowledge the other's rationality and take or try to take into account the other's point of view. That is to say, he must show respect for the other as a person.

I don't want to be misunderstood. I am not suggesting that doctors and electricians and politicians must, that is to say, logically must, show respect for persons. There is no reason why someone could not be a good doctor or electrician or politician yet show only contempt for persons. The point is simply that to the extent that these and other professionals deal with people, their activities have a moral dimension as well as a technical and perhaps a theoretical dimension, and that their professional education ought to prepare them for it. One good way to prepare them is to get them to see the need for explaining to others and to help them learn how to explain to others. Moreover, who knows what benefits might accrue to someone who took the norm of respect for persons seriously and tried to meet it by explaining something to someone. Provided he did not overdo it in the manner of the airline pilot who explained his every move to his passengers and, in view of some of his moves, succeeded in frightening them half to death, he would probably create some very good will. He might also find his job more interesting, for explaining is anything but a routine task. He might even find himself gaining understanding, for it is well known that there is something about having to organize and formulate one's ideas about some topic for another which leads to new sorts of enlightenment for oneself.

As I have noted, it has been said that "the function of educa-

---

[12] *Ibid.*, p. 210 (p. 132 of American edition).

tion is to get students to arrive at explanations and the grounds for making explanations on their own"; it has also been suggested that the educator's purpose is "to nurture the powers of explanation."[13] Although these statements are inherently ambiguous, I do not think they are meant to be assertions about the importance of explaining something to someone; rather, I suspect, they are concerned with explaining$_R$ something. One of the dominant themes in education today is inquiry, and these statements are best understood, I think, as reflections of that theme. To be sure, inquiry includes many things besides explaining$_R$ something, so that these claims about explanation in education ought not to be taken as coextensive with claims about inquiry in education.[14] Yet it is inquiry and its outcome, or one part thereof, whose praise the authors of these statements are singing. Explaining something to someone may be seen by educational theorists as a technique for the educator himself to use, or better still to avoid so that the student can figure things out for himself, but it is not seen as something to be learned by those being educated.

I would not want to deny that the educator ought to try to get students to explain$_R$ things or that he ought to help them become better equipped to explain$_R$ things. It is worth pointing out, however, that this cannot plausibly be considered to be *the* function or purpose of education. The scope or range of education far exceeds that of explaining$_R$ something. To view education solely in terms of getting students to explain$_R$ or to learn how to explain$_R$ is to abandon large areas heretofore considered to be the province of education or else to distort them beyond recognition.

No doubt explanation has *something* to do with the arts, but education in the arts can include both appreciation and performance, and neither of these is reducible to explaining$_R$ something. Even if explanations help one to appreciate a work of art or to perform a musical composition, they play at best a secondary role in both appreciation and performance. To make arriving at expla-

[13] Marc Belth, *Education as a Discipline* (Allyn and Bacon, Boston, 1965), p. 124.
[14] For an account of the role of explanation in scientific inquiry, see Israel Scheffler, *The Anatomy of Inquiry* (Knopf, New York, 1963), pp. 46–57.

nations *the* function or *the* aim of education is to ignore these areas of education or else to distort them beyond recognition. It could be argued, I suppose, that a work of art is itself an explanation$_F$ (explanation$_D$?) of something or other (for example, the artist's feelings), that artistic practice consists in trying to arrive at an explanation$_F$ (explanation$_D$?), that appreciation of art consists in finding out what the artist's explanation$_F$ is and in understanding it. This view of the arts assimilates them nicely to the sciences—or at least to some people's view of the sciences—and in so doing makes the educational claim at issue seem plausible. But the price of so arguing is high: the view taken of the work of art is quite unilluminating while the view of artistic practice and appreciation is downright misleading.[15]

In the case of professional education and technical education, explanation again plays *a* role but by no means *the* role. If education in the law, in medicine, in social work, in engineering were devoted solely or even primarily to getting students in these fields to explain$_R$, we would simply not have professional education in these fields—at least not if "professional education" is understood as the training of practitioners in the field itself. To be sure, research or inquiry in the various professions involves explaining$_R$, and some professions, for example, science, consist primarily in research or inquiry. But "research professions" such as science must be distinguished from "practical professions" such as law and medicine, and of course, the researchers within a "practical profession" must be distinguished from the practitioner of that profession. Furthermore, as we have already noted, it is not the case that research or inquiry consists solely in seeking explanations.

There is perhaps some plausibility in construing moral education, religious education, and civic or political education as serving to get the student to arrive at explanations, for example, explanations of moral principles, religious beliefs, political practices. But

[15] For an interesting discussion of teaching art appreciation which gives explanation an important role, see B. Othanel Smith, "The Logic of Teaching in the Arts," in Ralph A. Smith (ed.), *Aesthetics and Criticism in Art Education* (Rand McNally, Chicago, 1966), pp. 46–55. See also Monroe Beardsley, *Aesthetics: Problems in the Philosophy of Criticism* (Harcourt, Brace, New York, 1958).

in each case such education would be one-sided if viewed solely in this way, for these areas involve conduct as well as belief—teaching and learning *to* as well as teaching and learning *that*.

The view of education embodied in the claim under discussion is in a real sense overly intellectualistic. It is also too narrow even in those areas where explanation is relevant, for there are other aspects of inquiry worth the educator's attention and other things besides inquiry worth learning. But if getting students to arrive at explanations on their own, that is, getting them to explain$_R$ something is not and should not be *the* function of education, there seems to be no reason why it cannot and should not be *a* function of education. As an aim of education in particular contexts, in other words, this seems to be unobjectionable. This rather modest view of the role of explaining$_R$ something in education has the virtue, moreover, of leaving room for explaining something to someone. Educators who are advocates of explaining$_R$ something, and indeed, of inquiry in general, too often forget that explaining something to someone is both distinct from explaining$_R$ something and important in its own right.

3 Learning to Explain and Learning by Explaining

But, it will be asked, is it possible to teach someone to explain something to someone? I do not see why not. There is no guarantee that someone who is taught to explain will learn to explain or that, if he learns, he will learn to do it very well. But this is true whatever the activity being taught. Presumably, explaining can be taught in the manner of other activities: by providing demonstrations, practice, guidance, criticism, and so on. The conditions of explaining something to someone formulated in Chapter 6 above are surely relevant for this task. This is not to say that one who is learning to explain must necessarily be aware of these conditions or even that the teacher of explaining must be aware of them. They are there to be used, however, insofar as they are found to be helpful in teaching and learning this activity.

In a fascinating essay entitled "The Study of 'Politics' in a

University," Michael Oakeshott draws a distinction between a "language" (a manner of thinking) and a "literature" or "text" (what has been said in the language).[16] He then argues that a university education is properly an education in "languages" of a certain sort, namely *explanatory* languages, whereas a vocational education is properly a study of literature or texts and, perhaps, a study of nonexplanatory languages. This is not the place to evaluate Oakeshott's general thesis about university and vocational education, nor is it the place to investigate his claim that politics has no explanatory language of its own. His recommendation about the most appropriate way to study explanatory languages in a university does, however, deserve our attention.

According to Oakeshott, the proper way to study a language is in conjunction with the study of an appropriate literature or text. This is not to say that university education is, after all, vocational education, for "text" is to be understood in different ways in the two contexts: in the context of vocational education it is to be understood as an organization of information, while in the context of university education it is to be understood as a paradigm of a language.[17] But granting that "text" can be understood in two ways, the view that explanatory languages are best studied through texts which exemplify them is not without problems, first because the notion of an explanatory language is ambiguous, and second because what is to count as a text is not entirely clear.

For Oakeshott a language is a mode or manner of thinking. But is an explanatory language a mode of thinking connected with explaining$_R$ something or a mode of thinking connected with explaining something to someone? Now it would seem that whatever is meant by "a mode of thinking," both sorts of explaining involve modes of thinking. One suspects, however, that Oakeshott has in mind the inquiry-related notions of explanation. Thus university education is to be devoted to the study of the ways of thinking of those who engage in certain sorts of inquiry. But if this is so, is it really the case that the study of texts is so peculiarly appropriate? It is not clear whether Oakeshott's texts are texts in the ordinary

---

[16] Oakeshott, *op. cit.*, pp. 308ff.
[17] *Ibid.*, p. 313.

sense, that is, works written for some audience. If they are, and it is clear that at least some are, for example, Gibbons or Bagehot, we may at least wonder whether the mode of thought revealed by the text will be the mode of the explainer$_R$ or whether it will be the mode of the explainer$_T$.

Perhaps Oakeshott intends the language learned to be explanatory in a twofold sense. Whatever his intent, however, it is surely important to differentiate an explanatory$_R$ language from an explanatory$_T$ language. In some contexts it may be important or desirable to learn the one but not the other; furthermore, the most appropriate way to study one sort of explanatory language may not be at all appropriate for studying the other sort. For example, our interest here is in explaining something to someone, and whatever one thinks about the use of paradigm texts in relation to the study of explanatory$_R$ languages, it would seem to be quite appropriate to use such texts in relation to the study of explaining something to someone.

Oakeshott believes that different disciplines, for example, history and chemistry, have different explanatory languages. Although he may be thinking about differences in explaining$_R$ something, it is not too far-fetched to suppose that disciplines vary also in their explaining something to someone. But then, explaining something to someone can be illuminated by the study of texts which are paradigms of the different explanatory$_T$ languages, and the study of the disciplines themselves may be enhanced by studying their respective explanatory$_T$ languages.

The study of the disciplines at all levels of education normally proceeds without concern for explaining something within the discipline to someone. This seems to me to be a mistake on at least two counts. First, a person can learn a great deal about a topic by explaining or trying to explain it to someone. More will be said about this in a moment. Over and above the pedagogical benefits which may accrue from having students explain things to others, there is good reason for educators to make sure that at least some people who are proficient in a discipline are able to explain things in that discipline to the layman. For otherwise the potential usefulness of the disciplines for everyday life may go untapped.

The disciplines are relevant to a host of situations including matters of public policy and personal conduct. Indeed, the "transfer value" of disciplinary knowledge is often given as justification for studying the disciplines in general education. But to say that the disciplines are relevant to the problems and concerns of everyday life is not to say that one can know in advance which disciplines are relevant to which problems and concerns.[18] To be sure, at a given time t one may know that a given discipline D_1 is relevant to a certain problem P and that a given discipline D_2 is not. But disciplines change and since we cannot know at time t what disciplines D_1 and D_2 will be like at time t_1 we cannot know at t that at t_1 discipline D_1 will be relevant and discipline D_2 will not be relevant to problem P. Moreover, our everyday problems and concerns change too, so that even if we knew at time t what disciplines D_1 and D_2 would be like at t_1, we would not know at t whether D_1 and D_2 would be relevant to our problems and concerns at t_1.

The matter is even more complex than this. Suppose we could know at time t what the relevance of D_1, D_2, D_3, . . . D_n would be at time t_1 for our problems and concerns at t_1. New disciplines can come into being, and it might be the case that at t_1 discipline D_{n+1} had more relevance for problem P than any other discipline. We could not, however, know this at time t. Moreover, even if we could know at time t which disciplines at t_1, including new disciplines, would be relevant to problem P at t_1, we would not know which parts or aspects of the relevant disciplines would be relevant to P. We speak of the disciplines in general as being relevant to everyday problems and concerns, but given some particular problem P we do not normally find that the disciplines en masse or some one discipline as a whole is relevant to P; rather we find that some part of a discipline is, or perhaps that some parts of several disciplines are, relevant. But the parts of a discipline can change, so that a part of a discipline which is relevant to a problem

[18] For more on the question of the relevance of study of the disciplines for the concerns of everyday life, see Jane R. Martin, *Educational Philosophy and Theory*, 1:23–40, 1969; reprinted in Jane R. Martin (ed.), *op. cit.*

at time t may not be relevant at time t_1, and perhaps more to the point, a part which is not relevant at t may in fact be relevant at t_1. Moreover, as in the case of the disciplines themselves, new parts of a discipline may come into being at t_1 while old parts may fall by the wayside.

Surely enough has been said to make it apparent that there is no guarantee that even the most comprehensive of educations in the disciplines will equip people with everything the disciplines will have to say to the problems and concerns of their lives. Even if we taught every person every part of every discipline, success would not be guaranteed. And, of course, it is impossible to do this. Selection from the disciplines as a group and selection from within any given discipline is necessary. And if we select, we run the risk of excluding disciplines or parts thereof having relevance to everyday matters. Even the best-educated person in the disciplines, in other words, may find himself confronting a problem on which some discipline or discipline part which was missing from his education sheds light. He may fail to capitalize on that light unless there is someone who knows that discipline or discipline part well, sees its relevance for the problem at issue, and is able to get the relevant material across to—that is, *explain it to*—the problem facer. There is a need, that is to say, for people who know some discipline or discipline part and can explain things to the uninitiated from the standpoint of that discipline or discipline part. To be sure, where education in a discipline is concerned, explaining something to someone may not have first priority. I do not mean to suggest that it does. But it has *some* priority, and I am not at all sure that educators have recognized this.

The study of what, following Oakeshott, we have called the explanatory$_T$ language of a discipline can proceed through the study of appropriate texts, but if the aim is to be able to *use* an explanatory$_T$ language, practice in using it will be necessary as well. The student, in other words, will have to be put in the role of explainer in genuine explaining episodes; it will not be sufficient to expose him to the episodes of others. I can think of only one typical educational context in which today's student is put in what might be viewed as the explainer's position: that is when he is asked to write an essay examination. But of course the purpose of putting him in the explainer's role is in this case not to teach him to explain things to others but rather to find out whether he knows or understands. Moreover, the explainee in the typical essay examination is the teacher or grader who knows too much about the topic at hand for a pedagogically valuable explaining episode to take place. What is needed if a student is to learn to explain things to others is a wide range of genuine explaining episodes for him to participate in.

One can imagine a series of explaining episodes constructed in such a way that a student who is to learn to explain things to others would have experience with different sorts of underlying questions and different sorts of explainees in different sorts of predicaments. The series might be "programmed" so that one step was taken at a time. For example, the student might at the beginning be told what predicament his explainee was in relative to the underlying question Q; later on he might be required to figure the explainee's predicament out for himself. He might also be told at first what shift in question from Q was most appropriate, given the explainee's predicament relative to Q; later on he might be required to figure this out for himself. The underlying question could be kept constant while other important features of explaining episodes were varied. And of course the underlying question could be varied while other features were kept constant, and finally, they too could be varied.

Actually, explaining episodes with the student as explainer and with some uninitiated explainee can be used not only in the interests of teaching the student to explain, or at least teaching him how to explain, but also in the interests of increasing his understanding of the topic at issue. For a person can learn something or attain better understanding of something by explaining it to someone. This, it should be noted, is quite a different thing from his learning to or learning how to explain something to someone. When a student participates in explaining episodes in order to learn to explain, he is, in effect, practicing. The situation is comparable to that of a violin student who plays the violin in order to learn to play the violin. When a student participates in explaining

episodes in order to learn or understand better the topic of that episode, he is not practicing at all. The situation in this case is to be
compared not to the violin student, but to the student of, for example, history who learns why the Pilgrims came to Massachusetts
by reading a text or by reading primary sources and drawing conclusions from them.

I do not mean to suggest by this example that learning by explaining something to someone involves reading a text or figuring
things out from documents. Of course this is not so. The point is
simply that explaining can be a *way* of learning just as reading
texts and figuring things out from documents can be. It is often
said that to understand a subject you have to teach it. Taken literally this surely is false: we can all point to people who do understand a subject yet have never taught it. There is, however, something to this claim, and we should not dismiss it too hastily. For
although you can understand a subject without teaching it, teaching it is one good way to improve one's understanding of it.

Teaching is such a complex activity, however, and so many
problems attend it that one may doubt whether having students
enter into teaching episodes as the teacher in order to better their
understanding of what they are teaching is worth the trouble. On
the other hand, explaining something to someone, at least in comparison to teaching, is a relatively simple activity. To be sure, an
explainer must take into account his explainee's predicament and
must shift the question and decide on the appropriate facts in accordance with his view of that predicament. But the teacher has
this and more to do. Moreover, for the present purpose, explaining
has the advantage over teaching of requiring the explainer to do
the linguistic work. It is this work of answering or trying to
answer the underlying and subsidiary questions of an explaining
episode in terms simple and clear enough for another to understand
that would seem to provide the link that is said to exist between
teaching a subject and coming to understand it. However, the
teacher need not do this sort of linguistic work, whereas the explainer must.

I do not mean to suggest that an explainer's understanding of
a topic will benefit no matter what sort of explaining episode oc-

curs. There are explaining episodes and explaining episodes, and some may be of no use in improving the explainer's own condition vis-à-vis the topic at issue. Moreover, the sort of explaining episodes which may be of most value in *learning to explain something to someone* may not be so appropriate for *learning by explaining something to someone*. If A explains W to B in order to understand W better himself, he will not need to worry so much about whether his diagnosis of B's predicament is right; he will, however, have to worry about his mastery of the answers to a wide range of subsidiary questions. On the other hand, if A explains W to B in order to learn to explain, the accuracy of his diagnosis of B's state will matter a great deal. This is not to say that A can only have explained W to B if A was right about B's predicament. But if A is rational at the time of the episode—and since he must be rational in order to have explained W to B, he will have to learn to be rational if he is to learn to explain—A will have tried to be right about B's state. And of course if A is to be ranked as a *good* explainer, his marksmanship in this respect will surely be taken into account.

Students are sometimes asked to explain things to their fellows. But I wonder how often they are asked because it is thought that they ought to get practice in explaining or because it is thought that they will thereby increase their own knowledge or understanding. I suspect that anticipated benefits of student explaining rather different from these—for example, easing the teacher shortage, drawing an introverted soul out of himself, keeping an extrovert busy—may in fact lead educators to encourage student explaining. The reason for the use of explaining episodes in education will, however—or at least should—affect the nature and quality of the episodes. Just as an episode used in order to learn to explain may differ in important respects from one used to learn by explaining, so one used to draw out an introvert or keep tabs on an extrovert may be very different from either of these. Thus it cannot be assumed that the sort of explaining episodes there now are will do the jobs being discussed here. If learning to explain something to someone not only from the standpoint of a particular discipline but more generally is adopted as an educational objective—as I have been arguing it should be—then explaining episodes suited to it need to be constructed. And if explaining something to someone is adopted as a way of learning or improving understanding—and I certainly think educators ought at least to try it out in this role and see if it works—then explaining episodes need also to be suited to it.

Chapter 10

VERSTEHEN AS AN EDUCATIONAL DOCTRINE

Understanding as well as explaining has been the subject of all sorts of educational claims. It has been said that the purpose of teaching is to promote understanding that and understanding how [1] and that teaching aims at the acquisition of understanding in the learner through the promotion of knowledge.[2] Our discussion of the rationality theory of teaching in Chapter 5 touched on this sort of claim and I will therefore concentrate on a rather different sort of claim about understanding in this chapter. One finds educators claiming not simply that understanding should be promoted but that a particular kind of study is necessary if understanding of a particular sort of thing is to be achieved. In the last two

---

[1] Kingsley Price, "On 'Having an Education,'" *Harvard Educational Review*, 28:320–337, Fall, 1958.
[2] Reginald D. Archambault, "Teaching and Explanation," *Proceedings of the Philosophy of Education Society*, 21st Annual Meeting, 1965, p. 19.

sections of this chapter I will consider this sort of claim as it functions in the context of education in the arts and the disciplines. Since this sort of claim rests on a version of the *Verstehen* theory, I will begin the chapter with an account of the *Verstehen* theory as a doctrine with educational significance.

1 Taking the Agent's Point of View

One who explains something to someone must take the explainee's point of view into account. Does this mean that empathic understanding is a necessary condition of explaining something to someone? If so, then to the extent that explaining something to someone is part of the curriculum, the educator will have to attend to the question of whether his students have the required capacity and what to do about it if they do not. *Verstehen* theorists often talk as if empathy is the easiest state in the world to achieve: we understand others in this way for we too are human beings and that is that. I suspect, however, that this view of the matter is overly sanguine and that developing in people the ability to put themselves in the position of others is itself a major educational task.

Before we go any further, however, we must distinguish between taking someone's point of view *into account* and taking his point of view. Empathic understanding, that is to say, putting oneself in the other's position, may perhaps be viewed as taking his point of view, but it is not necessary to take someone's point of view in order to take his point of view into account. Given relevant theoretical knowledge, for example, of cognitive development, combined with knowledge about the particular situation, there would seem to be no reason why one could not know what the other's point of view was. Granted that to know someone's point of view is not necessarily to take that point of view into account, it is still not the case that to do the latter one must put oneself in his position. To take someone's point of view into account involves having knowledge of it and basing one's decisions or actions in part, at least, on this knowledge. To be sure, one way to get this knowledge is to put oneself in the other's position. But that in itself does not guarantee that the knowledge will be gotten, nor does it guarantee that, if it is, it will be taken into account. Moreover, and perhaps most important, it is not necessary to do this to get the knowledge.

Although we have given no reasons yet for supposing that educators should get their students to take another's point of view, granted our belief that explaining should be taught, it seems that educators do at least have to reckon with the problem of what is involved in taking another's point of view into account and how best to get students to do this. But as a matter of fact there are very good reasons for maintaining that education ought to be concerned not simply with students taking or being able to take the point of view of others into account but also with their taking the point of view of certain others. If the concern of education were simply that people come to understand things, including other people, this would not be necessary for, as we have seen, it is possible to understand people and their actions without taking their point of view, indeed without even taking their point of view into account. But education is not solely concerned with understanding. Pronouncements of educational theorists and philosophers notwithstanding, there are many things people ought to acquire, achieve, attain in the course of their education besides understanding.

Ways of living, acting, feeling, seeing, hearing, and so on are the business of education. Granted that one job of education might be to get people to understand various ways of living, acting, feeling, seeing, and hearing, another job is to get people to acquire or adopt these ways, and this job is not reducible to promoting understanding. It is because of this that the core argument of the *Verstehen* position—we are human beings, therefore we are in a special position vis-à-vis human behavior—has significance and force in the educational context that it lacks in the contexts in which the doctrine is normally presumed to be applicable. It is not the case that because we are human beings we must understand actions in certain ways, but it is the case that because we are human beings we must in the course of our education acquire certain ways of living, acting, feeling, seeing, etc.

How are we to acquire these ways if we do not put ourselves in the shoes of one who himself pursues these ways? We saw in Chapter 8 that, contrary to the views of Dray and others, one need not put oneself in the agent's position in order to understand his action. Nor need one put oneself in the agent's position to be able to go through motions like the agent's. Presumably one could learn these motions by observing, imitating, and so on without ever taking the agent's position. But if what is wanted is not simply that the agent's *behavior* be *copied* but that his *form of activity* or *way of life* be *adopted,* then one must put oneself in his position.

Verstehen theorists try desperately and not always successfully to show that history and the social sciences are to be sharply distinguished from the natural sciences because they study human beings. What people fail to realize is that regardless of the truth of this position, education in which human beings are the topic of study must be distinguished sharply from education in which such things as stones and stars are the topic of study. In the case of human beings, just because we too are human, the educational task can and should be twofold: we need to learn about their ways of living, acting, feeling, seeing, etc., but we also need to acquire at least some of these ways. This way of putting the difference between education in relation to human beings and education in relation to the stones and stars is a bit oversimplified, to be sure. For it is not the case that we can and should only learn *about* the stones and stars; we need, for example, to learn *how to* study them, we need to learn *to* utilize them well for our various purposes, and so on. Yet no matter how broadly one conceives of the educational task in relation to such things as stones and stars, there is one dimension missing—the one that is of crucial importance in relation to human beings, namely acquiring their ways of living, acting, feeling, seeing, etc.

So far as I can tell, curriculum theorists do not really make enough of the gap, or better still the gulf, between the educational task in which what is being studied is human beings and their behavior and the educational task in which what is being studied is everything else. There is, to be sure, a marked tendency today to make much of the differences between the various academic disciplines; thus the social sciences and history are seen as very different from the natural sciences and mathematics.[3] What is not seen as very different, however, is the educational task given the different sort of phenomena the distinct disciplines study. Thus, once it is granted that the disciplines themselves differ, room is made for the disciplines, or at least some of them, in the curriculum. But once in the curriculum, the same sorts of things are stressed no matter what the phenomena under study: the methods of the discipline, the key terms or concepts used in the discipline, the basic laws and relationships established by the discipline.[4] It tends to be forgotten that given certain phenomena, namely human beings and their behavior, it is not enough to learn about them and about ways of inquiring into them.

There is one sort of human activity which those who believe in the educational power of the disciplines have thought worthy not merely of being learned about but of being engaged in by students, namely inquiry.[5] I do not doubt that inquiry is an extremely important human activity, one that should be included in the curriculum. But it is not the only important human activity or endeavor, nor is it the only one worthy of being seen from the "inside" by the student in the course of his education. Students ought to get "inside," or at least ought to have the opportunity to get "inside," one or more of the arts;[6] they ought to make their own, or at least have the opportunity to make their own, some games or sports

---

[3] See, for example, Philip H. Phenix, *Realms of Meaning* (McGraw-Hill, New York, 1964); Arthur R. King, Jr., and John A. Brownell, *The Curriculum and the Disciplines of Knowledge* (Wiley, New York, 1966); Paul H. Hirst, "Liberal Education and the Nature of Knowledge," in Reginald D. Archambault (ed.), *Philosophical Analysis and Education* (Humanities Press, New York, 1965), pp. 113–138; reprinted in Jane R. Martin (ed.), *Readings in the Philosophy of Education: A Study of Curriculum* (Allyn and Bacon, Boston, 1970).

[4] For the by now classic statement of this point of view, see Jerome S. Bruner, *The Process of Education* (Harvard University Press, Cambridge, Mass., 1961).

[5] See Phenix, *op. cit.;* King and Brownell, *op. cit.;* Hirst, *op. cit.;* Bruner, *op. cit.*

[6] I do not mean to suggest that those who stress inquiry leave no room in the curriculum for the arts. This view of curriculum does, however, tend to give practice in art a subordinate role. For more on this point, see sects. 3 and 4 of this chapter.

or forms of exercise; they ought to learn to be responsible members of their community, to be intelligent consumers, and so on. This list is just a beginning. The point here is not to enumerate activities and ways of life worthy of being acquired and worthy of being part of the business of education but simply to urge on the reader that there are many such activities and ways of life and that to make them his own the learner must take the point of view of another.

I do not want to be misunderstood. I am not saying that in studying an activity or a human endeavor the agent's point of view is the only one worth taking. On the contrary, it may be important, at some points at least, in the course of acquiring a way of living or acting, etc., to get "outside" it and to examine it from the viewpoint of one or more spectators.[7] Thus, to learn to be an intelligent consumer, it may well be of help to take the point of view not only of a consumer but also of a manufacturer, a retailer, and an economist; to learn to be a responsible member of a community, it may well be of help to take not only the point of view of such a member but to take the point of view of a sociologist, a psychologist, a political scientist. My point is not that students must take *only* the agent's point of view, given that some activity or way of life, etc., is to be acquired, but simply that they must *at least* take this point of view.

Let me ward off another possible misunderstanding by making it clear that I am not proposing that the schools should be microcosms of society or that they must replicate real-life situations. For one thing, I am not saying that *all* human activities, endeavors, and the like are the business of education, but rather that *some,* inquiry being only one of them, ought to be. With respect to the ones that ought to be, I am leaving open the question of whether they ought to be studied in school or in some other educational context. I am leaving open also the question of whether the best

[7] Arno A. Bellock in his discussions of the curriculum has invoked a distinction similar to the inside-outside distinction I am using here, namely the distinction between a participant's language and an onlooker's language; see, for example, "What Knowledge Is of Most Worth?" in William M. Alexander (ed.), *The Changing Secondary School Curriculum* (Holt, New York, 1967), pp. 221–234.

way to go about this sort of education is to put the student in a real-life situation, for it is at least possible that he will acquire ways of acting, living, etc., more easily in a sheltered, "unreal" situation. One way to get someone to put himself in another's position is to apprentice him to some master. But practicums in everything from buying to courage can be avoided.

The claim being made here—that one educational task is to get students to acquire or make their own certain ways of living, acting, etc.—is neutral, in other words, on questions of institutional setting and method. It is neutral also on the organization of the curriculum. To be sure, I am arguing here that to learn ways of living, acting, etc., as opposed merely to learning about them or learning to go through the motions of them, a person must put himself in the position of one who lives that way or practices that activity. But this does not require some particular curriculum organization, for there are a variety of ways to get someone to put himself into another's position, involving the use of very different sorts of subject matter organized into very different subjects.

Finally, let me make it clear that I am not supposing that simply by taking another's position or point of view, one acquires his way of living, acting, etc. Taking the agent's position is a necessary condition for making his way of life, etc., one's own but it is not a sufficient condition for this. The *Verstehen* theory can be formulated so as to make this clear:

(4) Only by putting yourself in the agent's position can you make his way of living, acting, etc., your own.

Taking the agent's position is, then, but one step on the way to acquiring his way of living or acting. We will follow no further along that way here since our concern is simply to show the importance for education of taking the agent's point of view. It is well to point out, however, that although it is but one step, it is a necessary step. *Only if* one puts oneself in another's position can one make his way of life, his enterprise, etc., one's own.

It seems, then, that in the context of education, if not inquiry, the doctrine of *Verstehen* does have logical force. For (4) does not simply contain methodological or pedagogical advice to the effect

that one good way to make someone's way of living, acting, etc.,
your own is to put yourself in his position. Its message is stronger
than this: you *must* put yourself in the agent's position in order to
acquire his way of living, etc.

2   A Theory of Learning

The reader may be reminded at this point of our discussion in
Chapter 8 of the *Verstehen* theory as a doctrine of being under-
standing$_A$. We argued there, it will be recalled, that even if putting yourself in the agent's position is necessary for being under-
standing$_A$ toward his actions, the *Verstehen* doctrine would verge
on triviality unless being understanding$_A$ itself had some privileged position vis-à-vis human actions. And we went on to argue
that being understanding$_A$ has no such privileged position. May
not the same sort of argument apply here? Granted that putting
oneself in the agent's position is necessary for making his way of
living, etc., one's own, does not the doctrine again verge on triviality?

I think not. For being understanding$_A$, although it is an attitude one *can* take toward people and their actions, is not, at least
in the context under discussion in Chapter 8, namely inquiry into
human actions, an attitude one *must* take.[8] But one *must* make
some ways of living, acting, feeling, etc., one's own. Now it does
not follow from the fact that one must do something, that it is the
job of education to see that one does it. Yet in this case it seems to
me it *is* the job of education. Or rather, it is *one* job of education.
This is not to say that there is some one way of living, acting, etc.,
that education must foster or that there is some particular point in
the course of a person's education at which some way of living,
etc., must be fostered. I am arguing here merely that it is the job
of education to foster *some* way or ways of living, etc., at *some*
point or points. The question of which ways of living for which
people at which points remains open, which is not to say that all
ways or all points are equally good.

[8] I leave open the question of whether in some context other than inquiry
into human actions, for example, a moral context or some professional
context, being understanding$_A$ is an attitude one must take.

Actually, we take too limited a view of the educational significance of putting oneself in another's position if we conceive of it solely as necessary for making some ways of living, etc., one's own. For there is value in putting oneself in another's position even when this is not the objective. In many of our everyday relationships with others, it would be all to the good if we could put ourselves in their position, if we could see things as they do. In the social and political realm it might well be the better part of wisdom, if not virtue, if we could at least once in a while see the world, ourselves included, as the other fellow does. Because we too are human, education must not only help us make certain ways of living, acting, etc., our own, but it ought also to help us simplify to see things from the other's point of view as well as from our own. One value attributed to the study of the disciplines is that they can equip us with different viewpoints. This is no doubt true, yet if we take seriously Dray's distinction between the actor's and the spectator's point of view, we see that the disciplines, with perhaps one or two exceptions, equip us with spectator viewpoints.[9] There is no reason why the disciplines should do otherwise. There is, however, reason why education should do otherwise.

We need to distinguish two versions of the *Verstehen* doctrine, each one having logical force in the context of education:

(4.1) Only by putting yourself in the agent's position can you make his way of living, acting, etc., your own.

(4.2) Only by putting yourself in the agent's position can you come to see things or feel things as he does.[10]

One can think of many ways of living, acting, feeling, etc., which the student *ought not* to make his own: for example, ways which

[9] Dray, of course, would argue that history is one exception. Some would argue that anthropology is another; on this question, see Michael Martin, "Understanding and Participant Observation in Cultural and Social Anthropology," in R. Cohen and M. Wartofsky (eds.), *Boston Studies in the Philosophy of Science,* vol. IV (Humanities Press, New York, 1969), pp. 201–228.

[10] *Ibid.,* pp. 205–209, distinguishes two senses of empathy: an *adoption* sense and an *assimilation* sense. Thesis (4.2) would seem to involve the adoption sense but not the assimilation sense of empathy, whereas thesis (4.3) would seem to involve both senses.

are in principle wrong or immoral, such as gangsterism; also ways which, although not in principle immoral, would be harmful for him and others, such as piloting commercial airplanes given that he is an alcoholic; etc. One can think also of ways of living, acting, feeling, etc., which the student *cannot* make his own, for example, ways bound to other historical periods or to other cultures. Yet given an activity of either sort, it does not follow that the student might not benefit from putting himself "inside" that activity, that is, from taking the agent's position.

Seeing things or feeling as another person does may be valuable simply because it broadens one's horizons. But other benefits might accrue. Consider, for example, some way of life or some activity which is not in principle wrong or undesirable but which a given person cannot or ought not for some reason make his own. We might hypothesize that if the student sees things or feels as the agent does, he will come to appreciate such a way of life or activity more than he would otherwise, and in certain contexts at least such appreciation might well count as an educational benefit. But there is no reason to suppose that seeing things or feeling as another does in all cases breeds appreciation and admiration. It might for some students and some ways of life under certain circumstances breed contempt. But then, it might be the case that there would even be good reason for having students get "inside" ways of living, etc., that are in principle wrong or undesirable, for to see or feel as another does and as a consequence despise his way of life would surely count as an educational benefit with regard to some undesirable ways of life.

Despising an agent's activity or way of life upon seeing things from his standpoint is not, however, the only possibility to consider in relation to those activities and ways of life I have been calling wrong or undesirable in principle. One might hypothesize that the desire to change, modify, or abolish that way of life might develop in one who saw things through the agent's eyes. Indeed, one might go further and hypothesize not merely that seeing things or feeling as an agent does affects the *desire* to change his way of life but that it affects whether or not he *does* try to change it. And given that he does try to change it, one might hypothesize that seeing things or feeling as the agent does affects the *way* he goes about changing it and the degree of success he has. Needless to say, these are all matters for empirical investigation. We cannot say here whether and under what circumstances seeing things or feeling as another does breeds appreciation or contempt, produces the desire to reform or the desire to preserve, leads to wise or stupid, efficient or inefficient action. But if it is not the job of philosophy to determine what does happen to a person when he sees things or feels as another does, it is surely within our province to suggest that putting oneself in another's position simply to see things or feel as he does may have educational significance far wider than is normally supposed.[11]

In arguing that (4.1) and (4.2) need to be distinguished, I have been dwelling on those ways of living, acting, etc., which education for one reason or another ought not to try to get students to make their own. But those ways aside, there is still need to keep (4.1) and (4.2) distinct. For there are ways of living, acting, etc., which, although there is no reason why a student cannot or ought not to make his own, he is not obliged to make his own—ways which he can, so to speak, take or leave. Thus, for example, although a student may have to make *some* work his own, he can take or leave the practice of law. Thesis (4.2) has special relevance for ways such as this—ways which the student himself can choose to make or not to make his own. For seeing things or feeling as the agent does can help give the student the basis for a rational decision about whether to make the agent's enterprise his own. If what a person sees or feels when he takes another's position does not appeal to him, he would surely do well to consider carefully whether he should make that person's enterprise his own. I do not suppose that a rational decision on whether or not to adopt can be made solely on the basis of such seeing or feeling: other considerations might always be capable of overriding one's view from within, whether the view is such that it disposes one toward the enterprise or away from it. On the other hand, one won-

---

[11] I do not mean to give the impression that only good can come from putting oneself in another's position. There may well be agents into whose shoes some students at least ought not to put themselves lest admiration develop where contempt should, adoption follow where rejection should, etc.

ders whether, at least in those cases where such seeing or feeling is easily attained, a rational decision can be made in its absence.

I gave the practice of the law as an example of a way of life or enterprise which a student can choose or reject, but it should not be thought that the professions or vocations or, if you will, *work* [12] are the only things to fall in this category. The arts, forms of exercise, types of community or social action, and many many other things would seem also to fall in this category. For even if education ought to provide a student the opportunity to make *some* art, form of exercise, type of social action, etc., his own, it might well leave the choice of which *particular* art, form of exercise, type of social action, etc., up to the student. Thus to the extent that thesis (4.2) is relevant where the decision whether or not to adopt a way of living, acting, etc., is at issue, (4.2) is applicable to a great many different areas of education. If we add this breadth of application to all the other reasons we have given for supposing that (4.2) has educational significance and if we combine the resulting significance of (4.2) with that of (4.1), we see that although it may not be necessary to take another's point of view in order to learn to explain something to him, there is more than enough reason nonetheless for educators to try to get their students to put themselves in other people's positions.

3 *Training in Performance*

Having said that the *Verstehen* doctrine has educational significance, I want now to argue against what I take to be a misapplication of the *Verstehen* doctrine to education. I have in mind the view that it is virtually impossible to understand or appreciate an activity or its end products unless one has had training in that activity. This view crops up in discussions of art education: some training in artistic performance is necessary, it is said, if a person is to understand or appreciate a work of art. It is admitted that the amount of training need not be as great as artists themselves re-

---

[12] See Thomas F. Green, *Work, Leisure, and the American Schools* (Random House, New York, 1968), for an account of work including an illuminating distinction between work and job.

quire, but some training in the art is deemed essential. This view crops up also in discussions of science education, indeed in discussions of education in all the disciplines. The student, it is said, will neither understand nor appreciate the discipline in question if he does not receive some practice in it. To be sure, he need not receive as much training in the discipline as a practitioner of the discipline, yet some training or active engagement in it is deemed essential.[13]

Arguments of this sort would be of interest to us if only because they reflect a Rylean view of understanding. Ryle's belief that execution and understanding are merely different exercises of knowledge of tricks of the same trade is very much in evidence in these claims. We are, moreover, in a position to see now that Ryle's theory of understanding, which we discussed in Chapter 7, is in a real sense a *Verstehen* theory. Dray says that we can only understand someone's action if we put ourselves in his position, take his point of view; Ryle, in saying that we must have some degree of competence in an activity if we are to understand someone's actions, is, despite his placing one who understands in the spectator's position, in effect saying the very same thing. Ryle, however, is saying something more than Dray, for he is saying not merely that we must take the agent's point of view but also that we must have had training in doing what the agent is doing.[14]

Actually, the view under discussion has significance for us beyond the fact that it echoes Ryle and Dray. For when the Rylean

[13] "It is virtually impossible to understand, let alone appreciate, a work of art without some such training in performance"; Harry S. Broudy, "Aesthetic Education in a Technological Society: The Other Excuses for Art," *The Journal of Aesthetic Education*, 1:13–23, 1966. See Hirst's discussion of study of the disciplines, *op. cit.*, pp. 132–133; Robert Karplus and Herbert D. Thier's discussion of the science curriculum, *A New Look at Elementary School Science* (Rand McNally, Chicago, 1967), p. 30. In treating this view here I will not differentiate between understanding and appreciating, as I do not think it is necessary to do so for the present purpose. Needless to say, however, understanding and appreciating are different and ought not to be confused.

[14] On the other hand, Ryle is saying something less than Dray, for Dray is saying not only that to understand an action we must take the agent's point of view but also that we must give or have a rational explanation.

form of the theory of *Verstehen* is adapted to educational contexts, decisions which are normative and therefore the province of the educator masquerade as conceptual. As a result the educator's task is made to look easier, but also a good deal less challenging, than it really is. For given that understanding and appreciation are held to be important goals of art education and also of education in the disciplines, on a Rylean view of understanding, training in the arts and in the disciplines becomes an essential part of the curriculum. Now I do not want to be taken here to be denying the value of experience and training in various activities; indeed, the preceding section included a plea for more of this very thing. Yet it is important that such experience and training be included in the curriculum for the right reasons. A Rylean view of understanding does not provide these.

Let us briefly consider in relation to education in the arts, music in particular, the claim that some training in performance is necessary if a person is to understand and appreciate. What we say about the music case can be generalized, with appropriate substitutions, to the case of other arts and also to the case of the sciences and the various other disciplines.

Training in what sort of performance is necessary to understand or appreciate a musical work or the performance thereof? Training in some instrument? Which one or ones, or wouldn't it matter? Or would it be training in composition? But would that training be in some particular form or style of composition or in just any form or style at all? On the one hand, it would seem that there was no *necessary* connection at all between training in composing one sort of work, for example, fugues, and understanding another sort, for example, a symphony; nor would there seem to be a necessary connection between training in some instrument, for example, the flute, and understanding works for another instrument, for example, the piano. But then, on this view, training in the whole range of instruments and forms of composition, etc., would be necessary if the whole range of musical works, or even masterpieces, was to be understood and appreciated. Moreover, training in different sorts of instrumental composition and playing

—solo, chamber, orchestral—would be necessary, for presumably training is needed to "get the feel of the appropriate techniques," [15] and it is well known that, for example, chamber works and solo works are in important respects very different. We need not pursue this point any further, for the educational task would be an impossible one, and in any case no one supposes that all the people who do understand or appreciate music have all this competence.

Perhaps it is assumed that certain kinds of performance, for example, piano playing or singing or composing fugues, have great transfer value so that training in one kind of performance could serve, so to speak, as a substitute for training in many other kinds. One then wonders just what degree of training or competence there must be in performance for it to have relevance for understanding and appreciation. Even minimal training in composition or in some instrument requires considerable pedagogical time and effort, yet minimal training would scarcely be relevant here: one who could just barely play or sing or compose a simple song, for example, would seem to be in no better position vis-à-vis understanding or appreciating great works of music than one who could not play or sing or compose on this level at all and had never tried. Once we go beyond minimal training to a point where the training might have some bearing on understanding and appreciation, there is not only the problem of the time and effort that would have to be devoted to the task but the problem of whether a sufficiently large number of students could profit from the training.

I do not want to deny that training in composition or in some instrument *can* help someone understand or appreciate music. The question, however, is whether it is feasible to provide all the students we want to understand and appreciate music with the relevant sort of training. It seems to me that the kind of training we could provide them with would be meaningless for the present purpose, whereas the kind that might be meaningful could not in gen-

[15] Harry S. Broudy, B. Othanel Smith, and Joe R. Burnett, *Democracy and Excellence in American Secondary Education* (Rand McNally, Chicago, 1964), p. 227.

eral be provided or, if it could be, ought not to be since so many could not profit from it.

If a Rylean conception of understanding were tenable, music education, indeed education in art quite generally, would face an unpleasant predicament: either understanding and appreciation of works of art would have to be given up as a goal of general education, or students would have to be subjected to training which would overburden the educational system and for which they might be quite unsuited. As far as I can see, the same sort of predicament would face education in the various disciplines. Fortunately, the predicament is not a real one, for although *some* sort of competence is doubtless necessary for understanding and appreciating the arts and the disciplines, it need not be the competence of the artist or disciplinarian or the amateur artist or amateur disciplinarian. But then, training of the sort educators speak of is not necessary, and education does not have to take on a thankless task or else give up valued goals.

Understanding something requires having a certain sort of *knowledge that,* whereas training in performance, although it may in fact yield knowledge that, is not necessary for achieving knowledge that. Such knowledge can be acquired in other ways. Of course it might be argued that training is necessary for *knowledge how* and that understanding requires knowledge how as well as knowledge that. Perhaps understanding does; the account I gave in Chapter 7 of understanding was by no means complete, and it might well be the case that one necessary condition of understanding something is having some knowledge how. But if this is the case, there is still no reason to suppose that the knowledge how one must have is the knowledge how of the performer or the amateur performer. We noted that Ryle makes one who understands a spectator rather than a performer or agent. The spectator-performer distinction does not apply in all cases in which the term "understand" applies—for example, to engine seizures—but when the distinction does apply, Ryle's spectator characterization of one who understands is apt. The trouble with Ryle is that he does not carry through with the implications of this characterization. Having drawn a sharp distinction between one who understands a performance and one who executes it, he then weakens it by insisting that the two have the same sort of competence—the one simply an amateurish version of the other.

But one who understands a performance *is* in a real sense a contemplator or onlooker. This is not to say that he is passive. He must see things and make connections, and as I have argued, this is not a passive matter. But whatever the activity of one who understands and whatever skill or know-how or competence he must have, he does not have to know how to do the things the performer does. This is not to say that one who understands cannot have the competence of a performer. Of course he can. The point is simply that he *need* not have it. And fortunately so, for if only a performer or amateur performer could understand a performance or the creation issuing from it, the arts, the sciences, indeed the disciplines in general would have a much smaller audience than they deserve.

4 Knowing about Performances

Before we go any further, some clarification is necessary. As we saw in Chapter 7, Ryle's theory of understanding is a theory of understanding performances. The educational thesis under consideration here, however, is a thesis about understanding not merely activities and practices or performances of these, but also the product or work or creation growing out of them. I take it that a novel or a painting or a scientific theory or a historical reconstruction is not, at least in any ordinary sense of the term "performance," a performance. Perhaps the creation of a novel, etc., could be called a performance, although there is reason to wonder even about this. But performances are occurrences: they take place, they are over with. Novels and paintings and scientific theories are quite different. This is not to say that some performance might not be classified as a work of art nor that a work of art might not be the sort of thing that is performed. But works of art, indeed human creations, be they works of art, scientific theories, or whatever, ought not as a class to be confused with performances even though in particular cases the descriptions "It's a work of art" and "It's a performance" might both be true of a given thing.

Training in performance is necessary neither for understanding a performance nor for understanding the product or creation growing out of some performance. Since the same arguments against such training hold in both cases, I did not bother in the preceding discussion to separate the claim made by educators about the need for training in performance into two claims, one a claim about understanding creations and one a claim about understanding performances. Strictly speaking, however, two distinct claims are being made and it is well to recognize this, for there may be cases in which something is necessary for understanding the one sort of thing but is not necessary for understanding the other. And there may also be cases in which, although a given thing is necessary for understanding neither performances nor creations, rather different considerations apply, given the different objects of understanding.

One who receives training is acquiring, or at least is intended to acquire, some skills or know-how. Although there is no necessary connection between training and *knowledge that,* he may in fact also be acquiring some knowledge that in the form of *knowledge about* those skills. Perhaps it is the acquisition of some sort of knowledge about a performance rather than the acquisition of the skills or know-how exercised in that performance that educators are thinking of when they hold that training in performance is necessary for understanding both performances and the creations growing out of them. Whatever the intent of those who hold that training in performance is necessary to understand a performance or the creation issuing from it, to suppose that in order to have such understanding one must know about what the performer does is surely as plausible as to suppose that one must be able to do what he does.

There is all sorts of knowledge about a performance which one who simply receives training in that performance is not likely to get, for example, knowledge about its history, its social implications, etc. If one who receives training in a performance gets knowledge about it, the knowledge is likely to be knowledge about how to perform—that is, knowledge about the techniques or methods or strategies to use, when to use them, and why. Interestingly enough, this sort of knowledge about performances is very much in keeping with the spirit of the claims we have been discussing. I suggested earlier that the theory of understanding that underlies these claims is Rylean and that Ryle's theory of understanding can be viewed as a *Verstehen* theory. We may take the educational claims we have been discussing, then, as having a *Verstehen* component as well as a know-how or a competence-in-performance component. And we preserve the *Verstehen* component, although not of course the know-how component, when we interpret the claim made by educators about understanding performances and creations in terms of the sort of knowledge about the techniques and methods used that one who received training in the performance would be likely to have.

I say we preserve the *Verstehen* component of the claim when we give it this interpretation because what we have is, in effect, the sort of claim that Dray makes when he says that to understand an action we must have a rational explanation of it. And Dray, as we saw in Chapter 8, makes this claim in order to give the doctrine of *Verstehen* logical force. Dray, it will be recalled, argues that to understand why someone did what he did one must put oneself in the agent's position. On his view, although not ours, to do this is to give (or have) a rational explanation of the agent's action; that is to say, it is to give (or have) a reconstruction of the agent's calculation or deliberation about the means best suited to his ends in light of the circumstances.

The knowledge about performances which we have been talking about involves just the sort of knowledge Dray's notion of rational explanation encompasses: knowledge about what techniques or methods are used in a performance, what the techniques or methods are used for, when it is appropriate to use them, and so on. Let us formulate our knowledge-about interpretation of the claims that understanding performances and their attendant creations requires training in performance so as to make this clear:

(4.3) Only by giving (or being given) a rational explanation can you understand a performance.

(4.4) Only by giving (or being given) a rational explanation of a performance can you understand the creation growing out of that performance.

The need for keeping separate claims about understanding performances and claims about understanding creations becomes clear when we examine theses (4.3) and (4.4). We have already discussed and rejected thesis (4.3); thesis (4.4), on the other hand, is a new one. I say we have already rejected (4.3) because it is, in effect, a restatement of *Verstehen* thesis (2.2), which we discussed at length in Chapter 8 and found to be mistaken. According to (2.2), only by giving (or being given) a rational explanation can one understand an action. But a performance is an action. Thus if (2.2) is untenable, and it is, so is (4.3). A performance *can* be understood in terms of some rational explanations of it, that is, in terms of the performer's purposes, strategy, reasons, beliefs, etc., but it can also be understood in terms of other things. Hence knowledge about the techniques and methods used by the performer is no more necessary for understanding a performance than is the ability to use those techniques and methods. Plausible as a knowledge-about interpretation of the notion of training in performance may be, it fares no better when it is put to the test than does a know-how interpretation.

If thesis (4.3) is untenable we may well be suspicious of thesis (4.4). Yet (4.4) must be examined in its own right, for in one very important respect it diverges sharply from (4.3). Thesis (4.4) is what might be called a *historical* thesis in that it makes knowledge of the process *leading up to* a work or creation a requisite for understanding that work or creation. We may expect questions to arise about it, therefore, which do not arise about (4.3). It is also, of course, a *Verstehen* thesis. But we would do well to consider its historical component and not just its *Verstehen* component here, since the assumption that one must have some knowledge of the process leading up to a human creation if one is to understand that creation, even if not necessarily the sort of knowledge embodied in a rational explanation, is a widespread one.

If we learned anything at all from our discussion of understanding in Chapter 7, it was that one can understand a given thing without relating it to anything else. One can look "into" it rather than "around" it, single out parts of it, and see how the parts are connected to one another or to the whole. That is to say, one can have internal understanding of a thing. Thesis (4.4) is mistaken then, as indeed is any claim that knowledge of the performance out of which a creation grew is necessary for understanding that creation. Some people might want to deny that one must have a rational explanation of a performance to understand the creation growing out of it, while holding that *some* knowledge about that performance is necessary for understanding the creation. But since internal understanding can be had of a human creation, one can understand a creation without seeing connections to things outside it, let alone to the process by which it was created.

But, it will be objected, to look at the process by which a work was created is to look "into" the work and not "around" it. For a work of art, it will be argued, cannot be separated from the techniques by which it was produced; a scientific theory, a historical reconstruction, and the like cannot be separated from the methods used in arriving at them. To understand a work of art or a scientific theory, in part at least in terms of the ways it was created, is, it will be maintained, to have internal and not external understanding of it.

Now this sort of argument does not by itself reinstate thesis (4.4), for even if one cannot separate a creation from the process by which it was created and even if one would then have to have knowledge about the process to understand the creation, that knowledge would not have to be of the creator's reasons, plans, beliefs, etc. Be this as it may, it is simply not true that a work cannot be separated from the process out of which it came. This is not to say that a work would not have been different had the process been different nor that a work cannot be illuminated by knowledge of the process. But it is to say that whatever interaction between work and creative process there is as a matter of historical fact, in theory or in thought, if you will, the two can be distinguished.

A human creation is one thing; the process out of which it grew is another. We can of course construe the one so broadly that it includes the other, but we need not. Knowledge of the creative process is not, then, necessary for internal understanding of a creation. Actually it would not be necessary for such understanding even if the process and the creation were not separable. For internal understanding is selective: it requires focusing on some, but by no means all, parts of a thing. Thus even if the process and the creation were not separable, one of the things we could focus on in a creation in order to gain internal understanding would be the process, or aspects thereof, but we could focus on other things instead. Moreover, it would not be necessary to have internal understanding of a creation. External understanding could be had, and given that the creation and the creative process were not separable, such understanding could, presumably, involve connecting the work to things other than the process. Nor would it be necessary in connecting the work to something outside it to focus on connections between the creative process and something else. External understanding is selective too.

Thesis (4.4) is mistaken, then. One need not have knowledge of a creator's performance, let alone the knowledge specified by (4.4), in order to understand that creation. This is not to say that knowledge of a performance cannot yield understanding of the work growing out of it, nor is it to say that one's understanding of a work might not be enhanced if one had knowledge of the relevant performance. The point is that one can understand a work without knowing about its history, so that, although it might be very valuable to have knowledge of its history, a case would have to be made for its being valuable on grounds other than that it is *necessary* for understanding.[16]

What *is* necessary for understanding a creation is *some* knowledge of that creation. But this verges on triviality and should give comfort neither to *Verstehen* advocates nor to advocates of a historical view of understanding. *Some* knowledge of a performance

---

[16] W. B. Gallie makes such a case in connection with human institutions, practices, and the like, in *Philosophy and the Historical Understanding* (Schocken Books, New York, 1964), chap. 6; reprinted in Jane R. Martin (ed.), *op. cit.* Frederick A. Olafson makes a case—a different one from Gallie's—in connection with a different sort of human "creation," in "Philosophy and the Humanities," *The Monist*, 52:28–45, 1968; also reprinted in Jane R. Martin (ed.), *op. cit.*

is likewise necessary for understanding that performance. But if this makes thesis (4.3) look to be closer than (4.4) is to the truth, there is still a gulf between the view that some knowledge of a thing is necessary for understanding it and the view that one particular sort of knowledge is necessary. Thesis (4.3) makes the latter sort of claim and is mistaken.

5   Curriculum Decisions and the Nature of Understanding

Let me repeat that in saying that training in performance of a certain kind is not necessary for understanding or appreciating performances of that kind or the creations growing out of them, I am not saying that such training may not as a matter of fact get someone to understand or appreciate performances of that kind or human creations of that kind. Perhaps training in performance is for certain people in certain contexts the very best way to achieve these goals: but if so, it is still not the case that it is generally necessary for achieving them. Understanding and appreciation of musical works, for example, are open to people with no proficiency in composition or in an instrument, although not to people with no proficiency at all; to people without the capacity to compose or perform music, although not to people with no capacities at all.[17]

I am not saying either that training in performance has no place in the curriculum. To show that one way of justifying its inclusion in the curriculum is invalid is not to show that all ways are. Indeed, I think that education *should* provide people with the opportunity to learn the arts and the disciplines, or at least some of them, in the sense of gaining competence in them, but I would argue that this sort of education or training should be conceived of as relatively independent of the goals of understanding and appreciation. To justify training in the arts or disciplines on the grounds that it contributes quite generally to understanding and appreciation is to run the risk of excluding this sort of education from the

[17] Needless to say, I am not suggesting either that rational explanations of performances might not illuminate performances of that kind or the creations issuing from them.

curriculum on the grounds that it does not do the job assigned it.

If another good reason for divorcing competence in performance from the goals of understanding and appreciation is needed, it
is readily available, for one would hope that art education would
aim at understanding and appreciating works in the various arts—
music, painting, dance, and so on—and not just in one of the arts;
training in performance, however, might well be viewed more narrowly, with experience in one art—the one suited to the person's
talents and interests—being considered quite sufficient. Similarly,
one might hope that education in the disciplines would aim at understanding things from various disciplines; training in the disciplines, however, might also be viewed more narrowly, with experience in the one discipline suited to the person's talents being considered sufficient.

The question of just what sort of training or competence one
does need in order to understand or appreciate works of art is a
difficult one, and I could not begin to answer it here.[18] However,
I want to make clear that in denying that competence in performance (or knowledge about performance) is necessary I am not proposing that education in the arts rely solely or even primarily on
imparting theoretical and factual knowledge about works of art.
In the case of music, for example, all sorts of "doing," for example, moving rhythmically, playing percussion instruments, and lis-
tening, may help students understand and appreciate musical
works. The point is simply that these doings, even if they should
qualify as performances, are not performances of the sort the com-
poser or instrumentalist gives.

One thing should be clear from our earlier discussions of understanding: that there is no reason to suppose that one particular
sort of competence or knowledge is essential for understanding a
particular sort of thing. As we have seen, a given thing, and that
includes works of art and disciplines, can be understood in different ways, so that the sort of competence that may have bearing on

---

[18] For an illuminating discussion of education for "experiencers" of art,
see Walter H. Clark, Jr., "On the Role of Choice in Aesthetic Education,"
The Journal of Aesthetic Education, 2:79–91, 1968; reprinted in Jane R.
Martin (ed.), *op. cit.*

one sort of understanding may be quite irrelevant for another sort. There is always the possibility, however, that education has as its goal a particular sort of understanding and that for that sort of understanding a particular sort of competence is essential. Thus, for example, it may be granted that training in performance is not necessary for all understanding of works of art, yet it may be argued that it is necessary for a particular sort of understanding of artistic works, for example, artistic or aesthetic understanding.

As we know from our discussion of the *Verstehen* doctrine as a theory of historical understanding, to determine whether a limited thesis such as this is valid or not would require extensive investigation. It is important to recognize, however, that even if a thesis of this sort about training in performance were upheld, nothing very much would follow about art education. Art educators could choose to work for the special sort of understanding of works of art in question, but they would not have to; indeed, if the difficulties and drawbacks to providing the necessary sort of training were too great, they might decide to give up trying for this sort of understanding and try for other sorts instead. Discussions of curriculum often leave one with the impression that curriculum development is very straightforward: you set your goals and then you do whatever is necessary to achieve them. But as a matter of fact, this is a gross oversimplification, if only because what is necessary to achieve your goals may be so costly or undesirable that you give up your goals.

Analogous remarks apply to the study of history and the effort to produce historical understanding. Supposing *Verstehen* thesis (3.1) or (3.2) were valid, educators would still have to decide whether or not to work for historical understanding of actions: the benefits of this sort of understanding would have to be weighed against the benefits of other sorts, for example, psychological or sociological, and against the costs of achieving it. On the other hand, suppose that for one reason or another educators say "So much the worse for historical understanding," or suppose that theses (3.1) and (3.2) turn out to be false. It does not follow that rational explanation and putting oneself in the agent's position have no place in the curriculum. One good way to understand human actions is in terms of rational explanations, and we may therefore want to include in the curriculum the giving of such explanations quite independently of their connection with historical understanding. As we have already seen, putting oneself in another's position does have all sorts of values quite apart from its connection with historical understanding and can be justified for inclusion in the curriculum without recourse to the goal of historical understanding.

It cannot be stressed too much that philosophical analyses of understanding and explanation do not in themselves provide answers to questions about the proper role of understanding and explanation in education. For these are questions about the *right* thing to do, what *ought* to be the case, the *best* course of action. To the extent that in specific contexts such as history or the law or biology one way of understanding has preferred status, that way of understanding becomes something the educator can try to get his students to achieve. But it is never the case that he must set a particular way of understanding as his goal just because it has preferred status in some context. Nor is it the case that he must not set a particular way of understanding as his goal just because it does not have preferred status in some context outside education. The educator is in both an unenviable and an enviable position: unenviable because his freedom of decision means that he has his hands full; enviable because he has so much freedom. He has freedom to select and to discard ways of understanding as educational goals, and as if this were not enough, he has freedom to come up with interesting and novel combinations of ways of understanding. His task, although a complicated and even an awesome one, is also, potentially at least, a creative one.

INDEX

Actions:
  being understanding toward,
    181–184
  causal explanation of, 173–175
  rational explanation of, 171–193
  understanding, 173–194
    agent's point of view, 149, 176–
      181
    historical, 185–194
    internal and external, 174–181
    spectator's point of view, 148,
      176–181
Archambault, Reginald D., 11*n.*,
  29*n.*, 197*n.*
Art education, 231–243
Atkinson, R. F., 82*n.*, 89*n.*
Austin, John, 24

Beardsley, Monroe, 210*n.*
Beatley, Ralph, 70*n.*
Bellock, Arno A., 225*n.*
Belth, Marc, 29*n.*, 47*n.*, 209*n.*
Berlin, Isaiah, 3*n.*
Black, Max, 50*n.*
Brodbeck, May, 6*n.*, 7*n.*, 21*n.*, 26*n.*,
  143*n.*
Bromberger, Sylvain, 16*n.*, 26*n.*,
  47*n.*, 56*n.*, 60–86, 129*n.*, 131–
  133
Broudy, Harry S., 232*n.*, 234*n.*
Brown, Marcus, 202*n.*
Bruner, Jerome S., 117
Burnett, Joe R., 234*n.*

Clark, Walter H., Jr., 234*n.*
Cohen, Jonathan, 26*n.*
Collingwood, R. G., 5*n.*, 187*n.*,
  188*n.*
Cox, C. Benjamin, 27*n.*, 28*n.*
Croce, Benedetto, 5*n.*

Danto, Arthur C., 3*n.*, 45*n.*
Dearden, R. F., 117*n.*
Dilthey, Wilhelm, 5*n.*, 168*n.*
Disciplines:
  education in, 224, 228, 242–243
  explaining something to someone
    and, 213–215
  questions characteristic of, 151–
    152

Disciplines:
  understanding, 232–235
Donagan, Alan, 3*n.*, 4*n.*
Downie, R. S., 167*n.*
Dray, William, 3–7, 19*n.*, 26*n.*, 29,
  37–59, 133, 151, 153, 157*n.*,
  160, 170–192, 223, 228, 232,
  238

Education:
  explaining something, as goal of,
    209–211
  explaining something to some-
    one: as goal of, 206–219
  as method of, 198–206, 216–
    219
  significance for, 8–11, 197–198
Elton, William, 6*n.*
Explaining how, 115, 199
Explaining something, 15–33, 129–
  131, 139, 209–211
Explaining something to someone:
  being understanding, as aim of,
    144–146
  discovery method and, 117–119,
    122
  explaining something and, 15–18,
    129–131, 139
  explanations of something for
    someone and, 17–19, 117–
    129, 132–134, 138–139
  indirect questions and, 61–86,
    110
  language in, use of, 116–129
  question-shifts in, 44–49, 82–84,
    107–108, 127
  rationality and, 67–68, 79, 104–
    110, 124–129
  Socratic method and, 119
  teaching and, 70–71, 104–110,
    114–116, 123, 125, 131
  telling and, 76, 123–125, 131
  truth and, 63–73, 86, 120, 125–
    129
  tutoring and, 87–88, 123
  understanding, as aim of, 44,
    107, 114, 124–130, 144–146
Explanation:
  ambiguity of, 12–33

Explanation:
continuous series model, 37–59, 86, 89, 160–161, 188
context-free notion of, 21–33, 40, 134–138
covering law model (*see* regularity theory *below*)
deductive model (*see* regularity theory *below*)
demands for, 50–56, 62
familiarity of, 56–58
Hempelian theory (*see* regularity theory *below*)
historical, 8, 27, 31, 38, 202–203
laws and, 27–29, 33
nonpragmatic dimension, 21-25, 29–30, 39
Popperian theory (*see* regularity theory *below*)
pragmatic dimension, 8, 18–20, 29–30, 33, 39
pragmatic notions of, 13–33
puzzlement and, 50–56, 62
regularity theory, 3–8, 27–33, 42, 44–45, 135–138, 160
semantic dimension, 21–25, 29–30, 39
semantic notion of, 21–33, 40, 134–138
standard view (*see* regularity theory *above*)
"why" questions, 47, 61
Explanation of something, 22–33, 134–139
(*See also* Explanation, regularity theory; Explanation, semantic notion of)
Explanation of something by someone, 19–33, 137–139
Explanation of something for someone, 19–33, 40, 117–123, 125–129, 132–139

Flew, Anthony, 6n.
Frankena, William K., 28n.

Gallie, W. B., 3n., 88n., 170, 185n., 202–204, 241n.
Gardiner, Patrick, 4n., 6–7, 174n., 182n.
Garrette, Annette, 191n.

Goodman, Nelson, 23n.
Gorovitz, Samuel, 25n.
Green, Thomas F., 10n., 82n., 89n., 205n., 231n.

Hart, H. L. A., 6n.
Hay, William H., 10n.
Hempel, Carl G., 4n., 7n., 21n., 23n., 26n., 30n., 45n., 56n., 65n., 91n., 93, 159n., 169n., 170n.
Hirst, Paul H., 224n., 232n.
Hospers, John, 56n.
Hypothesis Four, 62–86, 89, 109–110, 120–121

Indoctrination, 100, 104

Karplus, Robert, 232n.
King, Arthur R., 224n.
Knowing how, 149–150, 235–237
Knowing that, 165–167, 235
Komisar, B. Paul, 10n., 30n., 117n., 202n.

Learning:
to explain, 211–219
by explaining, 201, 211–219
rationality theory of teaching and, 94–95, 100–103
Verstehen doctrine, as a theory of, 227–231
Learning how, 201, 211
Learning to, 201, 211

McClellan, James E., 30n.
MacIntyre, Alasdair, 6n.
Mandelbaum, Maurice, 45n., 156n.
Martin, Jane R., 214n.
Martin, Michael, 144n., 228n.
Massialas, Byron G., 27n., 28n.
Merton, Robert K., 91n.

Nagel, Ernest, 4n.
Nowell-Smith, P. H., 3n., 6n., 27n.

Oakeshott, Michael, 197n., 213–215
O'Connor, D. J., 50n.
Olafson, Frederick A., 241n.
Oppenheim, Paul, 4n., 30n., 47n.

Passmore, John, 50n., 56n.
Perry, Leslie R., 27n.

Peters, R. S., 89*n.*, 207–208
Phenix, Philip H., 224*n.*
Pitt, Jack, 26*n.*
Popper, Karl R., 4*n.*, 169*n.*
Price, Kingsley, 111–124, 150*n.*

Rawls, John, 92*n.*
Rickert, Heinrich, 168*n.*
Rudner, Richard, 169*n.*
Ryle, Gilbert, 15, 112*n.*, 146–150,
    163, 181, 201*n.*, 232–233, 235–
    238

Scheffler, Israel, 7*n.*, 10*n.*, 15*n.*,
    29*n.*, 30*n.*, 67*n.*, 89*n.*, 90,
    93*n.*, 95*n.*, 113*n.*, 166*n.*, 188*n.*,
    201*n.*, 205*n.*, 209*n.*
Scriven, Michael, 4*n.*, 20, 88*n.*
Smith, B. Othanel, 10*n.*, 112, 210*n.*,
    234*n.*
Soltis, Jonas, 11*n.*, 156*n.*, 163*n.*
Swift, Leonard F., 27*n.*

Taylor, Charles, 177*n.*
Teaching:
    conversation in, 95–97, 103
    explaining something to someone,
        as method of, 11, 166, 197–
        206
    language, role of, in, 89, 112–
        139
    learning, as aim of, 94–95, 100–
        103
    linguistic theory, 89, 112–139
    question-answering approach to,
        105–107, 201–204
    questioning in, 97–99
    rationality theory, 89–105, 112,
        166, 205
    reasons in, 89–103
    truth requirement, 67*n.*
    understanding, as aim of, 113–
        116, 166
Teaching how, 98, 105–106, 115,
    199–202
Teaching that, 98, 200–202
Teaching to, 98, 106, 199–202
Thier, Herbert D., 232*n.*
Toulmin, Stephen, 50*n.*

Understanding:
    being told and, 165–166

Understanding:
    being understanding versus un-
        derstanding something, 144–
        146
    belief, 107–108, 116, 144, 164
    classification, role of, 158–159,
        174–175
    complete, 53, 152–153, 175
    description, role of, 155–159,
        177–180, 188–190
    education and, 9–11, 166, 220,
        231–245
    external, 152–163, 174–193, 241
    historical, 185–193, 239–242, 244–
        245
    indirect questions and, 150–153,
        159–160
    internal, 152–163, 174–193, 241
    knowing how, 147–152, 231–238
    knowledge, 55, 108, 144, 164–168,
        231–242
    seeing connections, 44, 59, 146–
        147, 153–168
    truth condition, 126, 156
Understanding how, 113–115, 150*n.*
Understanding that, 113–115

Vendler, Zeno, 15*n.*
Verstehen doctrine, 169–193
    agent's point of view, 173–193
    education, significance for, 193,
        221–243
    historical understanding, 185–193
    learning and, 227–231
    logical force of, 169, 172, 184–
        185, 192
    methodological advice, 169, 172,
        184, 191
    rational explanation, 171–194,
        238–239
    standard criticism of, 169–170

Warnock, G. J., 119*n.*, 120*n.*
Weber, Max, 169*n.*
White, Morton, 7*n.*, 45*n.*, 135–138,
    190*n.*
Whitehead, Alfred North, 154*n.*
Williams, Ron G., 25*n.*
Winch, Peter, 170, 185*n.*
Windelband, Wilhelm, 5*n.*
Wittgenstein, Ludwig, 5*n.*